EDGE ENTANGLEME[ ]
MENTAL HEALTH ALL[ ]
RESEARCH, AND PRA[ ]

Edge Entanglements with Mental Health Allyship, Research, and Practice traverses the borderlands of the community "mental health" sector by "plugging in" to concepts offered by Gilles Deleuze and Felix Guattari along with work from Mad Studies, postcolonial, and feminist scholars. Barlott and Setchell demonstrate what postqualitative inquiry can do, surfacing the transformative potential of freely given relationships between psychiatrised people and allies in the community.

Thinking with theory, the authors map the composition and generative processes of freely given, ally relationships. *Edge Entanglements* surfaces how such relationships can unsettle constraints of the mental health sector and produce creative possibilities for psychiatrised people. Affectionately creating harmonies between theory and empirical "data," the authors sketch ally relationships in ways that move. Allyship is enacted through micropolitical processes of becoming-complicit: ongoing movement towards taking on the struggle of another as your own. Barlott and Setchell's work offers both conceptual and practical insights into postqualitative experimentation, relationship-oriented mental health practice, and citizen activism that unsettles disciplinary boundaries. Ongoing, disruptive movements on the margins of the mental health sector – such as freely given relationships – offer opportunities to be otherwise.

Edge Entanglements is for people whose lives and practices are precariously interconnected with the mental health sector and are interested in doing things differently. This book is likely to be useful for novice and established (applied) new material and/or posthumanist scholars interested in postqualitative, theory-driven research; health practitioners seeking alternative or radical approaches to their work; and people interested in citizen advocacy, activism, and community organising in/out of the mental health sector.

Tim Barlott is Assistant Professor in the Department of Occupational Therapy at the University of Alberta, Canada, and Adjunct Fellow and Co-Director of SocioHealthLab at The University of Queensland, Australia. He is interested in participatory, community-based, and applied postqualitative approaches to health research, particularly with psychiatrised people.

Jenny Setchell is Senior Research Fellow in physiotherapy at The University of Queensland, Australia and founder of SocioHealthLab, an interdisciplinary collective pursuing social transformation in healthcare through sociocultural research. Jenny enjoys using postqualitative and creative research approaches and has also been an acrobat and a human rights worker.

"The authors successfully take an obtuse line of theoretical inquiry from Deleuze and Guattari, and artfully make it accessible and engaging. They carefully avoid rehashing the now clichéd elements of this theory, in favour of more direct and grounded explanation. Specifically, the authors takes readers deep into relationships with eight participants - produced through a time-consuming process of relationship-building developed over several encounters – to clearly demonstrate the re-imaginative benefits of their theory-data entanglement."

Rebecca Olson, Associate Professor, School of Social Sciences, The University of Queensland, Australia

"In this powerful book, Barlott and Setchell demand we radically rethink the nature of friendship and (health)care. To reframe friendship through posthuman philosophy is to explore how our very being is made and remade in tiny moments of everyday life. Barlott and Setchell trace the genesis and unfolding of four such friendships, how they support, challenge, and resist dominant frameworks of mental health service. Health researchers, whether we like it or not, are part of this process. If we wish to affirm life in freely-given relationships, this book is the place to start."

Thomas Abrams, Assistant Professor, Department of Sociology, Queen's University, Canada

Postqualitative, New Materialist and Critical Posthumanist Research

Editor in Chief: Karin Murris (University of Oulu, Finland, and Cape Town, South Africa)

Editors: *Vivienne Bozalek* (University of the Western Cape and Rhodes University, South Africa)
Asilia Franklin-Phipps (State University of New York at New Paltz, USA)
Simone Fullagar (Griffith University, Australia)
Candace R. Kuby (University of Missouri, USA)
Karen Malone (Swinburne University of Technology, Australia)
Carol A. Taylor (University of Bath, United Kingdom)
Weili Zhao (Hangzhou Normal University, China)

This cutting-edge series is designed to assist established researchers, academics, postgraduate/graduate students and their supervisors across higher education faculties and departments to incorporate novel, postqualitative, new materialist, and critical posthumanist approaches in their research projects and their academic writing. In addition to these substantive foci, books within the series are inter-, multi- or transdisciplinary and are in dialogue with perspectives such as Black feminisms and Indigenous knowledges, decolonial, African, Eastern and young children's philosophies. Although the series' primary aim is accessibility, its scope makes it attractive to established academics already working with postqualitative approaches.

This series is unique in providing short, user-friendly, affordable books that support postgraduate students and academics across disciplines and faculties in higher education. The series is supported by its own website with videos, images and other forms of 3D transmodal expression of ideas – provocations for research courses.

More resources for the books in the series are available on the series website, www.postqualitativeresearch.com.

If you are interested in submitting a proposal for the series, please write to the Chief Editor, Professor Karin Murris: karin.murris@oulu.fi; karin.murris@uct.ac.za.

Other volumes in this series include:

For a full list of titles in this series, please visit: www.routledge.com/Postqualitative-New-Materialist-and-Critical-Posthumanist-Research/book-series/PNMR

EDGE ENTANGLEMENTS WITH MENTAL HEALTH ALLYSHIP, RESEARCH, AND PRACTICE

A Postqualitative Cartography

Tim Barlott and Jenny Setchell

Routledge
Taylor & Francis Group

LONDON AND NEW YORK

Cover artwork by Lauren Hermann

First published 2023
by Routledge
4 Park Square, Milton Park, Abingdon, Oxon OX14 4RN

and by Routledge
605 Third Avenue, New York, NY 10158

Routledge is an imprint of the Taylor & Francis Group, an informa business

British Library Cataloguing-in-Publication Data
A catalogue record for this book is available from the British Library

Library of Congress Cataloging-in-Publication Data
A catalog record has been requested for this book

ISBN: 978-1-032-26084-6 (hbk)
ISBN: 978-1-032-26089-1 (pbk)
ISBN: 978-1-003-28648-6 (ebk)

DOI: 10.4324/9781003286486

Typeset in Bembo
by SPi Technologies India Pvt Ltd (Straive)

To the incredible theorists whose work we have drawn on, or whose work the theorists we have drawn on have drawn on – thank you for the lively wilderness you have created. To Deleuze's wife (Denise Paul "Fanny" Grandjouan) and Guattari's wives and lovers (Micheline Kao, Nicole Perdreau, Arlette Donati, Joséphine Guattari, and). And their children (Émilie Deleuze, Julien Deleuze, Emmanuelle Guattari, Bruno Guattari, Stephen Guattari, and). They aren't mentioned enough.

And to those who don't fit in.

CONTENTS

ACKNOWLEDGEMENTS

We acknowledge and pay respect to the Traditional Owners and their custodianship of the lands on which this project occurred and was written, Meeanjin (also known as Brisbane, Australia). We recognise the country north and south of the Brisbane River, as the home of both the Turrbul and Jagera nations. We pay our respect to their Ancestors and their descendants, who continue cultural and spiritual connections to Country. We recognise their valuable contributions to Australian and global society. We also acknowledge that Tim worked on this book from Amiskwacîwâskahikan (also known as Edmonton, Canada), which is part of Treaty 6 and the traditional and ancestral territory of the Nehiyawak (Cree), Dene, Blackfoot, Saulteaux, Nakota Sioux, a diversity First Nations and also the home to the Métis people. We acknowledge the many First peoples, knowledge keepers, and elders who have lived on, cared for, and thrived on these lands for generations. We recognise their connection to these lands and their rich contributions to our communities.

Tim's acknowledgements

This book would not be possible without three dear friends and colleagues, who were also my PhD supervisors: Lynda Shevellar, Merrill Turpin, and Jenny Setchell. It has been an immense privilege to have your supportive and thoughtful mentorship over the years. Lynda, your kindness and care helped me feel a sense of belonging, not only as a PhD student but as a new staff member at UQ back in 2014. Thank you for your willingness to traipse through unfamiliar theoretical and methodological territory with me, and your ongoing critical engagement with my work. Merrill, you were such a natural addition to the team as a fellow "thinking with theory" faculty member. Thank you for supporting my development as a writer and educator – it has been a joy to have you as both an advisor and colleague. I miss getting stuck in the rain with you. Jenny, you joined us when I needed a theoretical push and a gentle nudge to be more experimental in my thinking and writing. Thank you, for mentorship not only during my PhD but also on my career development in the critical health and rehabilitation space. I have heaps of respect for you and love working with you – I am thrilled to co-author this book together.

To my friend Neil Barringham, I have a profound respect for both your work in the community and how you live your life. You make sorcery. Thank you for inviting me to learn with you and your community-based organisation on Thomas Street, A Place to Belong. I also want to thank you and Penny for befriending Denae and me – your kindness and friendship helped us adjust to our new life in Brisbane. The years have been tough, and I admire your courage, vulnerability, and commitment to reconciliation and community through it all.

I am thankful to other countless people that are part of my more-than-family, and want to specifically acknowledge my parents and mom-in-law – thank you for dropping everything in 2019 to come and be with us, we would have been utterly lost without you; my Brisbane family – especially the Lawson St crew and UQ family; Stanley – you are missed, dear friend; and budding relationships with colleagues at the UofA – Lindsay, thank you for your friendship and care.

To Denae – the last eight years have taken us through our brightest and darkest days. I could never have done any of this without you. My love. My best friend. Mo sheasamh ort lá na choise tinne – you are the place where I stand on the day when my feet are sore.[1] And my beautiful kids, Ella and Sawyer. Nothing brings me more joy than to have your warm little arms wrapped around me. I am so proud of you both.

Jenny's acknowledgements

First, I want to thank my co-author Tim for taking me along on this book-making journey. It's been an ongoing pleasure working with you on both your PhD and this book and our other projects. This book is first and foremost your work, Tim, and it has been an absolute treat to join you in this meaningful endeavour. I would also like to thank my partner, Sofia, who has supported me in so many ways during the ups and downs of academic life. Thank you also to the wonderful multiple people in our life who help me work and think every day: our families of origin and queer families and amazing friend families and colleague families – and all the overlaps between them. You know who you are – you make life and work wonderful!

Our collective acknowledgements

The book has incorporated sections from three articles we have published before, but have been revised to fit the context of *Edge Entanglements* and incorporate additional theoretical perspectives. Chapter 2 is based on Barlott et al. (2020a); our revisions have incorporated a brief historical excavation of the sociopolitical threads of psychiatrisation, as a backdrop to our discussion of dominant mental health approaches. We have also incorporated the work of Mad, postcolonial, queer, and feminist scholars in order to centre lived experience knowledge more and to draw out the sociopolitical elements in our analysis. Chapter 3 is based on Barlott et al. (2017), which was originally written for the field of occupational science. Our revisions have reoriented this theoretical chapter within the context of mental health research and practice. While this chapter draws mainly from the work of Deleuze and Guattari, we have tried to de-centre or trouble our use of these theorists by incorporating Mad, postcolonial, and feminist scholars, and also racialised scholars that use Deleuze and Guattari. Chapter 5 includes sections from Barlott et al. (2020b), which was a postqualitative cartography of a research interview. This chapter focuses on the methodological question of how to *do* a postqualitative cartography, something not covered in detail in our article. Substantial sections of the article are used as an example of doing this form of inquiry.

We'd like to express our gratitude to the people involved in the project from Chapter 5: Sarah Hutchens, Damian le Goullon, and Amanda Toivanen. Thank you for your contribution to this research and commitment to community practices that celebrate diversity. We'd like to thank the research participants ("Elliott" and all participants in the initial project), for their willingness to share their insights. We'd also like to thank Wendy Bryant for sharing her guerrilla activities with us (and providing the poem included in the paper), and Graham Potts for helping us refine (i.e., not totally mess up) our "story-telling."

Finally, to the people who participated in the *Edge Entanglements* project, we would like to express our sincere thanks and gratitude for your time and generosity. Tim in particular expresses gratitude for the time spent with you – for your hospitality, for the delicious pancakes, fish and chips, adventurous nights at the Monster Trucks, and laidback coffee conversations. Thank you for sharing about your relationships and showing us a glimpse of what allyship looks like.

Note

1 A phrase from West Kerry (Ireland), via poet Pádraig Ó Tuama.

INTRODUCTION TO THE SERIES
Postqualitative, New Materialist and Critical Posthumanist Research

Simone Fullagar, Series Co-editor

Edge Entanglements with Mental Health Allyship, Research, and Practice: A Postqualtitative Cartography is a deeply engaging book that takes up a central aim in this book series to think in transformative ways through research practices that seek to (un)imagine mental health service provision. Canadian and Australian authors, Tim Barlott and Jenny Setchell, invite readers to become curious about how research entanglements can contribute to an affirmative future for psychiatrised people. They push beyond the parameters of conventional research and humanist assumptions of selfhood that have been steeped in binaries of ill/well, us/them, professional/patient, normal/abnormal, clinical/social worlds.

By embracing a deeply relational and more-than-human approach to community-oriented support – allyship – this book enacts a postqualitative cartography that explores the transformative possibilities of social, rather than professional relationships. Each chapter pursues the multiplicity of relations that shape the lives of people with psychiatrised biographies, while also troubling the normativity of "helping" identities that limits how researchers in the allied health professions engage with the ontological, ethical, and epistemological dimensions of knowledge production (Tim as an occupational therapist and Jenny a physiotherapist). Drawing upon the philosophical insights of posthumanist scholars Deleuze and Guattari (1987), the book articulates a cartography that is less focused on individuals as atomistic subjects and is more interested in thinking "with" the profound entanglement of subjectivities, places, objects, and edges. These are transversal movements connecting ideas across Mad Studies, feminism and recovery movements, and minor everyday "freely given relationships" that occur on the edges of powerful major regimes of mental health and illness. By exploring the edges as productive zones for thinking about different kinds of connection, this book pursues a postqualitative practice that is informed by creative and critical desires that engage readers in imagining other possibilities.

This book will be an invaluable resource for doctorate students and more established researchers working across disciplinary perspectives as the theory-method approach pays attention to what happens in the spaces in-between. It provides an important point of departure for thinking about issues of privilege, marginality, and possibility in relation to mainstream and alternative approaches to mental health provision. Readers are invited to consider how postqualitative research can shift the conditions of possibility to enable different worlding practices that embrace justice, responsiveness, and a care-full vision for more inclusive futures.

1

THE EDGE OF THINGS

5 January 2021, 8:05 am

I (Tim) am sitting in my cubicle in the postgrad student study space – my fingers rubbing my eyes as I vigorously try to bring some energy into my body. I don't usually drink instant coffee, but it's the easiest option to kickstart my sedentary day of writing and thesis revisions.

I listen to the gentle *ping* of the granules on my porcelain mug. If only instant coffee tasted as delightful as it sounded. But this morning my coffee casts a spell – *ping*. I find myself lost at the threshold of the past/present; I swing to 2017 and back again.

I'm there – I'm here – I'm drifting.

10 January 2017, 4:45 pm

It's the end of my workday on a Tuesday in January 2017 – I'm walking up to my friend Stanley's rental, which is not far from the centre of Brisbane. I usually stop by on Tuesdays on my way home.

It's sweltering hot and muggy – my shirt is stuck to my back with sweat – moisture is dripping from my nose.

As I approach his house, I see a pair of eyes peering through the blinds – I look down at the ground and up again – his eyes are gone. Stepping up to the landing and towards the front door, I hear the deadbolt unlock and the door slowly swing open. Stanley waits behind a closed screen door, his silhouette slowly stepping backwards as if inviting me to come closer. As I open the screen door, I feel a refreshing rush of cool air from inside. Relief.

"Hiiii Tim," Stanley says in his slow and pensive tone.

"Stanley, how are ya?!" I ask as I step into his place.

DOI: 10.4324/9781003286486-1

"I suppose I'm ok for someone in my position," he replies, scratching his temple as he gazes away from me. Stanley is usually glad to see me but still emits an aura of sadness. He has a lived experience of trauma and distress, becomes quite anxious when around others in public spaces, has ongoing involvement with psychiatric and mental health services, and often feels quite confined in his home. Yet, his life has changed a lot in the last few years – it wasn't long ago that his treatment team deemed Stanley too dangerous/volatile to have a friend over to his home.

"Would you care for a coffee, Tim? I just picked up some fresh milk."

"Thanks, Stanley, I'm always up for a coffee," I reply, as I follow him through the living room towards his small kitchen. Stanley's place never smelled bad, just a tad funky. A mixture of old coffee, sitting food, and yogurt. In the middle of his living room is a dining table piled 10 centimetres high with mail, flyers, *National Geographic* magazines, and neuroscience and mental health books, all stained with coffee. Every three or four weeks, one of his support workers helps him clear it off, but within a day, the same items are back there on the table.

The two of us stand in the kitchen preparing instant coffee; sometimes I make the coffee, sometimes he makes it for me. Today Stanley prepares a mug for me while I wash a couple of dishes for him. He has a tremor in his hands (Stanley said the tremors are because of electroconvulsive therapy he received in the 1980s), and I am always nervous that he'll spill boiling water on himself or me. (He never did.) Stanley drinks about six to ten cups of instant coffee a day.

When I am with Stanley, I try to shed my professional status as an occupational therapist and academic, but Stanley is proud to have a friend that has status. Whenever he gets a phone call when I'm over, Stanley says something like: "I will have to call you back. I am with Tim – he's my ally and also a lecturer in occupational therapy." I rarely, if ever, offer any therapeutic advice, though he occasionally asks for it. And, just last week, Stanley's support team asked me to provide some recommendations about computer accessibility for him. But I just want to spend time with Stanley as a friend, not be his therapist.

Unsurprisingly, we talk about when Stanley visited the west coast of Canada in his 20s – he is now in his 60s.[1] We reminisce about a trip we took to Adelaide to visit his mother the previous year and talk about my recent travels to present at a conference. Travelling is one of Stanley's great joys. But today our conversation drifts to Stanley's frustration with his support services. So, we make a call together to provide feedback to his case manager and advocate for changes to his service schedule. Stanley looks relieved to have that dealt with as he sinks into his armchair with a deep breath.

After an hour or so together, before I get ready to leave, we get out his calendar and look ahead to an upcoming visit from his mother. She'll be staying in town for a few days and we decide that the two of them might come over to my place for morning tea. I write on January 22: "Morning tea at Tim's house? Tim will call in the morning."

I throw back the last gritty drop of my second mug of instant coffee and make my way to the door.

5 January 2021, 8:15 am

I'm back, sitting in my cubicle. I'm savouring this instant coffee, enjoying it with Stanley (in my mind). We first met in early 2015, in the early days of my PhD program, when the manager of a small community-based mental health organisation in Brisbane called A Place to Belong (APTB) invited us to meet.[2] This project and book is not about my relationship with Stanley, but my interest in relationships *like* the one I had with Stanley.[3] My interest is in the ways reciprocal social relationships might change the lives of psychiatrised people.

An introduction

In the early days of this project, Tim spent a lot of time thinking and reading about approaches in the mental health sector and noticed there was limited discussion about social connectedness for people diagnosed with "serious mental illness."[4] At the time, he didn't trouble the diagnostic categorisation of people who experience trauma and distress and/or have diverse sensory experiences (see Gorman, 2013) or the ways that people have been subjugated within the psychiatric apparatus (see Perry et al., 2017).[5] Yet, from the onset, following impulses of curiosity, Tim was drawn to the edges of the so-called "mental health" scholarship, searching for the "what else"; the scholarship that is yet to come.

> Is my friendship with Stanley unusual? Is it unusual for someone like Stanley to be cared for and cared about? How is that so?

Social connectedness is considered the sense of belonging that comes from having mutual relationships with others in the community (Lee & Robbins, 2000). Psychiatrised people are commonly reported to have limited social networks (Buhagiar et al., 2020; Cleary et al., 2014; Siegel et al., 1994) and experience a constrained and regulated participation in society (Barlott, Shevellar, et al., 2020a; Cleary et al., 2014; Sayce, 2015). Their social relationships often consist primarily of paid care providers and family members (Padgett et al., 2008; Siegel et al., 1994; Wong et al., 2011). While research and practice in the mental health sector has focused primarily on providing services (Barlott, Shevellar, et al., 2020a), this project pursues a community-oriented alternative. Freely given relationships (i.e., non-therapeutic, non-institutional, non-paid, non-familial relationships), such as the relationship between Stanley and Tim, have been underexplored in the mental health literature, particularly for people who have been psychiatrised and ascribed the label of "serious mental illness" (Boydell et al., 2002; Bredewold et al., 2016; Buhagiar et al., 2020).

Edge Entanglements (and the project it is based on) was born of a desire to experience/explore freely given relationships as a (potentially) non-dominating, community-oriented way to craft new worlds with psychiatrised people. We begin this introductory chapter by situating ourselves in the discussion and introduce some of the theory that seeps into the crevices of our writing. Next, we describe aspects of our writing style and offer an overview of the chapters that follow.

Situating ourselves (and the fascists within)

> Since each of us was several, there was already quite a crowd.
>
> *(Deleuze & Guattari, 1987, p. 1)*

Edge Entanglements began as Tim's PhD thesis, under the supervision of Lynda Shevellar,[6] Merrill Turpin, and Jenny. As most PhD students can attest, the final product was not a sole authored thesis but rather an arrangement of co-constructed ideas. Tim's supervisors, friends, family, history, socio-cultural positioning, (and instant coffee) are a part of him, their desires interconnected with his own. These connections carry forward into this book, which has new entanglements – publishers, special series editors, a deeper connection with Mad Studies, snow.[7] Here, we offer a glimpse into ourselves and how we are situated within *Edge Entanglements*.

Jenny

This is how Tim introduced me in the acknowledgements of his PhD thesis: "Jenny, you came onto my team when I needed a theoretical push and a gentle nudge to be more experimental in my thinking and writing." Although a gentle nudge/push might have been what Tim needed, I am not sure this was always what I provided. One of my harshest comments was on the first draft of what is now this chapter:

> Tim, this is a decent start. But its (*sic*) still pretty rough. Could do with a few more read throughs. I have only pointed out some of the more glaring places were (*sic*) it gets clunky or grammatically problematic. At this point it is not up to your usual standard, but I imagine it will get there with a bit more attention … basically the structure is ok, but it needs more finesse.

As one of Tim's supervisors I could provide feedback without having to enact it nor even having to apply the same standards to myself. Michel Foucault (1984), in the preface to Gilles Deleuze and Félix Guattari's book *Anti-Oedipus*, speaks to the importance of not only identifying fascism in society, but "also the fascism in us all, in our heads and in our everyday behaviour, the fascism that causes us to love power, to desire the very thing that dominates and exploits us" (pp. xii–xiii). We speak more about the fascist within, but it surfaces here.

So here I am, a fascist-within-the-thesis-production, known in this part of my life as "Jenny." The way I (Jenny) describe myself as a researcher is that I'm a physiotherapist with a PhD in psychology who is now more of a sociologist. Just as importantly, I'm "Divo" a renegade queer activist, acrobat, and arts worker. Although I rarely discuss this, the creative and anti-authoritarian ways of being I (Divo) learned inform my research at least as much as my formal education. Most of my research has been about healthcare professionals – how can they (we) be more (post)human. My work is entangled in my multiple histories (Jenny <-> Divo) bringing the anti-authoritarian aspects of activism and creative endeavours into relation with the hierarchies (fascisms) of healthcare. Although Tim's work is not about health professionals directly, I was intrigued by it from the start – his research challenges typical hierarchical healthcare approaches. When I was invited onto the PhD team, and later this book, I was thrilled, not the least because of the postqualitative methodologies Tim was intending to dive into.

As a white settler living on stolen land (Australia), I am both learning and unlearning postqualitative research (and the posthumanist/new materialist theory that underpins it). Postqualitative and new materialist research has been a welcome move away from rigid methodologies and an incitement to think and act outside the usual Western humanist foci and assumptions. Yet their more-than-human theoretical underpinnings are entangled in whiteness, elitism, and colonisation. Even though these philosophies may claim a different conceptual history to Indigenous and non-white engagements with more-than-human agencies, it is not possible that this is the case. As Rosiek et al. (2020, p. 332) aptly state, "[t]he pervasive context of settler colonialism cannot help but influence both the practice of new materialist scholarship and its reception." By failing to acknowledge and address this issue, white scholars such as myself contribute to ongoing erasure of Indigenous knowledges (Rosiek et al., 2020) and critical race scholarship in the new materialisms. There have been calls to attend to this erasure and the racism that underpins it. Discussing the work of theorist Sylvia Wynter, Erasmus (2020, p. 56) puts it this way: "stories we live and dream by" (including, unfortunately, racism) make our worlds and we must act to make the world/humans/health differently. Tim and I must engage with these concerns as best we can to attend to the ethical responsibilities of our postqualitative stories and their world making. We attempt to do this work in the pages that follow by engaging with Black and Indigenous scholars and attending to the whiteness of our perspectives.

Tim

Since the early 2000s I have practised, researched, and taught in so-called "helping" professions, initially as a youth worker and addictions counsellor, and for most of my career as an occupational therapist. I have been largely motivated by compassion for people who are struggling or disadvantaged in some way. I wanted to "help" people and to have expertise in "helping" – it felt good to "make a difference" in people's lives. "Helping" can at times be blind to the underlying, entangled relations of power that produce the need for "help" (McLennan, 2014). As if speaking to me, Nigerian-American novelist Teju Cole (2012) said:

> His good heart does not always allow him to think constellationally. He does not connect the dots or see the patterns of power behind the isolated "disasters." All he sees are hungry mouths, and he … is putting food in those

mouths as fast as he can. All he sees is need, and he sees no need to reason out the need for the need.

(para. 9)

Cole (2012) discusses the ways people with privilege (such as myself) can reduce and essentialise complex social situations to some sort of rescue mission. My point is not to vilify or essentialise my past actions or others in helping roles, but rather to acknowledge the complexity of power relations enmeshed in the situations I have worked in. I have been professionally socialised to avoid getting too close to my clients, to maintain boundaries between practitioner and client – frequently reinforcing dominant binaries of healthy/sick, helper/helped, us/them. Looking back, I recognise that I have sometimes unintentionally treated "clients" as objects of therapy rather than members of the community and contributed to their ongoing othering and marginalisation. And to some extent, this continued into my PhD work, where I consistently referred to people in my writing using their diagnostic labels (e.g., "people diagnosed with serious mental illness"), which fails to trouble the sociopolitical forces of dominant mental health services that permeate the lives of psychiatrised people. I try to shift this as we produce this book.

There is a song from my youth that I have returned to over the course of this project called "I Want to Conquer the World" by Bad Religion (1989). The song speaks to the underlying paternalism in the actions of a well-meaning people in (Western) society, mentioning, for example, "brother Christian," "sister bleeding heart," "man of science," "mister diplomat," and "moral soldier." The chorus brings to the surface the dominating tendencies in seemingly virtuous pursuits:

> I want to conquer the world,
> Give all the idiots a brand new religion,
> Put an end to poverty, uncleanliness and toil,
> Promote equality in all of my decisions.
> I want to conquer the world.
> (Bad Religion, 1989)

Is there an underlying paternalism in my work? Undoubtedly, yes. As a white, male, English-speaking, heterosexual, cis-gendered, non-disabled settler (of both Canada and Australia) I am a multiplicity of fascists.[8] I have not been psychiatrised or have a lived experience with psychiatric systems, yet here I am writing a book on "mental health." In exploring the (potentially) transformative power of freely given relationships in the lives of psychiatrised people, one of our tasks is to continually check and re-check, resist and re-resist the entangled fascism within, in pursuit of an affirmative future.

You

We do not know who you are, dear reader. Only who we imagine you to be. You might be someone we already know (hello!) or someone we might meet one day (hello!). We imagine you could be someone with lived experience of psychiatric systems, a researcher, a health professional or … we really cannot know. But of course, we are writing with you constantly in mind. Shawn Wilson's (2008) work on Indigenous methodologies introduced us to discussions on the importance of relationality in research including what the relations with you, the reader, might be. We hope that you find ways to dwell with us for a while in the edge of the forest and engage with our thoughts in ways that work for you.

The edge of things

The edge of two things is a place of enchantment, uncertainty, and mystery – the threshold between dreaming and waking, the haunting twilight between day and night when previously crisp forms lose their clarity, or the outskirts of town where abandoned lots meet the treeline of the forest. The edge of the forest is a liminal space, a precarious space of shape-shifting shadows. It is where controlled environments designed by (perhaps particularly white) humans start to come undone.

> There is a snake in my backyard.
> I can't type as the sound of cicadas[9] encroaches.

In ecology, the coming together of two ecosystems produces an *edge effect* or a "zone of tension," with a high concentration and diversity of wildlife and vegetation (Harris, 1988, p. 330). We are far from being ecologists but find the phenomenon of edge effects to be a compelling figuration for thinking about the edge of things and the creativity that can emerge when different things come together. Félix Guattari's concept of transversality (discussed in more detail in Chapters 3 and 10) refers to the praxis of cutting across rigid relational lines and producing creative zones of tension between things that are typically discrete and separate. When there is a high coefficient of transversality (an openness to cutting across rigid relational lines) there is an increased potential for creative desires and social production. Throughout *Edge Entanglements*, we pursue transverse lines that zigzag at the interface of theory/method, theory/practice, health/illness, research/practice, sanity/insanity, and practitioner/client. Thinking with theory, we seek to trouble lines of segmentation, erode distinctions, and play at the in-between of freely given relationships.

Across this book, we engage with the work of French philosophers Deleuze and Guattari (and many others, particularly those working in Mad Studies, postcolonialism, and feminist new materialisms) for imagining and re-imagining complex social processes and relationships, resisting the fascism within and pursuing a non-dominating way forward in the mental health sector. Two of the concepts we draw from are *major* and *minor*, which Deleuze and Guattari (1987) use to describe relational hierarchies in modern Western society. The major are the things (human and non-human, physical and non-physical) in the social world that have status and significance – the dominant bodies, systems, and structures (including values and beliefs) that have authority and power – whereas the minor are the things that lack status and significance and are often excluded and marginalised (Deleuze & Guattari, 1987). Within the context of the mental health sector, health professionals, mental health wards/clinics/organisations, mainstream practices, and mental health policies would be considered major; so too are pervasive attitudes such as the view that people psychiatrised with "serious mental illness" are dangerous (see Corrigan et al., 2002; McGinty et al., 2014), as well as beliefs about what is considered "normal" thinking and behaviour. The minor are the differential forces that are frequently "cast aside, overlooked, or forgotten" (Manning, 2016, p. 1), such as people with "abnormal" or deviant thoughts and behaviours, often diagnosed and categorised (by the major apparatus) with "mental illness."

Even though the major has power and unquestioned authority in society, it is governed by rigid expectations and structures (Deleuze & Guattari, 1987). By contrast, the minor may occupy marginal spaces in society, but have creative and liberating potential (Deleuze & Guattari, 1987). "[T]he 'minor' is not so much a stable form existing in opposition to something major, but relentlessly transformative and inextricably relational" (Katz, 1996, p. 489). The concept of the minor is not only a theory of the margins, but also a theory for what is less stable and susceptible to transformation. Thinking in terms of edge effects in ecology, major and minor are not a binary of two different ecosystems; the minor is also the asignifying and diffuse edge that the major desperately tries to control (see Chapter 2). Influenced by Deleuze and Guattari's work and Katz's (1996) pursuit of a minor theory, we desire to dangle at the edge of minor scholarship – a place of uncertainty, mystery, and creative experimentation. We want to be attentive to instabilities and transformations, and to minor movements in freely given relationships and how learnings might inform practices in the mental health sector.

Writing style and book structure

Pursuing the edge of things in our theory and analytic approach, our writing style and structure deviate somewhat from typical scholarship. The latter half of the book (particularly Chapters 5 and 7–10) is mainly written in a narrative style, at times resembling a piece of fiction more than conventional empirical chapters. We sometimes employ a writing style reminiscent of magical realism (see Arva, 2008; Coulter, 2020; Laws, 2017), invoking visual imagery to playfully bring a story to life. The imagery in magical realism is not a representation or a metaphor of what is real; rather, the imagery *is* what is real (Coulter, 2020; Laws, 2017). For example, we use Deleuze and Guattari's (1987) conceptual personae of a sorcerer throughout Chapters 7–10; she amplifies minor movements that are happening in the events. Most of the time the sorcerer or sorcery is embedded in the main text as we discuss aspects of freely given relationships. However, at times we have written short "fictional" accounts of the sorcerer without direct relation to the story being told, as if the sorcerer is in a parallel or unseen dimension. The formatting for these other-dimensional narratives is always right justified and italicised, such as this shortened example from Chapter 9:

At the edge of the forest the sorcerer paces. A snarling pack of wolves froth within her, like fire, burning in her chest, crawling up her throat and to the tip of her tongue…

Another formatting variation is the textboxes peppered intermittently throughout the book, as if something/someone were interrupting the narrator as they tell a story. Sometimes these take the form of actual interruptions that occurred during Tim's interviews with participants (e.g., a phone call), and at other times they are our own thoughts (e.g., a flashback). Here is an abbreviated example of a textbox in Chapter 7:

> I'm (Tim) having a flashback to riding in an outreach van in 2001 in city in western Canada. I was a student at the time doing an eight-week fieldwork for my diploma in Child and Youth Care – our shift would start at 8pm and run until about 2am…

The book can be read in order; however, in a number of places we offer alternatives for readers, such as an invitation to read Chapter 3 before Chapter 2, which would spur an additional theoretical interpretation of the background provided in Chapter 2. These instances of non-linear, "choose your own adventure" invitations are identified by endnotes. The book *can* be read front to back, in a linear fashion, but the reader can feel free to follow the lines of flight offered throughout. And, as you begin this book, we invite you to consider reading the Afterword before moving on to other chapters.

We have written this book collectively and use the first-person "we" and "our" throughout. But there are also times where the narrative is about Tim's personal encounters with people in the project (particularly in Chapters 7–9). In these instances we oscillate to first-person "I" with (Tim) in brackets.

Overview of the book

In partnership with APTB, a small community mental health organisation, *Edge Entanglements* explores freely given relationships (also referred to as "ally relationships" by APTB) between psychiatrised people and people in the community. Engaging with the philosophy of Deleuze and Guattari (and other theorists), this book attends to the disruptive and transformative processes in these relationships and the mental health sector. Over a four-month period, Tim spent in-depth time with four pairs of people, getting to know them through conversation and observation, and visually mapping the connections in their lives. Understanding these relationships as a Deleuzio-Guattarian ally assemblage[10] (complex interrelated and interconnected webs of sociomaterial), we wanted to explore: What are these assemblages like? How do they work? What do they do/produce? Using a postqualitative, cartographic approach, *Edge Entanglements* maps the composition and transformative processes of ally assemblages.

In Chapter 2, we use the Deleuze and Guattari's concepts of assemblage and deterritorialisation, along with the work of Mad, postcolonial, queer, and feminist scholars, to interrogate two pervasive and taken-for-granted assemblages in mental health: social inclusion and recovery. We consider how dominant (major) and transformative (minor) forces are entangled in the mental health sector and scholarship. Mental health assemblages have largely been dominated by institutional (major) mechanisms of authority and ongoing processes of control that have constrained the lives of psychiatrised people. We suggest that ongoing, disruptive movements on the margins of the mental health sector – such as freely given relationships – have transformative potential for psychiatrised people.

Building on some of the concepts introduced in Chapter 2, Chapter 3 outlines the Deleuzio-Guattarian concepts of *transversality, major* and *minor, becoming* (and *becoming-minor*), *transversality*, and the *rhizome*. We engage with these concepts throughout the book as they provide a useful way to think about inequities/marginalisation, challenge dominant ways of thinking/doing, and consider transformative processes in freely given relationships and the mental health sector. We conclude with a description of a cartographic approach (also referred to as rhizomatic cartography), the research processes, and analysis used in our postqualitative work. If desired, we invite readers to consider reading Chapter 3 prior to Chapter 2 as it offers a more detailed description of some of theory taken up in Chapter 2.

In Chapter 4, we outline our formation of a research assemblage that is entangled with our postqualitative approach and the remaining chapters of the book. We navigate the intersecting lines of connection in our community relationships/partnerships and the assembling of sociomaterial bodies for the collection/analysis of data. We also discuss some of the challenges we faced along the way – ethics applications, institutions, training – and how these do not always facilitate the production of postqualitative work. This chapter offers a comprehensive overview of the research project, including an exploration of the more-than-human relational affects that produced our in-process research assemblage. The chapter also includes a discussion about navigating institutional ethical clearance in postqualitative inquiry.

Chapter 5 then offers a detailed exploration of cartographic postqualitative processes, the *doing* of thinking with theory. We explore the affects of analysis, offering insights into what it means when St. Pierre et al. (2016) state, "our best advice is to read and read and read and attend to the encounters in our experiences that demand our attention" (p. 106). Rather than taking a systematic approach, we show how we entangled with theory to creatively experiment with data and the differential processes that occurred. We map the lines of movement and processes of social production and micropolitics in our more-than-human research assemblages. Our experimentation is centred on a research interview from another project that didn't "fit," and our cartography surfaced some of the ways interviews can be despotic. These learnings informed *Edge Entanglements* and our cartography of ally assemblages.

In Chapter 6, we commence our micropolitical mapping of ally assemblages. We provide an overview of the four ally assemblages we entangle with throughout the remainder of the book. Written primarily as four vignettes, we draw readers into the entangled lives of the ally relationships (who chose their own pseudonyms) – we meet Krispy and Chips (who connected when Krispy was living in a long-term secure psychiatric unit), Alan and Jack (who met when Jack was Alan's tutor in an adult literacy program), Carol and Julie (who met when Julie was a social work student working with Carol), and Batman and Robin (a dynamic duo that met when Batman was houseless and Robin was an outreach worker). This chapter provides an initial foray or entry point into these four assemblages. We try not to essentialise each into a set of key points or patterns that transcend each assemblage. Rather, we aim to remain amidst each assemblage as we introduce their elements, movements, and processes. This chapter sets the scene for the three cartographic chapters that follow.

Entering more deeply into the liminal space of the edge of the forest, Chapter 7 maps the territories of ally assemblages. We use the Deleuzian concept of *active/reactive force relations* and *becoming-reactive*, along with Erin Manning's concept of *minor gesture*, to entangle with the territories of ally assemblages. We begin by exploring the production of cramped spaces in the mental health sector and the entanglement of sociomaterial (human and non-human) in ally assemblages in our project. We then illustrate how reactive forces (such as those of psychiatrised people) have the potential to disrupt the dominating power of active forces through a process of becoming-reactive. The becoming-reactive of ally assemblages softened their relational territories (such as professional boundaries), producing a supple hierarchy between an ally and friend that was non-dominating and (potentially) transformative. Mapping an enticing and novel application of thinking with theory, we demonstrate becoming-reactive as a process produced through transverse movements and the collision of differing forces at the edge of the forest.

Gaining momentum from the previous chapter (Chapter 7), Chapter 8 surfaces the becoming in ally assemblages and conjures the conceptual personae of a sorcerer, the incorporeal and affirmative force produced in/among ally assemblages. Led by the sorcerer, we interrogate how these relationships were characterised by reciprocity, but more so how aspects of non-reciprocity had transformative (and magical) power. Flows of generosity opened new possibilities in the lives of psychiatrised people in this project. The flexible hierarchy of ally assemblages produced an affirmative (and collective) force of what we refer to as "careless generosity" and "care-full generosity." We conceptualise the former as gratuitous generosity that disregards convention and is not interested in payment or acknowledgement, and the latter as being full of intention, vigilantly working to bring benefit to another. Our conceptual development of careless and care-full generosity offers a contribution to the theory and practice of "care" and the relational ethics of "caring." The becoming of ally assemblages is also the production of kinship, a collective and unconventional union of (un)family that is produced rather than inherited. We conclude this chapter by mapping the reterritorialisations of ally assemblages, drawing attention to how these assemblages have changed/transformed over time.

A Deleuzio-Guattarian conceptualisation of desire is expansive; it is not (only) a human need or want but an(y) vital force, human or non-human, that propels creativity. In Chapter 9, we map the creative impulses of desire that are entangled with the production of affirmative forces described in Chapter 8. Drawing from the concepts of *desiring-machines* and *desire*, and the work of Simone Bignall and Rosi Braidotti with these concepts, we explore how desire both constructs and is socially constructed in ally assemblages. We suggest that desire in ally assemblages is at the threshold of becoming – it triggers/catalyses transformative flows in these relationships. Our analysis surfaces the ways that our community partner (a small community mental health organisation) operated at the edge of the forest and created space for desiring-machines to take flight. The discussion culminates in an illustration of how ally assemblages produce a particular form of Deleuzio-Guattarian desire, a desire for a people to come. While the cramped spaces and arborescence of the (major) mental health sector discussed throughout this book are imbued with disquieting and constricted affects, ally assemblages are dripping with joyful and collective affection for a people to come.

In Chapter 10, infused by the edge of the forest movements in Chapters 7–9, we engage with the micropolitics of allyship in the mental health sector. We fold our cartography into the scholarly landscape of befriending practices and allyship in the field of mental health. Ally assemblages in this project flow in an in-between space that is neither discretely befriending practice nor allyship. Using the concept of transversality, we consider ally assemblages in relation to emerging literature on accompliceship. Bearing in mind Guattari's "myth of togetherness," we suggest that allyship in mental health is an ongoing micropolitical process of becoming-complicit in ally assemblages. Allyship in these relationships involved ongoing movement towards taking on the struggle on another as one's own. This enticingly engages transversality in productive work with mental health research and practice, inviting a radical re-working of allyship and revolutionary practice processes.

As you read on in Chapter 2 (and throughout this book), we grapple with some of the historical and sociopolitical forces entangled with the everyday experiences of psychiatrised people and consider what else might be possible.

Notes

1 Tim is originally from Canada and moved to Brisbane, Australia, in 2014. Stanley enjoyed reminiscing with someone who was familiar with the areas he has travelled to.
2 For more details on Tim's partnership with A Place to Belong, see Chapter 4.
3 Stanley died in late 2017. He had a heart attack while out for dinner with friends.
4 Throughout the book, we have chosen to use the identity-first language of "psychiatrised people" in place of other identifications such as service-user, consumer, survivor, or diagnostic labels (e.g., people diagnosed with serious mental illness). This language choice centres the ways that the dominant mental health apparatus has imposed categorisations on people in the form of psychiatric labels. Our choice is informed by the field of Mad Studies and decades of lived experience activism and organising in the Mad movement beginning in the 1970s (see Beresford & Russo, 2022; Shimrat, 1997). See Chapter 2 where we engage more directly with the social processes in the mental health sector.

5   These are topics discussed throughout Chapter 2 and unravel throughout the book.
6   Lynda co-authors the Afterword, which grapples with some of the *knots* and *entanglements* that cut through this book.
7   Prior to writing this book, Tim relocated back to Canada from Australia.
8   "(T)he self is only a threshold, a door, a becoming between two multiplicities" (Deleuze & Guattari, 1987, p. 291).
9   An insect common in Australia, particularly in the summer months. Their call can be so deafening that it can be difficult to have conversation. It might even washout the sounds of an airplane flying overhead.
10 The concept of assemblage(s) is explored and defined in Chapters 2 and 3.

2

DESTABILISING MAJOR MENTAL HEALTH APPROACHES

Caught in the winds of dominant social forces, psychiatrised people are often funnelled to the margins of society. With little room to manoeuvre, their trajectory is frequently controlled and their participation constrained. In this chapter, we unsettle some of the dominant processes, namely recovery-oriented practices and efforts towards social inclusion, that are entangled in the lives of psychiatrised people (and those with experiences of trauma and distress). We seek a more liberating way forward.[1]

Before moving on, we want to do a brief historical excavation and surface some of the sociopolitical threads that are interrelated with the present-day experiences of people psychiatrised with "mental illness" (see Sayce, 2015). Following the so-called enlightenment in the 18th century, "mental illness" was understood as deviance from rational thought – in the "age of reason," people who deviated from the "norm" were viewed as morally corrupt and ethically flawed (Roberts, 2007). Echoing this view, the medical community through the mid-1800s diagnosed people with "moral insanity" which referred to the status of "depraved or perverted" minds, those whose "power of self-government is lost" (Dr J.C. Prichard in 1835, cited in Ozarin, 2001, para. 3). In the late 1800s, moral insanity was recategorised as psychopathic inferiority, a diagnosis believed to be an illness as well as an inferior moral state (Lewis, 1974). While most of these early diagnostic terms are no longer in use, the underlying assumption that psychiatrised people lack credibility and are morally suspect persists today (Sayce, 2015).

Throughout most of the 19th and 20th centuries, psychiatrised people experienced widespread involuntary confinement in institutions (Mayes & Horwitz, 2005) and forced medication adherence (Sayce, 2015). Institutions quarantined the "mentally ill" away from "normal" society. A cascade of factors (including public enquiries, government policy changes, civil rights movements, and advances in

DOI: 10.4324/9781003286486-2

psychotherapeutic medications) led to the deinstitutionalisation of psychiatrised people into the community in the 1960s, 1970s, and 1980s (Mayes & Horwitz, 2005). While deinstitutionalised, psychiatrised people remained tightly controlled through continued forced medication adherence, coercive community therapy, involuntary commitment, and ongoing monitoring (Schutt, 2016; Perry et al., 2017). Deinstitutionalised psychiatric patients often entered communities that were fearful of "mental illness" and ill-equipped to offer support (Hazelton, 2005). Without adequate support in the community, many deinstitutionalised adults ended up unemployed, houseless, struggling with substance use, and confined by the criminal justice system (Schutt, 2016). This chapter (and book) grapples with some of these historical and sociopolitical forces that are woven into the contemporary social fabric of the mental health sector and the everyday experiences of psychiatrised people.

Sociologists have tended to view "mental illness" as a label attributed to the behaviours, thoughts, and sensory experiences of people that deviate from societal norms and values (Bessa, 2012). "Mental illness" in contemporary Western society is primarily identified and categorised according to diagnostic criteria found in the Diagnostic and Statistical Manual of Mental Disorders (DSM), developed by the American Psychiatric Association (Bolton, 2008), and the International Classification of Diseases (ICD), developed by the World Health Organization (Clark et al., 2017). When a person's behaviours, thoughts, and sensory experiences deviate from societal norms in a way that is considered to seriously impair their "social functioning" (e.g., scoring below 60 on the Global Assessment of Functioning) it is categorised with "serious mental illness" (Kessler et al., 2003). Psychiatric diagnoses most commonly associated with "serious mental illness" include schizophrenia, schizoaffective disorder, bipolar disorder, major depression, and some instances of anxiety disorders (Ruggeri et al., 2000). The category of "serious mental illness" demarcates and pathologises those who are decidedly outside of what is considered "normal." There are instances in this book where we use the term "serious mental illness" categorically and acknowledge that this categorisation is one of the ways in which psychiatrised people are controlled and othered. Through this chapter, we aim to rethink dominant approaches in the mental health sector, utilising the theory of philosophers Deleuze and Guattari (along with Mad, postcolonial, queer, and feminist scholars) to envision transformational possibilities for psychiatrised people.

Deleuze and Guattari, and

Gilles Deleuze and Félix Guattari began collaborating in 1969, initially authoring a two-book project titled *Capitalism and Schizophrenia* (Colebrook, 2002). These books offered critiques of capitalism, modernity, structuralism, and psychoanalysis, providing a complex set of concepts useful for analysing the social world. Scholars have identified that rigorous engagement with philosophy and theory such as theirs has enabled researchers to think differently about issues, creating opportunities for social transformation (Mazzei & McCoy, 2010). While Deleuze and Guattari's work has been explored extensively in social, cultural, educational, and feminist theory and in the fields of art, film, and media studies, there is room for further engagement with this work in mental health research and practice and also in the field of Mad Studies.[2]

To analyse the dominant approaches in the management of psychiatrised people, this chapter employs Deleuzio-Guattarian concepts of *assemblage*, *major* and *minor*, and *deterritorialisation*. The idea of *assemblages* is used to conceptualise the interconnected nature of social formations, *major* and *minor* is used to examine social inequities and stratifications within assemblages, and finally, *deterritorialisation* provides a way to think about transformative processes. In order to draw out some of the sociopolitical elements of these concepts and turn our attention to non-Western and non-dominant perspectives (that are often overlooked), we have incorporated the work of Mad (e.g., Irit Shimrat, Rachel Gorman, and Peter Beresford), postcolonial (e.g., Frantz Fanon and Achille Mbembe), and queer and feminist (e.g., Jasbir Puar and Sara Ahmed) scholars. Following a discussion of the theory, we then use theory to think about two dominant mental illness approaches: recovery and social inclusion. Consistent with our Deleuzio-Guattarian theoretical orientation, for the remainder of this chapter we refer to the dominant approaches in the mental health sector as *mental illness assemblages*.

Assemblage

Social formations and processes are non-discreet and are made up of complex webs of interconnection, which Deleuze and Guattari refer to as assemblages. They assert that no single thing (be it human or non-human, physical or non-physical) can be defined unto itself; rather, all sociomaterial is entangled in a complex arrangement of interrelated parts (Deleuze & Guattari, 1987). No singular subject (e.g., an individual) can be understood in isolation "because a whole other story is vibrating within it" (Deleuze & Guattari, 1986, p. 17). Assemblages are continually changing as webs of interconnection fluctuate over time – their complexity grows as each is also a part of other mutually influential assemblages. The concept of assemblages acknowledges the "irreducible complexity" that characterises the social world (DeLanda, 2006, p. 6). Assemblages are not understood simply through the identification of interrelated parts; rather, they are understood by exploring processes of social production (Deleuze & Guattari, 1987). In other words, it is not enough to simply name the parts of an assemblage. It is the manner by which they are created, how they work, and what they do that is of interest. Describing the anti-structural qualities of assemblages, Puar (2017) outlines:

> assemblages allow us to attune to movements, intensities, emotions, energies, affectivities, and textures as they inhabit events, spatiality, and corporealities. … Assemblages are thus crucial conceptual tools that allow us to acknowledge

and comprehend power beyond disciplinary regulatory models, where "particles, and not parts, recombine, where forces, and not categories, clash" (Parisi, 2004, pp. 37, 215).

The notion of assemblage offers a way to weave and unweave relations of power, to diagram movements rather than name discrete mechanisms and identities. The figuration of an assemblage is the construction of a posthuman body – "What defines a body is this relation between dominant and dominated forces. Every relationship of force constitutes a body – whether it is chemical, biological, social or political" (Deleuze, 2006, p. 40). A (posthuman) body/assemblage is not defined by its organs (e.g., characteristics, structures, categories, and identities) but by affects and capacities for affect, relational movements and clash of forces.[3] *Edge Entanglements* joins conversations such as those developed by McLeod (2017) and Duff (2014), which draw from the concept of assemblage to explicate how health and wellbeing are inseparable from the processes of everyday life. For instance in their work on voice hearing, psychopathology (Blackman, 2011), and depression (McLeod, 2014), Blackman and McLeod consider how the assemblages of a person's life contribute to the in-process assembling of mental (ill)health (see also Blackman, 2012; Blackman & Venn, 2010; McLeod, 2017). Past experiences of trauma, socioeconomic circumstances, family situation, discrimination, physiological factors, and mental health systems are entangled in the production of bodily (and diagnosed) experiences. Assemblages are fluid and constantly changing – the mental illness assemblages analysed in this chapter are not static but an evolving arrangement of power, systems of thought, ideas, environments, things, and people, as will be shown later in our discussion.

Major and minor

The Deleuzio-Guattarian concepts of the major and the minor are useful for understanding power relations, social hierarchies, and our analysis of mental health assemblages. Before discussing these concepts, we would like to acknowledge the common use of dualisms in the work of Deleuze and Guattari, and draw attention to how they differ from modernist dualisms (e.g., healthy/sick). While Deleuze and Guattari frequently generate and discuss dualistic concepts (e.g., major/minor, molar/molecular, striated/smooth, active/reactive), they do so to problematise them, they work and rework them, they consider how dualisms and the boundaries between them can be disrupted. They play at the space in the middle of the dualism, at the threshold of power relations between the two where there is potential to fray the territory that separates them (Lundy, 2013). The major and minor are one of these dualisms, used to explore the organisation, structure, and significance of things (human and non-human, physical and non-physical) in modern Western society (Deleuze & Guattari, 1987). The major are all things that have status and significance at any given time, whereas the minor are things that lack status and significance. A parallel can be drawn to major and minor scales in music, where major scales/melodies are considered the "default" and minor scales/melodies are considered the variation (Halpern et al., 2008). Manning (2016) reminds us that "neither minor nor the major is fixed in advance. The major is a structural tendency that organizes itself according to predetermined definitions of value" (p. 1). The major, or majoritarian, are the dominant bodies, species, behaviours, objects, beliefs, and institutions that form the largely unquestioned authority in society (Deleuze & Guattari, 1987). The major is that which is established, clearly understood, and considered to be "normal"; it is the standard against which others are measured (Braidotti, 2011). A quality of the major is the propensity to categorise, code, and dominate things relative to the norm (Deleuze & Guattari, 1987).[4]

While writing this section, I (Tim) attended a focus group on "sense of safety" with Dr Johanna Lynch (see Lynch, 2020). Johanna mentioned meeting a tall male doctor that reported always feeling confident and safe – Johanna invited focus group participants to share their thoughts on why some people have an unwavering sense of safety. That night I was reading a couple of books with my kids before dinner, one was about ocean animals and another about dinosaurs. Both books mentioned apex predators (e.g., Great White Shark and T Rex) and how there were very few threats to them – they were generally "safe." This made me think of the tall male doctor Johanna spoke of and also of the major. We might think of this doctor (and the major) as an apex predator, where there are very few things to threaten their sense of safety. The intersection of diverse identity characteristics are entangled in one's sense of safety – race, gender, sexuality, ability, class, etc. In a way, that male doctor *is* the threat; he is the norm to which others are othered. He is (in a conceptual sense) the dominating man in domestic violence, the man that undermines the perspectives of women (and other gendered people) in the workplace, the upper class that benefits from the exploitation of the lower class, the heteronormative family structure that delegitimises other forms of "family," the diagnostician that marks psychiatric abnormality.

As the major codes and creates hierarchies, it organises binaries and oppositions: the norm (major) versus that which is other to the norm (minor). Examples of major binaries include man/woman, rich/poor, healthy/sick, straight/gay, right/wrong. The major privileges sameness, that which is normal, and deprivileges difference, that which is abnormal. "Man" is major; there is an ideal man, one that is strong, sane, intelligent, dominant, and successful (Colebrook, 2002); the ideal man is economically productive, non-disabled, white, heterosexual, property owning, and English speaking (Braidotti, 2011). In contrast, the minor is the site of difference, that which is considered "other," such as those whose mental health is determined by the major apparatus to be outside the norm – the "mentally ill." Deleuze and Guattari (1987) argue that, in a majoritarian society, people are ordered and organised categorically, each having greater or lesser value than others depending on their positioning in relation to the "norm." Major binaries and categorisations are not merely descriptive labels, but rank according to value and authority, to the benefit of the major. Adding political immediacy to how the major constructs the "other," Achille Mbembe (2001) describes the "other" as "not simply *not to be like* (in the sense of being non-identical or being-other); it is also *not to be at all* (non-being)" (p. 4, original emphasis).[5] The materiality of the "other" has a certain stickiness – Ahmed (2015) describes how, through repetition, signs, objects, and emotions become sticky. Through ongoing social processes, the "goodness" of the major and "otherness" of the minor becomes intrinsic, and interrelated emotions become entangled with things like "mental illness." For example, a male psychiatrist is intrinsically a credible authority and stirs (for some) emotions of confidence and trust, whereas a psychiatric patient intrinsically lacks credibility and stirs (for some) emotions of fear and distrust.

In addition to binaries and systems of categorisation, major assemblages are organised according to linear normative processes – straight, predictable, and expected pathways. For example: attending high school – getting further qualifications – having a career/trade; or boy meets girl – they date – boy proposes to girl – they marry – they have a family. These underlying habitual normative processes construct a social order that serves dominant interests – such how the heteronormative family structure[6] (and associated processes from which it is produced) serves patriarchal and capitalist interests. But these linear processes are difficult to comply with for many. The minor, the "others" in society, often struggle to follow (or reject) legitimate or expected pathways, occupying what Deleuze and Guattari (1986) refer to as the cramped spaces of society, where movement can be difficult and struggle is commonplace. Ahmed (2015) describes it in terms of comfort – normativity does not fit comfortably for those of us who are othered. If the minor is expected to traverse the expected path, it hurts. When spaces, places, and processes are reworked, there is a sense of relief – even celebration. But these transformative places are fragile. Akin to Fanon's (2004) postcolonial description of the colonised's sector, cramped spaces are a "disreputable place inhabited by disreputable people. … a sector on its knees" (p. 4). In contrast, "The colonist's sector is built to last, all stone and steel. It's a sector of lights and paved roads, where the trash cans constantly overflow with strange and wonderful garbage, undreamed-of leftovers" (p. 4). As will be discussed further in this chapter, it can be difficult for psychiatrised people to follow linear, normative pathways (e.g., expected pathways to mental health recovery) and often find themselves in the cramped spaces of society. Yet, it is not simply that psychiatrised people "fail" to follow normative pathways; the *other* pathway in many ways *is* the normative pathway and a product of the major apparatus. For example: person experiences distress and hears voices – person sees a psychiatrist – person is pathologised and marked "mentally ill" – person takes medications under the gaze of a mental health team – person is monitored and at times confined – person is marginalised, struggles to find gainful employment, experiences houselessness, etc. David Reville (2010), a Mad scholar, describes how he was confined for a year and a half when he was in university; on discharge the vocational rehabilitation team got him a job as a pot washer in a university residence hall. He described how the message was, "my aspirations needed to be adjusted downward" (Reville, 2010, 4:40).

The cramped spaces produce distress. Psychiatrised people not only find themselves in the cramped spaces because of their "mental health" differences or diversity – experiences of distress are also produced through macropolitical injustice. Colonisation, racism, heterosexism, transphobia, poverty, and houselessness (to name a few) are all entangled manifestations of normative major dominance. The stigma and discrimination (and cramped spaces) experienced by minorities and marginalised people "negatively impacts emotional well-being" and "compound(s) their experiences of mental distress" (Morrow, 2013, p. 326; see also Gorman, 2013). *Edge Entanglements* is not intended to analyse mental (ill)health, yet we want to trouble it's givenness and the power relations that give way to the "analytic of mental illness" (Gorman, 2013, p. 269). Our conceptual use of major and minor is immanently political, grounded in our desire to unsettle the dominance of major over minor.

The major and the apparatus of capture

One of the characteristics of the major is its desire to capture, absorb, and appropriate the minor: this is known as the *apparatus of capture* (Deleuze & Guattari, 1987). An apparatus of capture is any mechanism that seeks to territorialise the differential minor within the rigid segmentation of the major (Deleuze & Guattari, 1987); for example, psychiatrised people have a long history of being categorised and controlled (captured) by those in authority. Mental health classification systems such as the DSM or ICD operate as an apparatus of capture, both outlining criteria for "normal" experience and capturing those who cross the threshold into "abnormality" through pathologisation. The apparatus of capture grabs onto things that are outside of the norm (minor), and codes and overcodes them within the major (Deleuze & Guattari, 1986) – the "mentally ill" are coded with diagnostic labels, and then some are overcoded with labels such as "serious mental illness" or "concurrent disorders," which further orders the "mentally ill" in a hierarchy. The major "trolls the margins, defining, categorising and stratifying the unexplained" (Barlott et al., 2017, p. 526).

The apparatus of capture operates as a mechanism of social control, where interrelated and overlapping components within an assemblage forcefully swirl in unison, enveloping the minor. This forms what Deleuze and Guattari (1987) refer to as a *machine of resonance* (p. 248). For example, the constrained social participation and cramped spaces inhabited by psychiatrised people could be analysed as the product of interrelated major forces: the authority of healthcare professionals, expectations of medication adherence (and altered psychosocial function due to medication side effects), discrimination in the community/media, lack of employment (and general lack of access to economic capital), insecure housing (typically in the form of subsidised housing), and therapeutic nature of relationships (and lack of non-paid, non-therapeutic relationships). It could also be said that those within the major, those who are a part of the machine of resonance, may be unknowingly appropriated as agents of capture (e.g., psychiatrists), albeit rewarded (e.g., status, wealth, power) for participation in the apparatus of capture. Once captured (such as through adherence to mental health treatment), the minor "receive no adequate expression by becoming elements of the majority," only subjugation and control (Deleuze & Guattari, 1987, p. 547). While the most common relationship between the major and the minor is that of the dominant and the dominated, this is not a necessary or fixed relation – the dominance of the major and subservience of the minor can be disrupted, giving way to an affirmative future for people that are othered within major assemblages. We argue that, for practices to have transformative outcomes, there must be reflexive awareness of the major's propensity to act as an apparatus of capture, and a welcoming of disruptive minoring processes that unsettle major forces and segmentation. To this end, we employ Deleuze and Guattari's understanding of the process of deterritorialisation, whereby assemblages disrupt the apparatus of capture, break away from the rigid territories of the major, and transform into something different.

Deterritorialisation

Up to now, we have not spent much time offering an affirmative reading of the minor. As will be unfolded throughout *Edge Entanglements* (and this chapter), minor assemblages and minoring processes offer great hope. Deterritorialisation is one of these minoring processes where there is a break from the rigid territories of the major, forming what Deleuze and Guattari (1987) refer to as a line of flight. A line of flight (also conceptualised as a line of escape) is where the "system breaks down, or becomes transformed into something else" (Patton, 2001, p. 1153); it "manifests as something distinctly different, an 'intensity' that defies representation and categorisation" (Potts, 2004, p. 20). Deterritorialisation creates new possibilities and creative potential as the minor breaks from the confines of major segmentation (Deleuze & Guattari, 1987). Transformative processes do not necessarily involve the minor attaining power over the major, "when the weak triumph it is not by forming a greater force but by separating force from what it can do" (Deleuze, 2006, p. 59). Speaking to this notion of "separating force from what it can do," Bogue (1997) compares deterritorialisation to how a minor melody in music can "destabilise the harmonic order of a major key" (p. 105). Deterritorialising, minor processes disrupt and destabilise the rigid lines of segmentation of the major, transforming them into supple lines that accommodate and celebrate difference.

Deterritorialisation is a way to disrupt categorical and normative identities, disrupt systems of dominance and hierarchical control, and form a line of flight away from the major. The "cramped spaces" of the minor vibrate with creative and transformative potential, but this potential is not the "capacity to act within the stratified system of the majority, rather it is the capacity to act against or deterritorialise from the denumerable majority" (Barlott et al., 2017, p. 528). Processes of transformation occur when there is a rupture in the stratification of the major, forming differential lines of escape that evade the apparatus of capture and assemble new territories (reterritorialising) away from the major (Deleuze & Guattari, 1987). And it is to this idea that our discussion now turns.

Mental illness assemblages

Turning specifically to the mental health sector, we are interested in analysing the processes and movements of major assemblages, their apparatus of capture, and deterritorialising minor processes that generate new possibilities. The aim of our analysis is to look for ruptures, to illuminate possible lines of flight towards more dynamic, creative, and liberating minor assemblages. Our analysis focuses on two pervasive, "taken-for-granted" concepts in mental health work: *recovery* (including *social recovery*, *clinical recovery*, and *recovery-oriented practice*) and *social inclusion*. Both recovery and social inclusion are relatively recent assemblages, each emerging (and taking over) from assemblages of institutionalisation and biomedical psychiatric control starting in the 1960s and 1970s. Given that the context of our research and practice is in Australia, at times our analysis focuses on specific Australian examples (e.g., recovery-oriented policy). However, these examples are likely generalisable across other contexts that have focussed on recovery and social inclusion. In disrupting these major assemblages, we mainly discuss policies and practices in Western, Anglophone countries. However, at least in part due to the ongoing colonising practices of Western healthcare, there are elements of these concepts unfolding in policy and practice in much of the world, including South Africa (Bila, 2019), Latin America (Mascayano et al., 2019), China (Tse et al., 2013), and India (Kermode et al., 2021).

Recovery assemblage

Recovery is considered the most common approach in contemporary mental health practice and policy across Western countries such as Australia, Canada, England, Ireland, New Zealand, and the United States (McWade, 2016). Yet, despite the hegemony of contemporary recovery-oriented practice (in the West) and its growing influence in the majority world, there is both a lack of consensus about what the concept of recovery means and how it is best achieved (Sayce, 2015). Most definitions can be separated into two different (but entangled) assemblages: (1) clinical recovery and (2) social recovery (Davidson & Roe, 2007; Sayce, 2015; Stickley et al., 2016). These are "two very different forces" (Davidson & Roe, 2007, p. 460) – clinical recovery has been primarily a major assemblage, dominated by the apparatus of capture and led by mental health service providers, and social recovery has been primarily a minor assemblage, with prominent deterritorialising processes led by psychiatric survivors (see Morrow, 2013). Despite distinct differences, these two recovery assemblages formed around the same point in history and are inextricably linked. Thus, following an initial analysis of both social and clinical recovery, our discussion shifts to a critical analysis of contemporary "recovery-oriented practice" as an entanglement of both forms of recovery.

Clinical recovery

Clinical recovery acts as an apparatus of the major, closely interconnected with psychiatric diagnosis and treatment. Beginning in the late 1960s, through rigorous research and evaluation, the medical and scientific community began to discern that the "mentally ill" had the potential to recover from the symptoms of their "mental illness" (Carpenter & Kirkpatrick, 1988). Clinical recovery was firmly situated within psychiatry, conceptualising recovery as the elimination of symptoms, as determined by the psychiatrist and mental health team (Davidson & Roe, 2007). Clinical recovery reaffirms a normal/abnormal binary, asserts mental health services as a centralised axis of power, and establishes fixed linear recovery processes – but it also deterritorialises "mental illness" from its rigid stratification as a permanent (and progressive) disability (Davidson & Roe, 2007). Clinical recovery reterritorialises mental illness as a medical condition that a person can recover from. The individual, through dedication, perseverance, self-management, personal responsibility, and lifelong adherence to medication, can reintegrate into society, be independent, and free from symptoms (Silverstein & Bellack, 2008; Vandekinderen et al., 2012). Clinical recovery means becoming more "normal" (symptom free), less of a burden on the state (minimal, yet ongoing use of mental health services and less reliant on financial supports), and ultimately becoming a productive member of society (Davidson et al., 2010; Davidson & Roe, 2007; Vandekinderen et al., 2012). This reterritorialised assemblage remains a major configuration that serves (and is controlled by) dominant and neoliberal interests.

Social recovery

Social recovery emerged from the minor voices of psychiatrised people (in the West). Growing out of the civil rights movement, people categorised with "serious mental illness" sought to reclaim their lives, recover from the stigma associated with a diagnosis of mental illness, and recover from mandatory treatment (Davidson & Roe, 2007; Deegan, 1988). This is commonly referred to as the recovery movement, a grassroots social justice movement led by survivors of social marginalisation, institutionalisation, and harmful psychiatric treatment (Davidson & Roe, 2007; Morrow, 2013). The recovery movement emerged in the North America during the 1960s and 1970s; it was in the 1980s and 1990s that the recovery movement gained the most momentum (Ostrow & Adams, 2012; Piat & Sabetti, 2012) and quickly spread to other mainly Western countries (see Oades & Anderson, 2012). While recovery-oriented practice (see next section) has become a common approach in non-Western countries (see Bila, 2019; Mascayano et al., 2019; Tse et al., 2013; Kermode et al., 2021), the recovery movement was predominantly in the West.

The early recovery movement was a disruptive force, unsettling the territories of a biomedical psychiatric assemblage, which was dominant at the time, by challenging psychiatric labels and linear treatment pathways. Social recovery is defined by Davidson et al. (2005) as "a redefinition of one's illness as only one aspect of a multidimensional sense of self capable of identifying, choosing and pursuing personally meaningful goals and aspirations despite continuing to suffer the effects and side effects of mental illness" (p. 15). Social recovery does not require the elimination of symptoms or a return to "normal" functioning; rather, diverse and embodied responses to distress and trauma (often diagnosed as "mental illness") are considered an acceptable part of the person, not something to be left in the individual's past (Davidson & Roe, 2007; Vandekinderen et al., 2012). It is an ongoing process, where the individual asserts or recovers control over their life, learning to manage and live *with* their "illness." "It is not a perfectly linear process. At times our course is erratic and we falter, slide back, re-group and start again" (Deegan, 1988, p. 15). The early recovery movement disrupted and softened the rigid territories of the major mental health apparatus at the time.

We would be remiss if we did not acknowledge the co-occurring activism and community organising by psychiatrised people that was not directly related with the recovery movement, what has been referred to as the Mad movement (see Shimrat, 1997). The Mad movement (also referred to as the mental patients' liberation movement in Europe) can be traced back to the formation of psychiatric patient associations across North America and Europe (Starkman, 2013; Shimrat, 1997). The disruptive energy of the Mad movement was more radical than that of the recovery movement and distanced itself from the major apparatus – in contrast to the recovery movement, Mad activism confronted the paternalism of psychiatry and resisted pathologisation of trauma and distress. Where recovery has been entangled with the dominant apparatus, the lines of flight of the Mad movement has led to the assembling of Mad Studies, a field of study and practice led by psychiatrised people and with the support of Mad-affirming allies/scholars (Beresford & Russo, 2022).

Social recovery was described not as a solely individual pursuit, but rather as one that involves caring others, supportive environments, and flexible health providers (Davidson & Roe, 2007; Vandekinderen et al., 2012). Similarly, barriers to recovery are not considered to be only within the individual and their illness; social recovery acknowledges barriers within society such as social stigma (Williams et al., 2015). Processes of social recovery have deterritorialised "mental illness," and formed a line of flight away from individualistic, constrictive, and oppressive treatment practices, and centralised (major) medical authority. The early recovery movement was a minoring force, making way for people with diverse mental health experiences to pursue a life of their choosing (Rose, 2014).

Some forms of social recovery have been considered more radical, the trajectory of their lines of flight notably away from (and in resistance to) the pathologising practices of psychiatric assemblages. Peer support models emerged within social recovery, either informally through peer support groups or by formally employing service users as peer support workers (Repper & Carter, 2011). Peer support workers draw upon their lived experience of recovery to support people who experience mental health challenges (Repper & Carter, 2011; Stewart et al., 2019). Peer support models grapple with the micropolitics of mental health service delivery, destabilising boundaries and power relations between the major professional and the minor client. Rather than a relationship of dominance/expertise, peer support work reterritorialises the relationship as one of mutual support. People who received peer support reported feeling less like a traditional "mental patient," more connected with others, less likely to feel stigmatised, and more hopeful about their future (Repper & Carter, 2011, p. 396). The effectiveness of peer support work has led dominant mental health services to incorporate peer support as a legitimate treatment approach (Ostrow & Adams, 2012) – note that the process of legitimation (e.g., through systematic research, standardisation of peer support qualification) is a majoring force of segmentation. Legitimised peer support models have been slowly captured and appropriated by the major, and as such, the advocacy role and reciprocity of peer support has diminished in favour of roles sanctioned by the service provider (Ostrow & Adams, 2012). Moreover, as Rose (2014), a prominent scholar in the service-user movement, has noted, peer support staff have become a form of "cheap labour" (p. 218), and a part of the centralised state apparatus (see also Morrow, 2013). Another deterritorialising force alongside the peer support model was the hearing voices movement (Corstens et al., 2014). This movement does not consider hearing voices (a criterion for the diagnosis of schizophrenia) to be abnormal; instead it is considered a "natural part of the human experience" and a "meaningful and interpretable response to social, emotional and/or interpersonal circumstances" (Corstens et al., 2014, p. 286). Rather than pathologising and treating their experiences pharmacologically, voice hearers are encouraged, with support, to explore the meaning behind their experience and accept the voices (Corstens et al., 2014). The hearing voices movement deterritorialises the boundary of pathological human experience, and in welcoming diversity this movement disrupts major (biomedical) categories of normal and abnormal.

Recovery-oriented practice

Social and clinical recovery have become entangled in what is known as recovery-oriented practice, the current hegemonic form of recovery that dominates mental health policy and service delivery (McWade, 2016). Our analysis shifts from looking at each assemblage individually, to an analysis of the entanglement of these two forms of recovery. It can certainly be argued that clinical recovery has captured and controlled social recovery through recovery-oriented practice; however, we aim to disentangle some of the micropolitical tensions rather than oversimplify.

In 1988, Patricia Deegan wrote: "As professionals we would like nothing more than to somehow manufacture the spirit of recovery and give it to each of our program participants. But this is impossible. We cannot force recovery to happen in our rehabilitation programs" (p. 57). In a relatively short period of time, recovery has become the language and approach of the clinic (Harper & Speed, 2012; Rose, 2014), where a recovery-orientation has become a decidedly major orientation. For example, since Deegan's seminal work in 1988, research into the "effectiveness" of clinical recovery treatment methods has increased (Silverstein & Bellack, 2008), recovery-oriented outcome measures have been developed, and recovery-oriented treatment plans have become the norm in the mental health sector (Rose, 2014). The use of "recovery" language in mental health policy is also illustrative of how the major apparatus codes and overcodes – the meaning of the term "recovery-oriented" has become less clearly stated with each policy iteration. For example, in Australia, the early recovery movement of the late 1980s and into the 1990s shaped thinking and policy in the mental health sector (see the Burdekin Report and the First National Mental Health Plan in 1992). Initially, a recovery-orientation gave rise to a significant change in policy and government funding in mental health, shifting from primarily psychiatric hospital funding to (minimal) community-based funding in less than ten years (Rosen, 2006). However, 30 years since the release of Australia's first National Mental Health Plan, "recovery" is no longer explicitly defined in the plan and the term is only referred to in relation to service provision (Department of Health, 2017). This trend speaks to the assertion by McWade (2016) that recovery is not one thing, nor does it have multiple meanings; rather, recovery is enacted in different ways – recovery is often enacted in policy to assert the centralised authority of major institutions. Recovery acts as a floating signifier, a term that has legitimacy but no agreed upon meaning, and can be weaponised to serve the major apparatus. This can be seen most clearly in Australia's Fifth National Health Plan, where recovery for psychiatrised people is evidenced by improved "access to the clinical and community services (they) require to live a more contributing life" (Department of Health, 2017, p. 29). Recovery is reduced to service access and "contributions" (economic contribution to society). Similarly, new funding models, in an era of recovery-oriented practice, are underpinned by neoliberal ideology and the rhetoric of individual responsibility, choice, and autonomy (Harper & Speed, 2012; McWade, 2016).

Still, fragments of the recovery movement remain entangled in contemporary recovery-oriented practice. For example, elements of social recovery are present in the recovery model, the Recovery Star (a 10-point checklist of expected recovery outcomes), such as the emphasis on "social networks" and "relationships" (Lloyd et al., 2016). In addition, the routine inclusion of "consumer"/"service user" expertise in organisational and policy processes demonstrates the interrelationship of clinical and social recovery (Beresford, 2012). However, the (tokenistic) involvement of service users is believed to have had little influence on the direction of policy that affects them (Beresford, 2012).

In an era of recovery-oriented policies, psychiatrised people have remained marginalised and at times lack meaningful participation in society (Vandekinderen et al., 2012). The spirit of the recovery movement has been captured by the major apparatus, turning "recovery-oriented practice" into a mental health buzzword and a set of clinical processes (Rose, 2014). What was once a deterritorialising and liberating force has been captured and reterritorialised within the mental health sector as the dominant form of clinical practice. Given the emancipatory history of recovery as a grassroots movement, recovery-oriented practice has been difficult to oppose or critique (Rose, 2014).

Despite an awareness of societal factors such as social stigma, recovery-oriented practice often focuses on reducing stigmatising markers in the individual rather than addressing oppressive social forces (Harper & Speed, 2012; Rose, 2014; Sayce, 2015). The underlying assumption is that the challenges people face are due to an individual "illness," and can be resolved through recovery-oriented treatment. The identity politics of recovery "makes emotional distress an explicit problem of individualised identity rather than, for example, an effect of structural inequality" (Harper & Speed, 2012, p. 44). Constrictive majoritarian forces produce ongoing prescriptive emphasis on individual autonomy, choice, and reduction of stigmatising markers (Sayce, 2015).

Captured within a normative framework, contemporary recovery-oriented frameworks rely on standardised recovery outcome measures such as the Recovery Star or the Ladder of Change (a five-step change process) (Lloyd et al., 2016; Onifade, 2011). The "mentally ill" are expected to follow predetermined (linear) steps and achieve normative (primarily individualistic) outcomes in order to achieve recovery. However, a group of psychiatric survivors and activists have deterritorialised the Recovery Star, developing the Unrecovery Star as a line of flight, a 10-point model of social inequities that hinder (social) recovery (Recovery in the Bin, 2016). Rather than following a prescriptive recovery process, with normative recovery standards, the Unrecovery Star emphasises that "we need to not just pay attention to distressed people, but deal with the problems that exist in communities and wider society" (Recovery in the Bin, 2016, para. 3). Despite Deegan's warning in 1988, recovery has largely become captured and absorbed within dominant mental health policy and practice (McWade, 2016; Rose, 2014; Sayce, 2015).

Horwitz's (1982) theory of therapeutic social control further illustrates recovery-oriented practice as an apparatus of capture. People with mental illness are controlled through two primary mechanisms: coercion and conciliation. Psychiatrised people have been historically controlled with coercive practices (e.g., through the threat of force, mandatory medical procedures, forced medication use, or involuntary commitment) (Perry et al., 2017). We might consider coercive practices a thing of the past – yet in 2019, one in seven mental health service users in Australia were under an involuntary treatment order, one in five service users were involuntarily treated in residential care, and one in two overnight hospitalisations were involuntary (Australian Institute of Health and Welfare, 2019). Almost 20 in 1,000 residential beds involved a seclusion event (confinement), physical restraint, or mechanical restraint (Australian Institute of Health and Welfare, 2019). So we ask, what is at stake when a person receives a diagnosis of "serious mental illness"? Or, what might happen if they oppose or fail to adhere with (recovery-oriented) treatment recommendations? The era of institutionalisation has passed, but the threat of confinement is a part of everyday life for many mental health service users. This leads to the second mechanism of control, conciliation (persuasion by the major to adhere to a recommendation, often through relationship) (Perry et al., 2017). "Person-centred treatment plans" or "collaborative goal setting" used by recovery-oriented community mental health services may unintentionally persuade psychiatrised people to envision and work towards a normative vision of recovery (Perry et al., 2017; Vandekinderen et al., 2012). Through coercion and conciliation, psychiatrised people are led to believe that adherence with treatment recommendations will mean that they will be able to participate as productive members of society, and have decreased dependency on the state (Williams et al., 2015). But when the individual, likely burdened with additional stressors such as low-income and family challenges, is not able to manage their own recovery, "they become the objects of intensified surveillance, control and disciplinary practices" (Vandekinderen et al., 2012, p. 4). Psychiatrised people who require additional care and support gradually transform into "nonrecyclable and nondeserving citizens who become waste products in society" (Vandekinderen et al., 2012, p. 4).

Recovery-oriented policy and practice has de-emphasised social factors that contribute to the inequities experienced by psychiatrised people (Harper & Speed, 2012). A concurrent and interrelated major mental health assemblage, social inclusion, has been considered "a way of framing the social aspect of a recovery movement" that is focused on the individual (Thompson & Rowe, 2010).

Social inclusion assemblage

The concept of social inclusion initially emerged from a critical analysis of exclusionary structures in society (Pereira & Whiteford, 2013). Social *exclusion* was first introduced as a concept in 1974 by the French Secretary of State for Social Action, Rene Lenoir, who described various excluded members of society, including mentally and physically impaired, single parents, abused children, and, as quoted by Peace (2001, p. 19), other "social misfits." Addressing social exclusion became a policy focus throughout Europe towards the end of the 20th century (Stickley et al., 2016). Programs were created to address the disadvantage experienced by marginalised groups, such as psychiatrised people, providing them with opportunities to participate as productive members of society and less impeded by restrictive social practices (Pereira & Whiteford, 2013). Exclusionary processes and systems were exposed and reimagined in ways that were more affirmative and enabling for the minor. However, major forces have captured "social exclusion" and reterritorialised it into an individual "condition" that could be treated by inclusion (Spandler, 2007). The focus shifted from the analysis of social forces that exclude people to the analysis of excluded people that need including (Wright & Stickley, 2013). "The challenge now is to move away from conceptualising exclusion and discrimination as stigma and toward ways to support and promote the social inclusion of people with psychiatric disabilities" (Thompson & Rowe, 2010, p. 735). This quote illustrates the call to an individualistic approach to social inclusion and movement away from the analysis of oppressive social forces. Echoing the enthusiasm for strengths-based perspectives in allied health professions (see, e.g., Saleeby, 2006), social inclusion was believed to be a more positive way to frame the issue of exclusion by articulating the end goal rather than focusing on the problem (Pereira & Whiteford, 2013; Spandler, 2007). Central to the major's capture and recoding of exclusion in this assemblage is the production of an exclusion/inclusion binary and the assumption that these concepts cannot co-exist; inclusion was understood as the absence of exclusion (Spandler, 2007).

Social inclusion formally made its way into Australian policy in 2008 with the Social Inclusion Agenda, introduced by the Australian Labour Government (Pereira & Whiteford, 2013). Through this policy, the Australian Government aimed at improving the lives of people who experience disadvantage and marginalisation by enabling their participation in society (Pereira & Whiteford, 2013). However, social inclusion policy typically frames participation in terms of normative economic participation, emphasising the importance of enabling disadvantaged people to be productive members of capitalist society (Spandler, 2007; Stickley et al., 2016). Rather than highlighting and changing oppressive structures that contribute to chronic poverty and ongoing exclusion (see Wilton, 2004), social inclusion policy narrowly focused on improving economic participation (Pereira & Whiteford, 2013; Spandler, 2007). As a normative apparatus of capture, social inclusion policy reduced the experience of marginalisation to a problem of productivity.

Social inclusion in the mental health sector has not been well critiqued, with limited engagement in the micropolitics of power relations involved in deeming someone in need of inclusion (Wright & Stickley, 2013). This is in part because "inclusion is seen as a universal good and so any critique is constructed as resistance to change" (Spandler, 2007, p. 5). "Social inclusion is not only an approach but a moral imperative" (Thompson & Rowe, 2010), and as such, the social inclusion agenda has become a part of the unquestioned authority of major policy makers and service providers. Through this assemblage, psychiatrised people become targets for social inclusion, "another mechanism of reinforcing the social order [that] subjects people with mental health problems to both moral and social regulation" (Wright & Stickley, 2013, p. 78). Social inclusion covertly implies that there is an ideal common life that people wish to participate in – that inclusion in mainstream society is both lacking and universally desirable for psychiatrised people (Le Boutillier & Croucher, 2010). There is an assumption that a healthy life is one that does not draw from health services and mental health support, is not reliant on the welfare system, and that one's social networks should extend beyond those with a mental health diagnosis (Spandler, 2007). Further, when the "mentally ill" lack social connections, it is identified as an additional "defect" that is treated programmatically with paid friends, a form of counterfeit relationship (McKnight, 1995). The social inclusion assemblage is laden with the expectation that the person with a psychiatric diagnosis must meet certain expectations or conditions to be accepted and included into the majority (Gregory, 1994). Psychiatrised people are viewed as a risk to society, a "threat to social order" (Davidson, 2008, p. 305) that can be regulated through inclusion in the major. We are not suggesting that psychiatrised people do not want independence, employment, or other virtues of majoritarian society, but are highlighting that inclusion is a vehicle for the operation of power and is thus not neutral. Inclusion gives power to the dominant majority society to determine "whether to let them in or not" (Hamer et al., 2014, p. 206). The assemblage of social inclusion produces the conditions by which psychiatrised people are "subject to moral and social regulation," without addressing dominant structures that exclude people (Spandler, 2007, p. 3). Ironically, programs with social inclusion as their aim have tended to create ghettos, isolated or segregated spaces – service users have reported feeling as though they are not "good enough" for mainstream society and remain in major enclosures (such as drop-in centres) (Stewart, 2019, p. 1).

Parallel to the majoring of social inclusion policy, the concept and practice of community inclusion emerged in the mental health sector starting in the 1990s (Spandler, 2007). Policymakers, activists, and theorists collaboratively pursued community inclusion, a minoring pursuit that was less hierarchical, and focused on developing strategies for welcoming people who were excluded (Spandler, 2007; see Barringham & Barringham, 2002). These communities sought to generate a place in society for psychiatrised people and to "connect isolated and often vulnerable individuals into the richness of ordinary, everyday community life" (Shevellar & Barringham, 2016, p. 182). This approach manifests in countless ways that dominant members of society take for granted, for example, forming friendships, sitting in a café, or pursuing interests in the community (Barringham & Barringham, 2002). Community inclusion work involves coming alongside people with diverse experiences and challenges, developing alliances and networks of connection in places that are safe and welcoming (McGill, 1996; Shevellar & Barringham, 2016). The minoring processes of community inclusion decentre mental health work, loosening the grip of services in people's lives and fostering lines of flight into the community. Though this disruptive work generates a number of professional tensions, such as the development of reciprocal relationships between service providers and service users. The "conundrum is that it is likely that the more an agency builds a trustful and safe alliance with a service participant, the greater the danger of the agency itself becoming community for the service participant" (Shevellar & Barringham, 2016, p. 187). While community inclusion potentiates disruptive/deterritorialising movements that unsettle boundaries between the major and minor, the professional tensions in this work simultaneously give rise to overcoding movements by the major to contain these minoring processes. Major codes of ethics and codes of conduct have proliferated in order to ensure protection of the public, and also to establish and maintain a standard of acceptable professional behaviour (Banks, 2011; Shevellar & Barringham, 2016).

Deterritorialisation as a way forward

Major mental illness assemblages of recovery and social inclusion have centred on institutional and dominant mechanisms of authority, and ongoing processes of capture and control. Our analysis has highlighted several deterritorialising forces entangled within recovery and social inclusion, disruptive forces that challenge major systems of authority (e.g., the hearing voices movement, the early recovery movement, social exclusion, community inclusion). A starting point for transformation in the mental health sector may be to pursue deterritorialising processes that disrupt institutional control and encourage minor assemblages that evade the authority of dominant mental health services. But note that conceptually, Deleuze and Guattari (1987) do not suggest that we detach from the major entirely, for once detached we can no longer be a dismantling force. Rather, transformation occurs by cautiously dismantling and disorganising the rigid segmentation of the major from within, generating small fissures in the cramped spaces so that something might ooze through the cracks (Deleuze & Guattari, 1987). Minor "escapes and movements would be nothing if they did not return to the molar organisations to reshuffle their segments, their binary distributions" (Deleuze & Guattari, 1987, p. 253).

We now turn to additional examples of how deterritorialising processes might destabilise rigid territories in the mental health sector. These examples underscore three possible ways minoring processes can occur, by (i) disrupting binaries, (ii) decentring axes of power, and (iii) pursuing non-linear processes (Deleuze & Guattari, 1987). Starting with the disruption of binaries, there have been several recent examples that highlight how small subversive acts of reciprocity by service providers can be a deterritorialising force in the mental health sector. Hamer et al. (2019) describe how practitioners "break the rules" (p. 300), engaging in reciprocal relationships with clients so that service users will feel more connected and valued in their community. Examples included going to a café with a service user (rather than meeting in the office) or loaning a service user an outfit to wear to a funeral (as one would to a friend) (Hamer et al., 2019). Further to this example of reciprocity as a minoring force, Stewart et al. (2019) described how peer mentors were a "secret ingredient" in their recovery program. One participant in their study stated "they made me feel like I matter. I got a text message from [a peer mentor] when I missed a workshop – so many times so much in your life you feel no one misses you" (Stewart et al., 2019, p. 19). Here, peer mentors deterritorialise the boundary between service provider and service user in the act of sending a text message and "missing" the service user. Through reciprocity, service providers have the potential to destabilise the territories of the major – "missing" people (that we shouldn't miss) and being "missed" by people (that shouldn't miss us), and thus produce a deterritorialising line of flight.

Second, deterritorialisation can occur through decentring axes of power in the mental health sector, unsettling the machine of resonance. Alongside the previously mentioned "community inclusion" as a decentring practice, Mad Studies provides another example of decentring the axis of power in the sector. Mad Studies is an emerging area of minor scholarship, a "user-led challenge to biomedical thinking about distress" (Beresford, 2020, p. 1). Mad Studies grapples with the micropolitics of mental health scholarship, overtly challenging the authority of experts in the field through sociopolitical research that centres lived experience knowledge of people deemed "mad" by the dominant majority (Beresford, 2020; Rose, 2017).

Last, we look to the deterritorialisation of linear processes, with an example of an organisation that encourages non-linear methods of support. The Icarus Project (now called the Fireweed Collective), a community-based mental health support network in the United States, aims to respect the diverse ways that "people choose to navigate their distress" (The Icarus Project, 2019). The Icarus Project (2019) recognises that there is no formula for "navigating distress," and offers support, resources, and education for a wide range of people who may be in crisis, including those who do not wish to seek medical intervention. This network could also be an example for disrupting binaries (by challenging labels and diagnoses) and decentring axes of power (by encouraging alternative approaches to dominant services and enabling the development of community). Hua Fletcher (2018), reflecting on her time working with them, concluded "(The Icarus Project) allows us to think differently, to be differently, and to inhabit new spaces in profoundly different ways" (p. 42).

There is a small body of literature that suggests that non-institutional, reciprocal, and freely given community relationships may have transformative potential for psychiatrised people (Bromley et al., 2013; Pilisuk, 2001; Wong et al., 2014). Freely given relationships between psychiatrised people and members of the community, and their potential to produce minoring processes has not been well explored. Further, there is a lack of scholarship that explores the nuances of community connections outside the mainstream mental health sector (Wong et al., 2014). Schutt (2016) invites further exploration into how social relationships in the community can have an affirmative influence in the lives of psychiatrised people. The scholarship that does touch on community connectedness tends to couch it as a programmatic approach (Bromley et al., 2013; Pilisuk, 2001) or as a treatment plan priority (Townley, 2015). In one of the few studies that have used Deleuzio-Guattarian theory in mental health research, Tucker (2010) outlined how territories on the fringes of traditional institutional settings (e.g., drop-in centres), at the threshold of the major and minor, can act as a safe and affirmative space where people with diverse experiences can participate in their community. However, these spaces were inevitably at risk of becoming a "stepping stone" to capture by major institutional forces (Tucker, 2010). Freely given relationships *may* generate deterritorialising lines of flight, but if taken up as an "approach" it is susceptible to capture and appropriation within major health and human service assemblages.

Producing a machine of dissonance

While we have discussed a number of examples of deterritorialising lines of flight, we emphasise that the aim is not to develop a model for deterritorialisation. We are pursuant of a revolutionary force that does not recreate what it is fighting against – "if we revolutionaries are opposed to the status quo, then what kind of organisation can and could we give rise to, and how will we be able to avoid certain forms that we find detestable?" (Lundy, 2013, p. 236). We must remain cautious of "the pull of the major, the tendency to revert to given territories and practices" (Barlott et al., 2017, p. 528). We must reflexively be in the cramped spaces, at the threshold between the major apparatus and the confined minor, carefully wearing down and softening restrictive boundaries. Hamer et al. (2019) offer an example of how service providers advocated for acts of citizenship to be included in people's care plans, such as allowing a service user to buy the practitioner a coffee. This is an example of being at the threshold – invoking the apparatus of capture (appropriating a disruptive act as part of a care plan), but at the same time keeping tension in the opposite direction, stretching, pulling, and challenging the major to make room for diverse ways of being in relationship with people. This micropolitical struggle for territory is likely to bring to the surface the intersection of multiple vested interests in clinical practice (e.g., the authority of medicine and psychiatry) and policy – however, the analysis of these entangled vested interests is the topic for another conversation.

Disrupting capture is not something that is ever achieved, it is something that is always in process. The coding apparatus will inevitably capture and segment the lines again. Codes of conduct and practice guidelines will reassert professional boundaries, linear processes, and centres of authority; transformational and disruptive ideas will be absorbed and overcoded as treatment approaches or policy objectives. But, we shouldn't lose heart – the aim of deterritorialising lines of flight is not to conquer the major. Just as birds that fly in all directions are difficult to capture, so too are assemblages with multiple deterritorialising lines of flight. Let us continually generate "zigzag crack(s), making it difficult for them to keep their own segments in line" (Deleuze & Guattari, 1987, p. 252). Let us break the rules, miss our clients, stretch professional boundaries and practices, embrace the voices in our heads, and … and … and. Let us cautiously experiment in the cramped spaces – "should we go a short way further to see for ourselves, be a little alcoholic, a little crazy, a little suicidal, a little of a guerrilla – just to extend the crack, but not enough to deepen it irremediably?" (Deleuze, 1990, pp. 157–158). This deterritorialising way forward is the production of a machine of dissonance that separates the machine of resonance from what it is capable of. Deleuze (1988) does not call for a revolution, he does not suggest that a grand systemic change (in this case, mental health reform) will have a long-term transformative impact. Rather, transformation occurs through ongoing revolutionary processes – ongoing movement away from the major towards the margins (disruption and deterritorialisation of major assemblages) and movement on the margins (lines of flight of the categorical minor).

There's no need to fear or hope, but only to look for new weapons.

– Deleuze, 2017

Notes

1 We invite readers to consider reading Chapter 3 prior to continuing with Chapter 2. Chapter 3 offers a more detailed description of some of theory taken up in Chapter 2.
2 *Edge Entanglements* and our thinking about psychiatric and mental health systems have been informed by Mad Studies, and, while we consider ourselves allied with Mad Studies, we do not consider our work in this book to be a part of the Mad Studies project.
3 We re-turn to the formation of a posthuman body and the collision of forces in Chapter 7.
4 It is worth noting that segmentation and categorisation are not unique to major assemblages – all assemblages feature lines of segmentation (Deleuze & Guattari, 1987). However, compared to the major, minor lines of segmentation are supple, flexible and are not used to assert dominance and control (Deleuze & Guattari, 1987). This distinction will be carried throughout this chapter and book.
5 Deleuze and Guattari (1987) use the phrase "missing people" (p. 217) in a way that seems to be similar to the non-being described by Mbembe. In Chapter 9, we explore the transformative potential of missing people.
6 In Chapter 8, we agitate the notion of family in freely given relationship and the production of a diffuse form of kinship – family of choice rather than family of lineage.

3

BECOMING-MINOR, MAPPING TERRITORIES

In this chapter, we introduce some of Gilles Deleuze and Félix Guattari's theory, which offers onto-epistemological tools for exploring complex social formations and interrelated social processes in mental health research and practice. But we find it somewhat constraining to think about theory as (only) a set of tools – tools imply fixing something or solving a problem. We also think of theory as a toy-box – something that stimulates play and curious experimentation – for "crafting the conditions not to *solve* problems, or to resolve questions, but to illuminate regions of thought through which problems-without-solutions can be intuited" (Manning, 2016, p. 10, emphasis in original).

What would happen if I detached these blocks and build them in a different way?
What if this cape transformed me into a monster?
What if these glasses enabled me to see into another dimension?

We outline the concepts of the *major* and *minor*, *becoming-minor*, *transversality*, and the *rhizome*, which provide a useful and flexible set of ideas for challenging dominant ways of thinking/doing and attending to transformative processes in mental health research and practice. The major includes the dominant things in the social world (both human and non-human, physical and non-physical) that are established, clearly understood, and considered normal. The minor is the site of difference, that which does not align with the norm. The major has a propensity to categorise and stratify the minor, constraining the minor and limiting its potential. To resist the capture of the major and pursue social transformation, Deleuze and Guattari (1987) introduced the concept of becoming-minor, a collective process that disrupts categorical/normative identities. The process of becoming-minor is illustrated through the concept of the rhizome, a non-hierarchical figuration of entangled social processes

DOI: 10.4324/9781003286486-3

and interrelationships. These concepts were used in Chapter 2 to interrogate the mental health scholarship, and will come up in Chapters 7, 8, and 9 where we look more closely at ally relationships. This chapter concludes with a description of a postqualitative cartographic approach, a Deleuzio-Guattarian inspired way to think about micropolitical movements and social processes that we use in Chapters 7, 8, and 9. These concepts and approach provoke us (and, we hope, our readers) to (re)conceptualise inequities/marginalisations, challenge dominant ways of thinking/doing, and consider transformative processes in mental health research and practice, and in the freely given relationships discussed in this book.

Theory matters – matters of theory

The theory presented in this chapter is an invitation for creative exploration, transformation, and an analysis of the social world that is pursuant of what Katz (1996) referred to as minor theory. Minor theory is theory situated on the margins of dominant practices and theories; it is purposefully disruptive of typical ways of practicing and enquiring. For Katz (1996), dominant perspectives and theories are unable to see the landscape of the margins, whereas minor theory is "produced in a different register" (p. 488). The pursuit of a minor theory is not only about theory that can be transformative and liberating for those we deem marginalised, but for the transformation of all sociomaterial that is entangled in the assemblages of everyday life. Minor theory offers a way "to be worthy of our times while resisting the times and for a love of the world" (Braidotti, 2011, p. 298).

The theories and theorists we draw from matter – and the theories and theorists we draw from contribute to their mattering (Haraway, 2016). As we assemble and disassemble the conceptual toybox in this book we consider Audre Lorde's statement, "the master's tools will never dismantle the master's house" – at once we are attracted to the dismantling possibilities within the philosophy of Deleuze and Guattari, but what is it that attracts us?

TIM: Why is it that I am enamoured by their work? Why is it that I have found less kinship with minority scholars? Do Deleuze and Guattari offer a minor-ing opportunity that is accessible to me, a white, male settler? Or do I privilege their authority? Can we pursue a minor theory using the theory of two white men? I'm not entirely certain of the answer to these questions.

JENNY: White European men have been given too much airtime, so I find it challenging when working with a student who focusses on their work – yet my PhD did too (Foucault and Goffman were my key influences). These men's privilege has afforded them time, funds, and facilities to develop and hone their theories, and priority when it comes to publications and subsequent citation – so their work is hard to avoid. Since my PhD, I have worked hard to shift my citation practices to account for this issue, and I now almost entirely work with female or non-binary and often with racialised theorists. Deleuze and Guatarri are put to good work in this book I believe, but we build on their work by citing more broadly, and with attention to less heard perspectives.

One of critiques of new materialism and critical posthumanism (that often draws from Deleuze and Guattari) is the Western and colonial orientation whereby the "seemingly flattened ontology, emphasis on vitality of matter, and privileging of relations can erase subjectivity, become apolitical, and inadvertently recenter humanisms through a focus on predominantly white Euro-Western theories and theorists" (Truman, 2019, p. 8). And so, we have intentionally woven Mad Studies, postcolonial, and feminist new materialisms into our book event to go some way towards addressing some of these harms. The philosophy of Deleuze and Guattari remains a dominant thread throughout our book (and particularly this chapter); however we (hope to) use it (and others) as a stimulus for our own crafting and theoretical imagination rather than an authoritative and rigid framework.

Major and minor

We first introduced the concepts of major and the minor in Chapter 2 and build on that discussion here, with links to the concept of the rhizome later in this chapter. As mentioned, the major and minor are used conceptually to describe the hierarchical organisation and structure of things (human and non-human, physical and non-physical) in modern Western society (Deleuze & Guattari, 1987). Major and minor for Deleuze and Guattari (1987) are not determined by quantities or numeric values, but by significance. For example, take the profession of social work in the non-profit social sector; while there are far more women in those workforces, it remains dominated by men (Baines et al., 2015; McPhail, 2004). Men in social work receive higher pay than women (McPhail, 2004), and are more likely to hold leadership positions and influence the profession (Baines et al., 2015). The major have status and significance in society; they act as the unquestioned authority (Deleuze & Guattari, 1987).

As we described in Chapter 2, one of the characteristics of the major is its propensity and desire to capture, absorb, and appropriate the minor (Deleuze & Guattari, 1986). This dominating practice of the major is referred to as the apparatus of capture (Deleuze & Guattari, 1987). The minor, bodies deemed "other," are often captured by the major, categorised and territorialised within the major (Deleuze & Guattari, 1987). For example, psychiatrised people (minor) have a long history of being categorised and controlled by those in authority (the major) as noted in Chapter 2. The major apparatus of capture contains and constrains;

it prevents movement and flexibility (Deleuze & Guattari, 1986; Gilbert, 2010). Turning back to the social work and non-profit social sector, Baines et al. (2015) warn that male-dominated and managerialised approaches may lead to less caring (masculinist) practices pervading the profession: "some of the aspects of the non-profit sector such as social justice practices and strong connections to service users, may be lost as technical and managerialised approaches colonise more relationship-based, interactive practices" (p. 473). Major forces can constrain the dynamism of minor assemblages, and with the example from social work above, quell relationship-based, social justice practices. In Chapter 2, we offered a detailed account of some of the ways the major apparatus of capture habitually smothers minor practices in the mental health sector.

Research and practice in the mental health sector has the potential to act as an apparatus of capture, unintentionally constraining the experiences of the minor and stratifying them within our major assemblages. We argue that, if those in the mental health sector want to bring about transformative social change, they need to question the major within, consider ways they act as agents of capture (see Chapter 2), and make destabilising movements towards the minor. To this end, for the major to resist the urge to capture and stratify the minor, and for the minor to resist the capture of the major, Deleuze and Guattari (1987) outlined the process of becoming-minor.

Becoming-minor

Becoming-minor is a process of displacement, a process that unsettles major stratification in pursuit of more liberating assemblages for minor bodies. Deleuze and Guattari (1986) identified the following three characteristics of becoming-minor: deterritorialisation, connection of the individual to a political immediacy, and collective assemblage of enunciation. First, deterritorialisation refers to when the territories of the major break down or when the minor resists and breaks away from the stratification and rigid territories of the major, forming what Deleuze and Guattari referred to as a line of flight (Deleuze & Guattari, 1987).[1] Deterritorialisation frees the minor from the confines of the major, birthing creative potential and new possibilities (Colebrook, 2002; Deleuze & Guattari, 1987). There is always an "other" message within the major, a message "cast aside, overlooked, or forgotten in the interplay of major chords" (Manning, 2016, p. 1). This message in the shadow of the major is the site of potential deterritorialisation – the minor vibrates with transformative and creative potential to "(unmoor the major's) structural integrity, problematizing its normative standards" (Manning, 2016, p. 1). Second, the minor is characterised by connection to a political immediacy, where "everything in them is political" (Deleuze & Guattari, 1986, p. 17). The minor is found on the margins of society, in the "cramped space" where life flow is limited (Deleuze & Guattari, 1986). Becoming-minor involves recognising and engaging in these cramped spaces and the micropolitical power relations that produce marginalisation.

Becoming-minor is also a collective assemblage of enunciation, characterised by interrelatedness and connections (Deleuze & Guattari, 1986). Each non-unitary subject (such as a person) is always more-than-one's-self, what Deleuze and Guattari (1987) referred to as a multiplicity. All matter is non-discrete and entangled with other forms of matter (e.g., humans, flora, fauna, social structures, and historical contexts) in an ongoing affective process – affecting and being affected by other multiplicities (Deleuze & Guattari, 1986). No singular units of analysis (e.g., individuals, activities, contexts) can be viewed in isolation "because a whole other story is vibrating within it" (Deleuze & Guattari, 1986, p. 17). This does not negate the study of singular units of analysis; rather the "individual concern thus becomes all the more necessary" as it can illuminate the interrelated multiplicities (Deleuze & Guattari, 1986, p. 17). The collection of interrelated multiplicities makes up an assemblage. The theory of assemblages acknowledges the "irreducible social complexity" that characterises the "contemporary world" (DeLanda, 2006, p. 6). Assemblages are continually in flux as their constellation of interconnections is constantly moving/shaping/forming (Tamboukou, 2010). The complexity grows as each multiplicity within an assemblage is also a part of multiple assemblages, each mutually influential (Tamboukou, 2010).

The major seeks transcendence and individual significance, whereas the minor is a collective assemblage that does not seek individual significance or mastery; the minor is political in nature and acts in resistance to or is disruptive of the major. Since the minor is always moving and always becoming, minor assemblages and multiplicities are never categorically minor, but are always becoming-minor (Deleuze & Guattari, 1986). The major attempts to limit and contain the minor through the apparatus of capture, such as through psychiatric diagnosis. The process of becoming-minor involves ongoing processes of deterritorialisation (as discussed in Chapter 2), unsettling categorical/normative identities and oppressive major practices.

The creative potential of the minor is not the capacity to act within the stratified system of the majority; rather, it is the capacity to act against or deterritorialise from the denumerable majority (Deleuze & Guattari, 1987). Deterritorialisation frees the minor from the oppression of the major, creating new possibilities and creative potential (Colebrook, 2002; Deleuze & Guattari, 1987). Becoming and becoming-minor are the processes of rupturing from the stratification of the major, forming a line of flight and reterritorialising away from the major (Deleuze & Guattari, 1987). Becoming-minor is the collective pursuit of different processes and ways of thinking/doing that are outside of the normative, individualistic, hierarchal majority.

The becoming of the minor and becoming of the major may have very different starting points. Braidotti (2011) describes that the minor's first deterritorialisation may be to disengage with their identity as "other," as imposed by the majority, whereas for the major to enter a process of becoming, it may first deterritorialise itself from its identity as the norm and recognise how power has shaped the (re) production of "normal." For instance, Mad Studies, in its reclaiming of the pejorative "mad," cultivates affirmative understandings of Mad identity and experience (Diamond, 2013). The affirmation of difference, and dismantling of norm/other, is a key characteristic of becoming. The formerly "dialectical opponents" have the potential to turn into "allies in a process of becoming" (Braidotti, 2011, p. 31). The line of flight/escape of both the major and the minor is an undoing of the axiomatic that confines both identities respectively – norm and other, same and other of same. Thus, becomings – processes of social transformation – require a rupture of the boundaries that rigidise our lives and professional practices (Braidotti, 2011).

As I (Tim) write, I consider my own potential for engaging in an ongoing process of becoming and deterritorialisation, as a citizen of the major. I re-turn to my friend Stanley, a man psychiatrised with several mental health conditions. One of Stanley's strategies, when he is feeling overwhelmed or challenged by intrusive thoughts, is to sing in his head the James Taylor song "Carolina in My Mind":

> Now with a holy host of others standing round me, still I'm on the dark side of the moon.

> And it seems like it goes on like this forever, you must forgive me if I'm up and gone to Carolina in my mind.

> In my mind I'm going to Carolina. Can't you see the sunshine, can't you just feel the moonshine?

> Ain't it just like a friend of mine to hit me from behind? Yes, I'm gone to Carolina in my mind.

> *(Taylor, 1969)*

I find myself thinking of this song often (and am listening to it now as I write), likening my own becoming to "going to Carolina in my mind." I find it a difficult practice to continually deterritorialise from the major; I am entrenched in a majoritarian assemblage that consumes most of my waking day. Deleuze and Guattari (1986) cautioned against the pull of the major, the tendency to revert to given territories and practices. I hope to one day more easily break into lines of flight, more naturally strip myself of my rigid and stratified identity. For now, something that is helpful for disrupting the major that confines me is to sing in my head "Carolina in My Mind."

Transversality

The deterritorialising process Tim describes above is an entanglement of multiplicities; it is an event of (be)coming together and movement at the edge of major and minor. Central to our postqualitative, edge entanglements is the concept and praxis of *transversality*, the production of lines/movements/encounters that cut across difference or bring different things together in new (and destabilising) ways. Transversality is a concept developed by Guattari (2015) amidst his experimental psychotherapy in Clinique de La Borde clinic in the 1950s and 1960s. For Guattari (2015), transversality is the state of cutting across rigid relational lines, in particular, vertical lines of relationship (e.g., practitioner/client[2]) and horizontal lines of relationship (e.g., peer relations). Experimentally, Guattari sought to erode the hierarchical division between therapist and patients (and other non-medical staff), in hopes of producing a radical collectivity that could unsettle and mutate dominant power relations (Genosko, 2002). One example of transversality from his work in institutional psychiatry was the creation of the *grid*, a work rotation schedule where everyone in the institution (patients, non-medical staff, and medical staff) were responsible for the everyday tasks of the institution (e.g., cleaning, cooking, dishwashing) (Guattari, 2015). This was an experimental cut aimed at bringing precarity to the fixed identities of people in the institution. There was also a certain transversality to how Guattari's family was entangled with La Borde.[3] Guattari's daughter, Emmanuelle Guattari (2014) revisited her experience living at La Borde in her book *I, Little Asylum*: "We were the kids from La Borde" (p. 20). She described moments of kinship between children and "Madmen" at a period in the 1960s when a "fear of the *Insane* was palpable" (Guattari, 2014, p. 20).

> It was their aptitude for conversation, their care for others, their kindness or their impatience, the quality of their greeting, their aptitude for small talk, or to show genuine interest; the smiles, the insults, the absences and distractions, a worrisome or ravaged *faciality*, nervous behavior, atony or even catatony, the odd bodies, the gracious ones, the tortured hands, the outfits, the smells.
>
> *(E. Guattari, 2014, p. 21, original emphasis)*

Through transverse encounters, Emmanuelle developed a non-pathologising posture and came to see people not as "mentally ill" but as having "varied degrees of reactivity to oppression and porosity to trauma" (Rainsford, 2018, para. 4).

The degree of openness of an assemblage to unsettle hierarchies is the "coefficient of transversality" – the degree to which relations cut across and unsettle vertical hierarchies and horizontal ties (Guattari, 2015, p. 112). When there is a low coefficient of transversality, identities are fixed, and hierarchical relations remain and continue to reproduce cramped spaces such as the experience of psychiatrised people. For example, Guattari (2015) specifically refers to hierarchies in the mental health sector that "[block] any expression of the desire" of mental health service users (p. 110). Interestingly, Guattari also notes that with a low coefficient of transversality, self-organising peer groups have limited power. But, with a high coefficient of transversality, where hierarchies are flexible, there is potential for revolutionary becomings (Van der Tuin & Dolphijn, 2010).[4]

Guattari (2015) likened adjusting the coefficient of transversality to adjusting the blinkers on a horse – increasing the coefficient of transversality widens the gaze of the horse and allowing them to "envision [themselves] moving about more easily.... In (institutional psychiatry), the 'coefficient of transversality' is the degree of blindness of each of the people present" (p. 112). This is an intriguing metaphor given that the blinkers on horses are often considered protective, used so that horses do not become frightened – blinkers are also a means to keep horses focused and controlled (Genosko, 2002). We might consider policies around risk management or codes of conduct in the mental health sector (see Chapter 2) as a form of blinkers that prevent lines of flight that can come from transverse events.

Transversality, however, is not anarchy or the elimination of hierarchies. It is intentionally cutting across lines of segmentation, an ongoing awareness of existing lines of segmentation, and the softening of hierarchy. "One must not lose sight of the fact that, even when paved with the best intentions, the therapeutic endeavour is still constantly in danger of foundering in the besotting mythology of 'togetherness,'" wrote Guattari (2015, p. 118). We are struck by what Guattari refers to as the "mythology of 'togetherness'" as a reminder that processes of becoming (such as becoming-minor) do not eliminate hierarchies; rather, they serve to disrupt and soften the oppressive qualities of persistent forms of hierarchy. Throughout our postqualitative analysis, we demonstrate the value of attending to micropolitical relations and how collective enunciations remain a continually assembling entanglement of power relations.

Speaking to the ways in which transversality is implemented in practice, Guattari (2015) suggests: "what I am now proposing is only a temporary measure" (p. 106). In this sense, transversality is not a model, but an experimental movement or alignment. When we produce spaces with a high coefficient of transversality, we can produce a kind of sorcery that primes bodies for impulses of desire and potentiates the formation of affirmative forces of becoming.[5] We are forming what poststructural anarchist Hakim Bey (1991) refers to as temporary autonomous zones or the formation of a Deleuzio-Guattarian war machine (deterritorialising and disruptive machines that disrupt hierarchies). Duff, 2014, in his analysis of recovery and mental (ill)health, argues for the "articulation of novel assemblages" that can produce transformative becomings (p. 120). Transversality offers an experimental movement towards the construction of novel assemblages in mental health research and practice. Our book explores processes of transversality and how revolutionary forces are produced through transverse processes of becoming.

The rhizome

Becoming and transversality can be further illustrated through the concept of the *rhizome*, which Deleuze and Guattari (1987) introduced to describe the interrelation of things within an assemblage. Rhizomes are plants that are unlike arborescent trees with typical root structures; they grow horizontally and have no beginning or end. A rhizome cannot be controlled, has no organisational principles, and has multiple points of connection in any direction at all times. Every point of a rhizome is necessarily connected with another point and can be connected with any other point, regardless of location. "The rhizome is alliance, uniquely alliance" (Deleuze & Guattari, 1987, p. 26); its very nature is interconnection. The arborescent tree is very different, in that its roots have a starting point and the organisational structure is fixed and upward. "Arborescent systems are hierarchical with centers of significance and subjectification" (Deleuze & Guattari, 1987, p. 16).

The rhizome has lines of segmentarity, which are stratified and territorialised, and resemble arborescent structures, but also offshoots where it ruptures and grows in other directions. These offshoots, where the rhizome breaks away from the strata in a line of flight, is the process of deterritorialisation identified earlier as a characteristic of becoming-minor. Deterritorialisation frees the rhizome from its segmentarity, creating new possibilities, then reterritorialising into a new strata. The rhizome is always creating, never doing the same. Characterised by an ongoing process of interrelated and entangled social production, all elements within a rhizomatic assemblage (including human and non-human, animate and non-animate, physical and abstract) have the capacity to affect and be affected.

The rhizome is made up of lines, not points of significance, with these lines of interconnection also referred to as flows. There are lines of stratification, which may be lines of tradition, custom, and commonality, and there are also lines of flight / escape bursting from the stratification. The rhizome is constantly fleeing from its segmentarity and changing the nature of each interconnected multiplicity. "The rhizome is an acentered, non-hierarchical, non-signifying system without a General and without an organizing memory" (Deleuze & Guattari, 1987, p. 22). An entrenched anthropocentrism may influence us to think of the interconnected multiplicities as solely relationships between people. The rhizome is posthuman in that it is characterised by flows between all manner of things (e.g., animals, plants, environments, concepts, organisations, policies, discourses). One need look no further than the experience of people who are on the margins to see the interrelated flows of multiplicities fleeing from the confines of the major – whether it be people risking their lives to flee conflict areas to seek asylum and sustainable livelihoods for their family (Kirkwood et al., 2016), psychiatrised people rejecting the label placed on them and forming hearing voices groups (Adame & Knudson, 2007), or the whistleblowing of former United States soldier Chelsea Manning (Capuzza, 2015) (which is an example of interrelated flows of deterritorialisation – lines of flight both from the state apparatus and dominant gender discourses). Another example is the work of graffiti artist Banksy, whereby transformative and creative flows act in resistance to major assemblages – the artist transgresses social norms through an act of vandalism to create a political piece of art, which in turn generates dialogue and innumerable additional interconnected flows (McAuliffe, 2012). Yet with the example of Banksy, we also see how creative and rhizomatic flows can be captured, such as through processes of capitalist commodification.

The rhizome is always spilling to the edges, lines of flight to the margins, always growing and always producing new creative flows. The rhizome is always affirmative and hopeful; even in times of oppression and suffering, there is always potential for becoming. "We're tired of trees. We should stop believing in trees, roots and radicles. They've made us suffer too much" (Deleuze & Guattari, 1987, p. 15).[6] The concept of the rhizome enhances our understanding of the major and the minor, demonstrates the explosive potential of transversality, and illustrates a non-hierarchical structure for analysing social formations.

Rhizomatic cartography

> To write is to struggle and resist; to write is to become; to write is to draw a map: "I am a cartographer."
>
> – *Gilles Deleuze, 1988, p. 44*

Theory is creative; it can "fray the fabric of the given" (Barlott, Shevellar, et al., 2020b, p. 651) and produce new ideas and practices. As an agitating force, "theory is a form of organized estrangement from dominant values" (Braidotti, 2013, p. 104). One of the ways to creatively play with the concepts we have described is through mapping assemblages. This section introduces a cartographic approach, which uses rhizomatic thinking to inform research processes. A cartographic approach offers a way to analyse social formations, explore social transformations, and to engage politically and creatively in research.

A cartographic approach is not a method; rather, rhizomatic and cartographic thinking "is the method of the anti-method" (Zourabichvili & Aarons, 2012, p. 208). Guided by Deleuzio-Guattarian theoretical frameworks rather than method-ological steps, a cartographic approach offers a way for researchers to think differently about data collection and analysis, create experimental research encounters, and act creatively in the production of research texts (Honan, 2007; Paulston, 2000; Renold & Ivinson, 2014). In order to resist the apparatus of capture and make new transformational discoveries "we may well have to give up the comfort of method" (St. Pierre et al., 2016, p. 106); as Deleuze (2006) stated, "thought does not need a method" (p. 110). A cartographic approach involves a commitment to a process orientation, a commitment to experimentation, and an ongoing resistance of the given (Ulmer & Koro-Ljungberg, 2015). Cartographic research may draw from a wide variety of qualitative and quantitative approaches, ranging from (but not limited to) traditional ethnography, interviews, observation, surveys, statistics, art, photography, news media, documentary sources, and researcher memories (Fox & Alldred, 2015). But like a nomad, the cartographer is always moving amidst the rhizome, traversing through space without predetermined notions of the assemblage that is being mapped (Ulmer & Koro-Ljungberg, 2015).

Charting a cartography requires attention to "processes and flows rather than structures and stable forms"; the rhizomatic assemblage is the unit of analysis rather than individuals (Fox & Alldred, 2015, p. 407). "Assemblages can be made up of manner of matter: corporeal, technological, mechanical, virtual, discursive and imaginary, that carry affective charges" (Renold & Ivinson, 2014, p. 364). Cartographers in this tradition explore the nuances and intricacies of affective flows within an assemblage, identifying territorialisations, deterritorialisations, lines of flight, and reterritorialisation (Cole, 2013; Fox & Alldred, 2015; Masny, 2013; Renold & Ringrose, 2008). Compiling and making sense of the unravel-ling events in an assemblage, the cartographer is in search of destabilising flows, difference, and transformative change (Stivale, 1984; Taguchi & Palmer, 2014; Tamboukou, 2010).

Cartographies do not simply dissect, define, and categorise the parts within the rhizomatic assemblage; rather, they articulate the social production of affective flows and processes (Stivale, 1984). Mapping of rhizomatic assemblages opens up new realms of creativity and offers a productive process for exploring complex assemblages (Renold & Ivinson, 2014; Taguchi & Palmer, 2014). For example, in their cartographic study, Renold and Ivinson (2014) mapped the interrelated flows in the everyday life of a group of teenage girls in an ex-mining community in South Wales. Deleuzio-Guattarian theory facilitated their analysis of interconnections between these teenagers, their relationship with horses, heteronormative gender roles, and a post-industrial sociopolitical context. In another example, Motala et al. (2022) mapped a cartography of the subjectivities of Black academics in South Africa. Their cartography traced the micropolitical movements of racism and racialisation in the academy and the affirmative flows that "are possible through micro-instances of activism" (p. 8).

The cartographic mapping of assemblages is also a way for engaging politically in the research process. The researcher tracks "the offshoots, the expanding root systems, the ruptures, and the detours that are continually producing new relations of power and all manner of becoming(s)" (Martin & Kamberelis, 2013, p. 671, emphasis in original). This approach requires the identification of repressive stratifications that capture the minor and the pursuit of deterritorialising lines of flight that escape the major (Martin & Kamberelis, 2013). "A cartography is a theoretically based and politically informed reading" of rhizomatic processes, one that is grounded on "philosophical accountability" (Braidotti, 2011, p. 4). The researcher becomes entangled with the rhizomatic assemblage, affecting and being affected by the research assemblage (Honan, 2007). The researcher's own multiplicity is inseparable from the assemblage being mapped. This approach provides an approach not only for analysing social formations and identifying transformative flows, but also for rethinking how researchers engage politically in their research in pursuit of social transformation. A cartography reorients the researcher in a way that "opens up new ways of organizing political resistance (praxis). Praxis-oriented research is research that offers up different ways of organizing reality so that new *becoming(s)* (both for individuals and for social formations) are possible" (Martin & Kamberelis, 2013, p. 671, emphasis in original). Engaging in the micropolitics of the mental health sector, our book attempts to map out the lines of movement in freely given relationships.

A cartography offers a process for engaging in activist scholarship and the growing call for politically engaged research, such as the call for occupational scientists by Farias and Laliberte Rudman (2016):

> The next steps and challenges that occupational scientists who aim to embrace a critical turn towards transformative approaches need to confront are: to take an activist standpoint, to break the barrier between science and action, to reconfigure their positions and the way in which they negotiate with the institutional and political demands in which they are immersed, and

to reconfigure the sensibility underpinning their work within the discipline to a transformative approach.

(p. 46)

Cartographic work offers an avenue for activist scholars to engage with the political, for not only identifying disruptive flows, but also creating them. Guided by theory rather than method, there is the hope for discovering new and transformative territories in mental health research and practice. This pursuit is no straightforward task, as "we can't tell someone how to do this new work, how to think, how to experiment … Our best advice is to read and read and read and attend to the encounters in our experiences that demand our attention" (St. Pierre et al., 2016, p. 106). And so, in the pages of this book we experimentally map the lines and flows in the assemblages of freely given relationships in search of transverse moments and liberating processes of becoming.

★★★

In pursuit of a minor theory in mental health research and practice, we invite a shift, where discrete individuals are not the principal unit of analysis. Rather, we aspire to search for the ways that individuals are entangled in innumerable flows that intersect everyday life. With *Edge Entanglements*, we hope to sink into (and map) the micropolitical arrangements of dynamic rhizomatic assemblages – the assemblage is the unit of analysis rather than individuals. The concepts of the major, minor, becoming-minor, transversality, and the rhizome provide a useful and playful way for scholars and practitioners to engage in affirmative political modes of thought, challenge dominant and oppressive hierarchies, and seek transformative processes.

Notes

1 See Chapter 2 for more conceptual details on deterritorialisation and lines of flight.
2 See also active/reactive hierarchies as described in Chapter 7.
3 Guattari was a staunch anti-authoritarian and resisted the normative family structure, yet demonstrated dominating tendencies as a father and was often absent, including leaving his first wife Nicole Perdreau to care for their children (Dosse, 2010). In drawing attention to the transversality at La Borde, we do not want to glamorise or valorise Guattari. In a position of power at La Borde, Guattari was romantically involved with a number of junior staff, including a person he was charged to "care" for, and had multiple affairs that were distressing to his partners/wives. His children experienced a tumultuous upbringing that was unsettled by multiple relationship breakdowns – Micheline Kao (one of Guattari's partners) stated: "Things were awful" (Dosse, 2010, p. 67).
4 Mad Studies is an example of a transverse field, where there has been a cleaving of hierarchies and psychiatric authority, and alliances between Mad-identifying and Mad-affirming scholars.
5 See Chapter 7 for a discussion on relations of force in ally relationships.
6 For the record, we love trees.

4

ASSEMBLING

In this chapter, we outline our formation of a research assemblage, a dynamic and relational process. Producing postqualitative research within health fields is not a simple endeavour. There are many research practices that constrain and chorale research processes away from the edge of the forest. We hope this chapter helps others to consider how to navigate such issues. Our research draws from a cartographic approach (introduced in Chapter 3) which is briefly described here and elaborated in Chapter 5. Postqualitative research involves significant departure from traditional humanist research practices as it is underpinned by quite different ontological and epistemological assumptions. Aligned with postcritical and posthumanist theories, postqualitative approaches are used to deprioritise rationalist human thought and experiences (Fullagar, 2017). Deleuzian cartography fits well with this endeavour – as an "antimethod" (Zourabichvili & Aarons, 2012) that seeks to avoid predetermined pathways, ossification, and stability – following movements, flows, and shifts. We set out with the noble intention of aligning each aspect of the research approach with this antimethod, but this was not always easy. We describe the entanglement of researchers, community partnerships, study aims, participant recruitment, data collection, data analysis, and ethical considerations.

Assembling partnerships

All facets of a research project can be considered part of an interrelated and interconnected research assemblage – each element affecting and being affected in relation with other elements (Fox & Alldred, 2015). In keeping with our postqualitative cartographic approach, we describe how partnerships and research aims have (been) assembled in this research, and how elements of this research assemblage have become entangled in rhizomatic processes of social production. We follow the

DOI: 10.4324/9781003286486-4

trickle of water as it flows through crevasses and grooves in the ground, connecting with other flows of water, carrying a seed that eventually lodges in the ground and begins to grow.

> Go first to your old plant and watch carefully the watercourse made by the rain. By now the rain must have carried the seeds far away. Watch the crevices made by the runoff, and from them determine the direction of the flow. Then find the plant that is growing…
>
> *(Deleuze & Guattari, 1987, p. 11)*[1]

In what follows, we outline two parallel but interrelated processes that have helped shape the research assemblage which started as a PhD project: finding supervisors and community partners.

In mid-2014 Tim began the awkward search for a PhD supervisor that felt more like dating than an academic exercise. "Would you be interested in grabbing a coffee sometime?" he would ask over and over in email introductions. Then, as Tim sat with each potential supervisor, he wondered: "Are they the *one*? Do they like me? What if I don't find the right supervisor?" But this was an arborescent fantasy, a singular/terminal desire for what is lacking, in this case a supervisor. What Tim actually desired[2] was an assemblage, a constellation of entangled affects: a supervisor that is kind, but challenges him; a community partner that is excited to work with him; positive impact on a community; connection with research participants; intellectual stimulation; pleasure; career advancement; and and and.

In late August 2014 Tim met with Lynda Shevellar. It was a lovely coffee encounter where they had good conversation and some research-interest synergy. While he admired her scholarly work and interests, it was her kindness that drew him to her. Tim was somewhat apprehensive about doing his PhD at the time, and he recalls himself softening and relaxing as they spoke together – she was someone that he would like as a mentor, someone that he would like to spend more time with and learn from. As they parted ways, he was hopeful that Lynda might become one of his advisors.

At the same time as meeting with potential supervisors, Tim was having coffee with people out in the community development sector and developing relationships with people in the community. His past research has used community-based participatory research (CBPR) methods (see Barlott et al., 2015, 2016; Barlott, Shevellar, et al., 2020a) and while the project (that this book is based) does not explicitly use these methods, he was still influenced by a number of CBPR principles such as the involvement of community partners in the formation of research aims and study design, and ensuring research outcomes contribute back to the community in some way. So, Tim sought out relationships with people, following "the encounters in [his] experiences that demand [his] attention" (St. Pierre et al., 2016, p. 106).[3] One of these encounters was in late August 2014, quite possibly the same week that he first met Lynda. He was out for coffee with an experienced community development practitioner and author by the name of Dave Andrews. Dave is a charismatic and passionate citizen and is well-connected in the community development sector.

As they talked, Tim thought to himself: *"great, we're getting somewhere."* Then, at the end of the conversation, Dave said, "I think you should meet Neil over at a little grassroots mental health organisation, I think you two would get on well." So, Tim hopped in Dave's ageing white station wagon and drove down to an old house in the inner-city suburb of West End that housed the office of A Place to Belong (APTB). It was in the front garden of this house that Tim first met Neil Barringham, someone who became a dear friend and colleague.

Over the next couple months, Tim had multiple conversations with Neil, learning about APTB and doing some volunteer work with them at a small community event. APTB works alongside people who are involved with psychiatric services and "who experience mental and emotional trauma," people "who are 'on the edge' of our society" (Barringham & Barringham, 2002, p. 11). Their work supports people to develop connections with others in the community and encourages the development of inclusive communities. As an unfunded part of their work, Neil and APTB connect people in the community (referred to as "allies," "companions," or "bridge-builders") with people who access their services in order to promote freely given relationships (i.e., non-paid, non-familial, non-therapeutic relationships) between people (Barringham & Barringham, 2002). What struck Tim was how the promotion of freely given relationships was not a program within APTB – this was not a volunteer program and these relationships were not closely monitored by the organisation. Tim recalls Neil saying that he did not want risk management protocols to get in the way of genuine relationships. In an early publication about their work, Barringham and Barringham (2002) wrote: "Volunteers provide services. Friends provide friendship. A volunteer is not a friend – although they may become a friend. Further, we cannot fabricate or manufacture *'friends'"* (p. 10). Through his interactions at APTB, Tim learned of a number of these freely given ally relationships and how they have developed into long-term friendships over the years. Tim recognised that these relationships might be an example of a minoring process in the mental health sector (as discussed in Chapter 2) and a potential focus for this project.

Tim soon discovered that Lynda and Neil knew each other quite well and have done some work together. Together, Tim, Lynda, and Neil discussed the possibility of working together on a project. They were all interested in deepening an understanding of freely given relationships, how they work, how they influence the lives of both the ally and APTB service user, and how this might inform practices in the mental health sector. In early 2015, Tim partnered with APTB and began his PhD with Lynda as a supervisor, exploring freely given relationships in the lives of psychiatrised people.[4]

Adding to the supervisory assemblage

The assembling of supervisory teams varies from university to university, but the habitual pattern at the University of Queensland involves adding two co-supervisors. Merrill Turpin was a colleague of Tim's and quickly became a fellow "thinking-with-theory" ally and friend when he moved to Brisbane in 2014. "Is it appropriate or 'wise' to invite a colleague and friend to join my supervisory team?"

Tim thought. Determining the direction of the flow – following the encounters that demand his attention – finding the plant that is growing there. Tim invited Merrill to come on board, throwing caution to the wind.

The trickle of water. Over a year into Tim's PhD, Jenny and Tim had still never met. Jenny was working at the same university as Tim – they had worked in the same building for years – never meeting but were stacked one above the other, two floors apart. Brushing past perhaps in hallways and elevators, breathing the same air as the trickle of water flows through crevasses and grooves in the ground. Tim's home country is Canada. The flows connecting with other flows of water. Jenny was in Canada doing postdoctoral work on healthcare. And Deleuze. Posthumanism. Postqualitative inquiry. When at a multi-day workshop on "Educating for Critical Reflexivity" Jenny meets Shanon Phelan, a past colleague of Tim. Following the workshop, Shanon sends an email to Tim: "you have to meet someone named Jenny who works at UQ." The flow carrying a seed eventually lodges in the ground and begins to grow. Jenny and Tim exchange a few emails and decide to meet for a coffee.

Jenny sends an email on the morning of their coffee meeting: "I'm at Darwin's [a café] but with no idea of what you look like! I've got short grey hair and glasses – in the cue (sic) for coffee."

Tim replies: "Great I'll watch for you. I'm outside by my lonesome with a number 17 on table :)"

In 2017, Jenny joins Tim's supervisory team.

Dreaming forward – "research aims"

Tim had hoped (with this PhD) to pursue minoring processes/approaches in the mental health sector. It was his *hope* that freely given relationships would shed some light on minoring processes and allyship with psychiatrised people. Rosi Braidotti (2011) describes *hope* as "a sort of 'dreaming forward' that permeates our lives and activates them. It is a powerful motivating force grounded in our collective imaginings" (p. 298). Jenny's hope is to inspire healthcare professionals to join in minoring processes – creating more openings for those they work with. By maintaining an attention to power and history through this postqualitative work, we hope to produce both "generative and subversive" reworkings rather than closure or erasure (Gerrard et al., 2016, p.10). Our "collective[5] imagining" is for an assemblage (with you too, reader) that produces zigzag cracks in the major mental health apparatus, one that creates room to manoeuvre for people in the cramped spaces. Deleuze (2004), in his essay *Desert Islands*, conceptualises dreaming of new social imaginaries as *pulling away* or *starting new*:

> Dreaming of islands – whether with joy or in fear, it doesn't matter – is dreaming of pulling away … or it is dreaming of starting from scratch, recreating, beginning anew. Some islands drifted away from the continent, but the island is also that toward which one drifts.

(p. 10)

And so, as we undertook this research, we explored the ways that freely given relationships pull away from the major apparatus or perhaps the ways in which their potential is yet to come – an island "that toward which one drifts" (Deleuze, 2004, p. 10).

Employing the work of Gilles Deleuze and Félix Guattari and multiple entangled others as theoretical drivers for this postqualitative work, we aim to chart a cartography of ally relationship assemblages, mapping the interrelated processes of sociomaterial production in/of these relationships. Traversing the affective flows of social production, we considered how/if transformative processes unfold in ally assemblages, and what this suggests as possibilities for encouraging transformative assemblages in mental health work. In pursuit of minoring processes in the mental health sector, we wanted to explore the ways that ally assemblages resist or disrupt dominant/constraining processes (if at all). We sought to sketch the micropolitical movements of becoming in these relationships, looking for ruptures, lines of flight, and (hopefully) the production of liberating new territories. Mapping a cartography of ally assemblages, we sketch the ways that they pull away from major assemblages, the ways they create new territories, and the ways their potential may still be yet to come.

We have continually turned and re-turned to the following cartographic questions in this research:

- What are ally assemblages like?
- How do ally relationships assemble/disassemble?
- What do ally assemblages do? What do they produce?
- How do transformative processes unfold in ally assemblages (if at all)?

(More than) bodies

In this section, we outline how four pairs of people (four ally relationships, eight total participants) were selected to participate in the research assemblage. Each pair included a service user (with a psychiatric diagnosis) of APTB and a community ally who freely offered support and companionship to this person. Dividing people up in this way was problematic – this starting point involved identifying a minor/major pair, a minor person in need and a major person who could help. However, when Tim met each pair, he did not discuss diagnostic categorisations. Given the in-depth and theory-driven nature of the research, four pairs appeared sufficient to produce rich and complex "data" for analysis. In the following section, we provide details of the step-by-step recruitment process used in the project, as approved by the research ethics board. We also detail how the processes of seeking ethical approval (from both the university and the administering organisation for APTB) informed the research. The processes had agency – tidying up the cartography – which we resisted where we thought we could.

Through discussion with Neil at APTB and his advisors, Tim began to seek out pairs of people in "ally relationships," potential participants to engage in this research assemblage. We decided to include only those that had been in a relation-ship for longer than six months because there would be more relational history to draw from and the pair would potentially be more comfortable together. One person in each pair had to be a service user of APTB and have a psychiatric diagnosis (e.g., schizophrenia, schizoaffective disorder, bipolar disorder, major depression, or anxiety disorder). In additional efforts to appease the ethics boards, APTB con-firmed that service user participants had not been hospitalised for their "mental health" in the preceding six months and we agreed to develop a risk management plan with each pair of participants. Another stipulation added was that each service user participant was to have decision-making capacity in the domain of personal life (i.e., does not have a guardianship order) and the ability to communicate in English. Some of these additions to our ethics applications felt heart wrenching, such as having to inquire about recent hospitalisations that would "disqualify" someone or deem them "unstable" through risk management, whereas the "stability" or "cred-ibility" of the community ally was never in question. At times the ethical review process contrasted starkly with our hopes for generative and subversive action (Facca & Kinsella, 2021). Our actions were re-producing minoritising practices (Olson, 2021). We were participating in the medicalisation of service users and assumptions that they did not have sufficient agency for this research. Ethics applications become unethical at times.

Based on the above criteria, Neil reviewed all ally relationships that were known by APTB. By talking with relevant team leaders who were in weekly or daily contact with service users and support workers, he also considered whether or not potential participants were at risk of experiencing significant distress. This was another stipu-lation we added to our revised ethics application; they did not want Tim spending time with people who were "unwell" or "dangerous," only "stable" people and those sufficiently "recovered." While Mad Studies welcomes and embraces instability, dis-tress, messiness as part of the Mad experience (Shimrat, 2013), research ethics boards do not. The reality was that we included at least one person who had routinely accessed acute psychiatric services (including one time during the project – men-tioned in Chapter 6) but not technically hospitalised.

When Neil invited pairs of people to participate in the project, he made it clear that participating in the research was voluntary and would in no way affect the services they received from APTB. Neil arranged for interested pairs to meet with Tim to learn more about the project and was a part of each initial meeting with people. Each pair had a longstanding and trusting relationship with Neil, so Tim gained some credibility through his association with Neil – Neil was a part of Tim's multiplicity of sorts. "Recruitment" was a straightforward process, but our ethics application had a convoluted six-phase flow diagram on how participants were to be recruited.

Tim chose four ally pairs (eight people) to participate in the project with varied length of relationship (2 years to over 15 years) and gender. The first three pairs that drew his attention were men, so he purposefully sought out more gender diversity – the fourth pair chosen was a relationship between two people who were women. Neil and others at APTB were not informed about which pairs of people were selected to participate, but many participants chose to share this on their own.

Shapes, movements, vibrations (of data)

As is evident from our discussions in this chapter so far, one of the tensions of doing postqualitative research in the context of health is the need to gain human ethics approval. Such approval processes usually require known research techniques and conflict with postqualitative efforts to disrupt traditional methodologies (Lather & St. Pierre, 2013), data collection methods (Jackson, 2017), and the notion of what is data (Mazzei, 2016). During the processes of garnering ethical approval to conduct this project, it was necessary for us to constrain the data collection by giving it known and citable "methods" – rather than "staying outside of method" (Brown et al., 2021). The data collection was thus constrained and categorised – oriented rather than disoriented (ibid). We offer readers our reflections on this process in the hope that this might be useful for you, if you wish to follow similar research pursuits in health.

The initial thought was for Tim to simply spend time with participants. He envisioned coming alongside their relationships in ways they were comfortable with, following their lead of where and when to meet and joining in on the activities that they do together. Aligning with feminist and postcolonial "post-" openness (Gibson, 2019) or rhizomatic ethics (Facca & Kinsella, 2021), Tim's involvement would be responsive and attentive to the rhythms of each relationship. There would also be an ongoing attention to Tim's "partial perspective" (Haraway, 1988, p. 583) and work with Jenny, Lynda, Merrill, Neil, the participants, Deleuze (and other theorists) to disrupt his majoritarian positioning as "researcher" and "health professional." However, this was not the kind of detail the ethics committee required, so we constrained what Tim and the participants would do together, fitting intended actions into particular "data collection methods" and "defending" them with citations. Yet, there are spaces within ethics documents where flexibility might be woven in – the edge of the forest.

We framed Tim's data collection as "ethnographic methods," where the researcher:

> participates, overtly or covertly, in people's everyday life for an extended period of time, watching what happens, listening to what is said, asking questions; in fact collecting whatever data are available to throw light on the issues with which he or she is concerned.
>
> *(Hammersley & Atkinson, 2007, p. 2)*

[See what we did there? We cited existing work to legitimise the research processes.] Ethnographic data collection, we went on to say, typically features collection of data in everyday contexts or "in the field," use of a range of sources (most often observation and in-depth interviews), and unstructured data collection without a rigid research design, and it often focuses on "a small number of cases"

(Hammersley, 2015). This highly flexible approach [see what we did? – we provided ourselves possibilities to shift and change] enabled Tim to follow the flows of each ally assemblage. The data collection in this project resembled the ethnographic methods employed by Renold and Ivinson (2014), who also used a cartographic approach based on the work of Deleuze and Guattari. Their study utilised interviews, observation, field notes, and photography. [Again – citations to help "legitimise" not only the methods, but the theory.] So in the end, Tim spent time participating in the everyday life of each ally pair, meeting approximately two times per month over a four-month period [which was similar to what we wrote in the ethics application]. In their first meeting, Tim and the pair discussed what each ally pair liked to do together and discussed when Tim would be able to "tag along."

We described our research as drawing from the following three data collection methods.

(Less than) interviews

Tim conducted in-depth interviews [this is what we called them for the ethics application], saying that we were using a "conversational style" [citing Whitehead, 2005]. Whitehead describes that, with this interview style, the researcher is an active participant in the conversation rather than, for example, the facilitator of an unstructured interview. Participants, he says, have some freedom to disclose information at their discretion rather than having the interview topic and questions dictated by the researcher. We used Whitehead's interview description, because it gave us both a citation for legitimacy (for ethics) and provided us the most flexibility to engage with participants in something resembling just spending time together. Likely there are other citations that could be used similarly. We also said that this interview style has multiple natural breaks and pauses throughout, and as a result, is less demanding on participants than more structured interviews. Through conversation, the participants and Tim explored aspects of their relationship such as where and how often the pair usually met; what sort of regular activities they did together; the history of their relationship; how they met; what the relationship is like; what does it mean to be/have an ally; flow-on outcomes from their relationship (e.g., meeting other people, new interests, and activities); and changes to the relationship over time. Quite often the conversations meandered to other topics (such as the happenings in each other's lives) as they spent time together.

Whenever possible, and with consent from both members of the ally relationship, Tim audio-recorded and transcribed these (less than) interviews. Given that encounters with ally pairs did not always occur in ideal environments for audio recording (e.g., some were in a café), Tim took notes afterwards when recording was not possible. The discussions lasted between 45 and 120 minutes, with opportunities for the aforementioned breaks throughout. Breaks were rarely structured or overt since natural breaks occurred throughout their conversations (e.g., a break to refill a teacup during a get-together). These conversations were also an opportunity for Tim to seek participant feedback on the analysis as it was being produced (e.g., confirm understandings of their relationship, explore curiosities, discuss aspects of theory being lived).

Observation and field notes

Being immersed in the everyday life of ally pairs, Tim's intention was to make observations throughout each encounter: he was attentive, observant, curious. He looked for the intra-actions/affects/lines/movements. Gold (1958) describes four types of observation: *complete observer* (objective, the researcher does not engage in the activity of the observed), *observer as participant* (the researcher participates in activities with participants, but their main role is to be an observer and collect data), *participant as observer* (the researcher is fully involved in the activities of participants, and participants are aware that the researcher is also completing a research activity), and *complete participant* (the researcher is fully immersed in the day-to-day activities of participants, and the participants are unaware of any research objectives/identity of researcher is concealed). The observation style in this study was similar to *participant as observer*, as Tim observed the relationships as they spent time together, but also *observer as participant* when out in the community together (e.g., when out at a Monster Truck show with participants). Framing Tim's observations in the above categorical way gave legitimacy to his approach. Given our "thinking with theory" approach (discussed later in this chapter and throughout *Edge Entanglements*), Tim's observations were informed by and aligned with the theories we have discussed in this book. Tim made notes on elements of the encounter that he was drawn to as part of understanding what was happening in these relationships. This included consideration of the environment where the observations were made; verbal or non-verbal communication between participants and with Tim; anyone's emotions, levels of comfort, or signs of agitation, body language; interaction in relation to context; and Tim's own interpretations, feelings, and distractions.

Posthuman social mapping

We said in our ethics application that we "utilised social mapping (Hammersley & Atkinson, 2007) during interviews to supplement the ethnographic methods." Social mapping[6] is a participatory method that visually depicts interconnections between people, places, objects, and other structures (Kathirvel et al., 2012; Rockloff & Lockie, 2004) [here we go again, using existing methods and legitimising our approach with citations]. It identifies the intersection of human and non-human things in relationships, exploring physical, social, cultural, and institutional connectivities (Kathirvel et al., 2012; Minkler & Wallerstein, 2010). In this research, the social mapping process used was based on Tracy and Whittaker's (1990) social network map but incorporated additional (posthuman) elements to the mapping process such as objects and memories to align with our theoretical approach. Using post-it

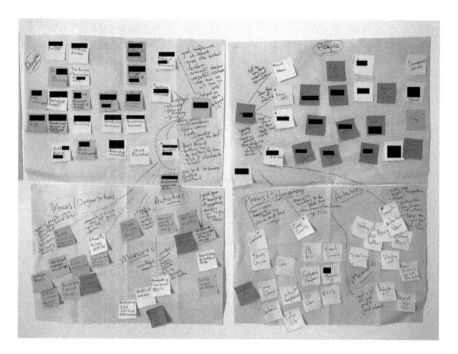

FIGURE 4.1 Example of a social map used in this project.

notes, markers, and poster paper on a wall, Tim invited participants to individually write or draw things in their life across the categories: people (past and present, alive and deceased), animals, places, organisations/institutions/social structures, activities, objects, and memories. As each item was placed on the wall, the pairs and Tim discussed what their connection was like for that particular item. They then talked through the interrelationship of each of their social maps (see example in Figure 4.1). Social mapping typically took three sessions (2–3 hours total) to complete. These social maps served as a useful approach to get to know each participant and to make sense of their relationship assemblage. Although it is an established (and categorical) method, we chose it because it had the fluidity to be adapted to suit the unbound-edness of our postqualitative approach. What is missing from the visual in Figure 4.1 are the parallel conversations on the intermingled elements – for example when a childhood summer camp (categorically mapped as a "place" and "memory") had lines of affect across people, current pursuits, and was entangled with their relation-ship. Each post-it had the potential to rupture into a line of flight.

Analysis: Cartography

As discussed, this research was principally informed by a cartographic, postquali-tative approach to research. Thinking with theory, we worked and reworked the (non-discrete) data created by the (somewhat unbounded) methods outlined above to produce a cartography. Introduced in Chapter 3, a cartography is a theory-in-fused re-presentation of the processes and relational affects of an assemblage. We used Deleuzio-Guattarian and other theories to agitate our thinking and produce zigzag encounters between theory and data (Fullagar et al., 2019; Springgay & Truman, 2018). Tim did the bulk of the work to map how territories were formed and broke down, how flows were constrained and opened up, and how disruptive processes created fissures and gave way to lines of flight. Situated within a postqualitative research tradition, a cartography is what Lisa Mazzei (2021) refers to as an "improvisational inquiry," where "theoretical concepts and data constitute one another in our analytic practice of thinking with theory" (p. 1). Postqualitative inquiry is not a systematic research method; rather, it is a commitment to (rigorously) think with theory (Fullagar, 2017; Mazzei, 2021; St. Pierre et al., 2016) – in our case (as with other cartographic research), primarily the work of Deleuze and Guattari. Postqualitative inquiry is akin to Deleuze and Guattari's (1987) notion of a pack of wolves, which we have described elsewhere as being:

> at once singular (pack) and multiple (wolves), porous and shifting, a unity exceeding its parts. Each wolf has its own body, its own mind, but at the same time it senses and acts as, and with, the other wolves in the pack. It is at once one and many – a singular multiplicity. The individuality of each wolf leaks and flows. It oscillates between wolf-pack-wolf, always becoming the other. Various inter-relationships shift and change within the pack. New members are born or die, hierarchies are challenged and couplings are made and unmade. The pack is one and many, fluid and becoming.
>
> *(Setchell et al., 2017)*

As a pack of wolves, postqualitative inquiry is not a stratified and clearly demarcated research methodology, but a pluralistic constellation of research that draws from poststructural, postmodern, posthumanist, new materialist, critical, feminist, and other theories to re-present research data. As Fullagar (2017) notes, "the Deleuzian-inspired research" of numerous researchers "has not identified with a unified methodological identity, rather these scholars articulate more specific thinking with theory practices" (p. 251). Examples include the cartographic work of Taguchi and Palmer (2014), Ulmer and Koro-Ljungberg (2015), Renold and Ivinson (2014), Dalgleish, Everett, and Duff (2019), Motala et al. (2022), and Abrams et al. (2019). While this project is situated within a postqualitative tradition (pack), our emphasis is on practices of thinking with theory (cartography). Chapter 5 further outlines how to *do* a cartography and offers an example of operationalising and experimenting with this (un)method.

Entangled ethical considerations

What does it mean to do ethical research? Earlier, we have drawn attention to some of the ways we crafted the project to be acceptable to our institutional ethics board and the administering organisation of APTB (and we did receive approval). Despite receiving full approval from relevant ethics boards, we wanted to carefully be cognisant of the ongoing ethics of our work. We wanted our project to be full of care. Feminists Fisher and Tronto (1990) refer to care as:

> everything that we do to maintain, continue, and repair our "world" so that we can live in it as well as possible. That world includes our bodies, our selves, and our environment, all of which we seek to interweave in a complex, life-sustaining web.
>
> *(p. 40)*

Ethical, caring research is responsive to the ways that power manifests (and dominates) and seeks to repair the worlds of people we involve as participants. Maria Puig de la Bellacasa (2017) describes care as an "ethico-political obligation" (p. 42) and "commitment to neglected things" (p. 66). Here, de la Bellacassa (de la Bellacasa, 2017) invites us to consider the ways research participants have been "neglected" (marginalised, devalued, and cast off) and commit to repairing our world. We are not sure how well we rose to the occasion, but we have identified a couple additional examples below.

For ethical approval we legitimised ourselves as capable of taming undomesticated madness. We highlighted, that, as a research team, we brought extensive experience of working with people who are considered vulnerable and marginalised. Tim spoke of his formal training and experience as an occupational therapist, a background as an addictions counsellor, community healthcare practitioner, and community-based researcher, current experience in an ally relationship, and extensive experience working with people who have disabilities. Lynda discussed her extensive experience working with people with disabilities and mental health challenges, and she has training in mental health first aid and counselling, as well as postgraduate qualifications in psychology, education, and community development; Merrill mentioned her experiences an occupational therapist in mental health and a variety of disabilities; and Jenny as a physiotherapist with extensive clinical experience working with "vulnerable populations," including people with mental health issues, and her a doctoral qualification in psychology. It made us cringe to re-read how we legitimise our authority and credibility. If we had talked about being psychiatrised ourselves, we may not have been permitted to do this work (see LeBlanc & Kinsella, 2016; Bellingham et al., 2021). Yet, perhaps our lack of lived experience with psychiatric systems is what we should be highlighting – is it okay that we do this work?

During the ethical approval process, there was considerable discussion about the level of risk in the project. The partner organisation, APTB, viewed the project as very low risk given that Tim would talk with people about a relationship that seemed to be positive in their lives. However, the administering organisation for APTB argued that the uncontrolled nature of the study and natural environment (e.g., community/private residences versus institutions) posed significant risk. We argued that the most ethical (and caring) approach would be to meet with participants in locations of their choosing rather than in institutional settings. In a research ethics board meeting with the administering organisation for APTB, Tim was asked things like "what will you do if someone has a psychotic episode in your interview?" and, "how are you, as an occupational therapist, qualified to deal with the mentally ill?" These questions bring to light some of the sanist assumptions in both the mental health sector and the academy. It seemed as though they were also suspicious of Tim, sceptically stating that the theories used in the study "sound like anarchy." Approval was eventually granted with the addition of a safety and risk management framework. The major apparatus attempts to contain and constrict our minoring approach. Placing emphasis on monitoring and risk management is a common practice in major mental health assemblages (as discussed in Chapter 2). With Neil, we created the following guiding questions for Tim to ask during his first meeting with participants to assist in establishing a "safety and risk management plan": How will we work together to make sure our research is safe? What could happen? How will we know if you are experiencing distress? What can you do to help? What can we do to help? Tim felt some discomfort asking these questions since their presence was rooted in the sanist assumptions of the ethics board. However, the questions developed with Neil were trauma-informed and communicated care for wellbeing rather than control.

Research assemblage

In this chapter, we have outlined the development of our research assemblage, a complex network of processes and relationships that forms the milieu we discuss in this book. We have outlined the collaborative community partnership with APTB, how we worked together to invite allyship pairs into the research as "participants," and the various processes we used to construct a cartography of ally assemblages. Using (less than) interviews, posthuman social mapping, and observation, Tim spent in-depth time with each pair to entangle with and learn about their relationships. Thinking with theory, we sketched a cartography of ally assemblages. Chapter 5 further outlines this cartographic approach, experimentally playing with data to show what a cartography can *do*. The remainder of *Edge Entanglements* (Chapter 6–10) is dedicated to our mapping of the micropolitical flows and social processes amidst ally assemblages. In a few pages, you will meet Crispy and Chips; Alan and Jack; Julie and Carol; and Batman and Robin, and become a part of the research assemblage yourself.

Notes

1 We return to this quote in Chapter 8 as we sketch processes of becoming in this research.
2 Deleuzio-Guattarian desire is a socially infused impulse to create. See Chapter 9 for a comprehensive description of desire and how desire surfaced my study.

3 This is a part of a quote that we have incorporated throughout this book. While St. Pierre et al. (2016) were not discussing the formation of research partnerships when making this statement, their words communicate how theoretically infused thinking can influence how scholars nomadically follow the flows of everyday life.

4 The Afterword explores some of Lynda's multiplicity, tensions, and sociopolitical entanglements with this work.

5 "Since each of us was several …" (Deleuze & Guattari, 1987, p. 1).

6 Despite the language of "mapping," this data collection method is unrelated to my overarching cartographic approach/methodology.

5
DOING A CARTOGRAPHY

In this chapter, we offer an in-depth exploration of our cartographic postqualitative process, the doing of thinking with theory. We traverse the lines of affect in our analysis, offering pragmatic insights into what it means when St Pierre et al. (2016) state, "our best advice is to read and read and read and attend to the encounters in our experiences that demand our attention" (p. 106). Rather than offering a systematic approach, we show how we used theory to creatively experiment with data in a postqualitative project that preceded the project that this book is based on. This experimental encounter with data is presented as asystematic transverse movements. We diagrammatically follow the lines of movement and processes of social production in our more-than-human research assemblages. The chapters that follow (especially Chapters 7–10) also demonstrate our cartographic processes, yet with less attention to the doings of a cartography (re)presented here.

Cartographic approach

As discussed in the previous chapter (Chapter 4), the sociomaterial assemblages of health research often work to constrain and ossify research practices. Health research training is frequently confined to quantitative methodologies and qualitative methodologies that are highly systematic, methods-driven, and post-positivist – ours certainly was. So how, when desiring a less constrained approach such as a cartography, might a health researcher work against this training? We said in Chapter 3 that a cartography involves moving amidst the rhizome, traversing through space without predetermined notions of the assemblage that is being mapped. In practice, how can this be done?

One of Tim and Jenny's early methodological discussions explored the possibilities of escape from the constraints of our training – how it might be possible

DOI: 10.4324/9781003286486-5

to achieve a more rhizomatic exploration. We explored the moments in our lives when we are less constrained in our thinking, able to move with "processes and flows" rather than "structures and stable forms" (Fox & Alldred, 2015, p. 407). For Tim it was when playing or listening to music, for Jenny when dancing or when doing "improvisation" exercises in their theatre training. In the giddiness of love? when exhausted? when drunk?

Throughout this chapter we discuss how we enacted a cartography. To do this, we unravel an early experimental encounter that informed the cartography of the freely given relationships in *Edge Entanglements*. We begin by introducing the project and the lines of movement in our analysis and what it was like to undertake, tracing the affective processes. In the second half of the chapter we then demonstrate how these cartographic doings were re-presented in the form of an academic publication. Our intention with this chapter is not to simply describe what a cartography *is*, but to demonstrate what a cartography can *do*.

The experimental encounter in this chapter began before Tim connected with the pairs of people for this book project. It started with us wondering together about how to "analyse data" cartographically. The exploration involved writing a paper as a rhizomatic experiment (which is now published in *Qualitative Inquiry* and parts of it are reproduced here with their permission, see Barlott et al., 2020b). At this stage, we had both read a lot of Deleuzio-Guattarian inspired research, but neither of us had done a cartography. We wanted a chance to play with data prior to "collecting data" for this book project. So, using data Tim had generated from an earlier project, we experimentally "played" with an interview that had previously caught Tim's attention.

TIM: I had no idea what I was doing, I had never done anything like this before. I could handle the first step ("read and read and read"), but what came next was a mystery to me. Still, I felt an openness to being affected by the "data" and an impulse to create. It reminded me somewhat of times where I was moved to pull out my guitar, usually by an emotion or a swirling melody in my mind. I recall sitting with my guitar on my lap and just playing, not quite sure what would happen next. (I feel the need to confess that I'm not a very good musician and haven't played a guitar in years.) I went into this cartographic experiment with an openness to experiencing something very different than in my previous research. But turning to my emotions, I was feeling quite nervous. What if Jenny doesn't like what I come up with? Does that even matter? Am I creative enough? What if I fall flat? Should I have a backup plan for my methodology? I was in-between: safe enough[1] to play without thinking about the outcome and simultaneously constrained by the expectation of an "acceptable" outcome. At the same time I also wanted to know, what will Jenny be like?

Will I enjoy doing this with them? Will I feel safe experimenting and being vulnerable? I tried to let go and just see what happens.

JENNY: I felt a little anxious at this point – could Tim actually do it? Would his analysis be tied down, obvious, uninteresting? Or perhaps worse – unbounded, obvious, and uninteresting. And I was worried that I might not be able to support Tim to stay in the edge of the forest – would the pragmatic parts of myself make neatly fenced lawns of his work? I was aware from experience that many PhD students are keen to eschew convention, and that doing so can sometimes cause difficulties when the result is challenging for others to untangle. I tried to relinquish control and support Tim to experiment, to stay in the wild. But I knew I was taking a risk to do this.

Thinking with theory as a transverse, edge of the forest encounter

Drawing from the work of Deleuze and Guattari, we experimentally charted a cartography of a peculiar interview (an "off-topic" and "dissident" interview that disrupted the agenda of the interviewer). We aimed to traverse the micropolitics of the interview, the entangled relations of power and resistance. We intentionally charted the intensive topography of the peculiar and re-presented what was once missed (or passed over). Thinking with theory rather than method, we used Deleuze and Guattari's conceptualisation of social machines, deterritorialisation, and desire to interrogate and experiment with the dissident interview. Much of the process happened in Tim's office. The office was an irregular shape, crowded with teaching materials, stacks of books, empty cans of energy drink, chairs (that didn't really fit), picture frames, and boxes of things that Tim still hadn't unpacked from Canada. Tim printed out the errant interview transcript, cleared his desk (by stacking stacks onto other stacks), sat down, and spread it out in front of him. As he read the interview, concepts came to mind, stirring him to flip to sections of the books around him, which stirred him to turn to other books, which stirred him to re-turn to the transcript, and. He sat, he stood, he paced, he stared out the window at the eucalyptus trees in the distance, he paused, he slowly walked through the university grounds with the transcript as his companion, carefully going through the process of reading – thinking – writing. He often broke away from his analysis to do other work, placing student papers and rubrics on top of the cartography. As if these major stratified documents tainted the cartography, it usually took a couple of hours (or days) to claw his way back into the theory-infused mapping of the interview.

Despite Deleuze and Guattari's book *A Thousand Plateaus* being the focus of his reading at that time, it was their book *Anti-Oedipus* and the concept of social machines that demanded his attention. Tim spread out dog-eared books on his desk beside/on top/below the interview transcript – the interview led his reading of theory, the theory led his reading of the interview transcript. Reading – thinking – writing, Tim began to think of the interview as an act of guerrilla warfare (affected by Deleuze and Guattari's description of a war machine) – he went to the library and took out every book on the topic. He cut up the transcript, re-ordered it, moved it, shuffled it, diagrammed the movements with post-it notes and drawings – "what would happen if I put this here? What would happen if I used this concept instead of that one?" Theory and data became entangled as Tim mapped the data with his writing. Movement and stillness.

Tim and Jenny met up to discuss Tim's initial thoughts. Tim brought a messy pile of post-it notes (see Figure 5.1, taken in 2022 when Tim found these notes while unpacking boxes in his new office) and thoughts about guerrillas to the meeting. Over coffee we discussed guerrillas and our initial ideas for how a paper might take form … and it did. Books, post-it notes, transcript, Tim, and theory swirled around producing various affects, and the discussion of the interview was eventually performed as a nine-movement guerrilla encounter. In this way, Tim re-presented the peculiarities of the interview as unconventional guerrilla tactics that deterritorialised and disrupted the interview. He mapped micropolitical flows – the experimentation surfaced some of the ways an interview could be despotic and stifle affective production. He also traced how a Deleuzio-Guattarian war machine prevented the capture and appropriation of the interview and produced a new creative machine. We share excerpts from the paper produced from

FIGURE 5.1 Cartographic diagramming of the dissident interview.

this experimental encounter below, and how theory is interwoven into our analysis and re-presentation of our cartography.

The dissident interview, a deterritorialising guerrilla encounter

A place to start. Tim was the principal investigator for a qualitative descriptive study that looked at the use of information and communication technology among people with learning disabilities (Barlott et al., 2020a). In that study, a research assistant ("Heather") interviewed ten people using a semi-structured interview technique aiming toward understanding the experiences of participants with learning disabilities using technology (e.g., mobile phones, tablets, computers) and their connectedness with others. One of the interviews always stood out to Tim – it was off-topic, tangential, and often difficult to follow. Heather said she struggled to keep the conversation focused on the research aims during the interview, with Elliott interjecting with different topics and questions of his own. For example, Elliott turned a discussion about technology use into a conversation about being "locked up in a sci-fi prison." Heather was apologetic for going off topic in the interview, "I'm not quite sure how useful it'll be," she reflected. But, to Tim, there was something intriguing about the interview – yet he was unsure of how to incorporate it within the analytic framework used in the study (thematic analysis), and only a small portion of the interview was used in the analysis and write up. However, thinking with theory, we re-turned to this dissident interview as an opportunity to "begin with the too strange" (St. Pierre, 2017, p. 307), that we might "produce different knowledge and produce knowledge differently" (Lather, 2013, p. 635). In doing so, we are mindful of the ethical tension in turning to the "too strange." A fascination with the unusual has not only the potential to deepen our appreciation of difference but also the potential to exotify and other (Newman, 2019; Ross & Setchell, 2019). Thinking with Deleuzio-Guattarian theory, we aim not to voyeuristically analyse an individual but rather take an atypical interview as a starting point for our cartography of the micropolitical relations among things.

We have reached the edge of the town, weeds proliferate and seedlings of forest trees establish themselves where they can. What is guerrilla warfare?

> I'm tired. My favourite vein is getting a bit knackered from repeated cannula insertion – I always have them use my right hand because I crochet left-handed. I choke back my breakfast – a pharmaceutical kaleidoscope. Forced to leave work.
>
> Weak – lethargic – resenting – melting I started crocheting when I got sick. I often imagine what I could vandalise as I walk my dog – the brick railway viaduct could use some knitted flowers and butterflies.
>
> Tomorrow we yarn bomb the village fair. There is nervous energy among the women in the group – "what will people think?" I feel like my head is going to explode from the vasculitus, but muster the energy to strategise the placement of squares over the tree trunks.

> Yarn bursts from my hands: single stitch –double stitch – treble stitch –repeat.
>
> Strong –revived –gratified – expanding
>
> In a small rural community where women are known for conventional roles, I am an artist, I am an activist.
>
> *– Wendy Bryant on her guerrilla activities*

The subversive activism of our friend Wendy (who provided the text for the epigraph above for the paper we produced from our experimental encounter) is not what would usually come to mind in relation to guerrilla warfare – yet we've been drawn to her yarnbombing as a performative example. Her story not only illustrates the ethos of the concept of the guerrilla but also subverts the masculinity of guerrilla warfare. Guerrillas are a paradox; although they often have limited power and resources, they can overthrow far more powerful adversaries (Boot, 2013). We love the idea of guerrilla tactics – we are drawn to its subversiveness – the bitumen-sabotaging-greenery-invasions of the guerrilla gardening movement, the Guerrilla Girls' feminist art protests, and our connections with freedom fighters (guerrillas) fighting oppressive regimes in East Hankor and Timor Leste.

The guerrilla is an icon of resistance – Rychetta Watkins (2012) highlights that it is both an ideology and practice aimed at disrupting oppressive social practices. She illustrates how guerrillas operate on the periphery of society or the battlefield (Watkins, 2012). "No one chooses to fight as a guerrilla, a lifestyle that has always come with great hardships" (Boot, 2013, p. 43). The guerrilla emerges as a response to oppressive forces (Watkins, 2012).

Guerrilla ontology was a term used by the author Robert Anton Wilson (2012) in his book *The Illuminati Papers*, first published in 1980. Unsettling the view that there is one reality, he writes, "guerrilla ontology is breaking down this one-model view" and "shaking up that certainty" (p. 2). Ontological (poststructural) anarchist Hakim Bey (1991) has conceptually used guerrilla tactics as modes of resistance for destabilising rigid ways of thinking. Bey (1991) speaks of guerrilla tactics (such as sabotage and hit-and-run, described later in the article) as generative/destructive practices for achieving Temporary Autonomous Zones – zones where hierarchies are destabilised, making way for creative events and encounters. Guerrilla tactics fray the fabric of the given and open up the possibility that something different will break through the holes. In our article, we operationalised the concept of guerrilla warfare, framed within the theoretical work of Deleuze and Guattari, to interrogate an interview in qualitative research.

A guerrilla-like move in itself, thinking with theory offers a way to traverse and potentially subvert the micropolitics of research encounters: "the internal movements of power and resistance" (Fox & Alldred, 2017, p. 198). Although some conventional qualitative methods tend to privilege common and recurrent patterns in data, a theory-driven approach can illuminate and rethink the micropolitics of the unusual (MacLure, 2013). "Plugged in" to our data using Deleuzio-Guattarian theory, we became enchanted by the peculiar, the strange "glow" of the unusual

(MacLure, 2013, p. 661). Taking a peculiar interview as a starting point for our experimentation, we began "with the too strange" and trusted "that something unimaginable might come out" (St. Pierre, 2017, p. 307). A cartographic un-process charts the nuances and intricacies of relational affects, tensions/differences, and unravelling and interconnected events (Stivale, 1984; Taguchi & Palmer, 2014; Tamboukou, 2010).

Thinking with theory, we continually asked the questions: "what is being produced?" and "how is it being produced?" rather than "what are the commonalities, categories, or themes?" Mapping research encounters opens up new realms of creativity and offers a productive tool for exploring complex, posthuman social formations (Barlott et al., 2017; Renold & Ivinson, 2014; Taguchi & Palmer, 2014; Motala et al., 2022).

Attending to the encounters that demanded our attention, we were drawn to a particular interview as the basis for this cartography – our theoretical experimentation with the data. We chose (or did it choose us?) to analyse a "deviant" interview that splintered away from the study objectives. A handful of qualitative researchers have analysed such interviews (sometimes referred to as "failed" interviews), citing that interviews that are driven in different directions by research participants often generate new ways of thinking (Jacobsson & Åkerström, 2012; Nairn et al., 2005).

In what follows, we introduce the Deleuzio-Guattarian concepts we used in our experimental analysis before turning to discuss the interview itself.

Social machines

To think and rethink the peculiar within the dissident interview, we employed Deleuze and Guattari's conceptualisation of social machines (also simply referred to as "machines") to generate a cartography of its complex relations and social production. They present social machines as aggregates of the interrelationship between the physical/nonphysical, human/nonhuman, past/present, actual/possible (Deleuze & Guattari, 1984, 1987). Social machines are always in flux, always in the process of forming new relations and assembling in new ways – the elements within a machine continually affecting each other and being affected (Deleuze & Guattari, 1984). The interview, as with any encounter, is the intersection of different social machines and is a machine itself. All materiality within the interview machine are mutually influential, constructed through a process of social production (see Honan, 2007; Mazzei, 2013). Affective relations (flows, interruptions, differences in intensities) within a machine influence the capacity to produce new flows and the actualisation of virtual possibilities (Deleuze & Guattari, 1987). Charting the cartography of affective relations within the interview machine has the potential to shed light on the intricacies of molecular ruptures, the micropolitics of the encounter. The capacity for production within an aggregate machine is desire – desire is the intensity and drive to create (Deleuze & Guattari, 1987). Desire is the potential to affect – it is a force, "the creative capacity of a body to act, feel or otherwise engage with other bodies and the physical and social world" (Fox & Alldred, 2017, p. 101). Social machines also follow patterns of recurring flows, which are referred to as territorialisations. When generative flows, desiring production, break away from or disrupt territorialised patterns, this is referred to as deterritorialisation (Deleuze & Guattari, 1987). The new trajectory, the creative/generative flow away from territorialised patterns, produced through desire, is a line of flight (Deleuze & Guattari, 1987). Bearing in mind the concept of social machines, desire, territorialisation, and deterritorialisation, we seek to understand and analyse the interview machine by asking the questions: What does it do? What does it produce?

Deleuze and Guattari's (1984) social machines take on several forms. Three particular types of machines are of interest to our cartographic analysis of the dissident interview: *territorial machine*, *despotic machine*, and *war machine*.

Territorial machines follow habitual patterns, typically following lines of filiation (lineage and inherited patterns) and alliance (existing connections and associated patterns; Deleuze & Guattari, 1984). Territorial machines are lateral; the relations produce patterned territories. Patterns of affect are predictable. For example, we could consider Jenny's house-buying experiences. Many people plan to create homes by buying or renting a house or apartment with their partner. In Australia and Canada at least, this usually involves fairly standardised elements and relations: location, property prices, negotiations processes, calculation of deposits, employment, forms from banks, dreams of ideal dwelling layouts, interest rates, and housing laws. Fairly predictable (if somewhat exciting and stressful) sociomaterial processes entangled in the micropolitics of capitalism. There are existing lists provided to check off and expected reactions from family and friends. Yet Jenny chose to buy a house with their partner, another couple and another adult – they planned to convert it into three separate living spaces with shared elements. Yet the banks had no forms that suited Jenny's situation, were hesitant to loan money, and friends and family reacted in multiple ways, often with concern. Difference can bring precarity and instability to territorialised machines.

Despotic machines reterritorialise the lateral relations of territorial machines with hierarchical relations (Deleuze & Guattari, 1984). The despot, a deity, person, or form imposes a new alliance with themselves as filiation (Buchanan, 2008; Deleuze & Guattari, 1984). The despot acts as a tyrant, controlling the affective flows into relation to themselves as master. The despot permits and facilitates relations and flows within the machine as a conduit to their own ends. Desire is constricted and production limited to affect that benefits the despot. Despotic machines are violent in that their affect limits the affective capacity of other bodies in the machine, constricting desire and stifling creative production. Despotic machines domesticate and civilise those that are under the control of the despot. Those under the despot are indebted to the despot. The territorial machine continues to exist, but the machinic parts (cogs and wheels – physical/nonphysical, human/nonhuman, past/present, actual/possible) are overtaken by the despot. Continuing with the example of Jenny's territorialised home-creation machine. The banks emerged as a despot when Jenny and co-owners tried to create a home that suited them. "How can we trust you?" – the bank manager said – "it would be different if you were married" (at that stage none of us could legally be married as we were all considered women).

The territorialised home creation machine has deviated from the preferred habitual patterns. "How can you trust each other?" friends and colleagues cried. Forms were added and adapted, Jenny and the others squeeze themselves into shape for the despotic machine, often making compromises, paying more, and expending considerable time and energy. The despotic machine controls the lines of affect to benefit the capitalist machine – less risk, compliance, order.

War machines, in contrast to despotic violence, are machines of disruption. These are insurgent machines that resist the reductive violence of the despot and deterritorialise patterned territories (Deleuze & Guattari, 1987). The war machine is a machine of resistance that "wages the violence of war on existing orders of knowledge" (Deuchars, 2011, p. 8). The war machine is a "conceptual tool of politico-cultural resistance" that creates lines of flight, creating conditions for generative transformation (Deuchars, 2011, p. 9). Although the despotic machine seeks to capture that which is beneath it, and to categorise and appropriate things that are abnormal, the war machine is a conceptual tool for resisting the violence of the despot. The war machine resists dominance but is not interested in dominating; the war machine resists normativity and the oppression of those that fall outside the norm that are captured by the despot. The war machine is a smoothing force, disrupting hierarchies, deterritorialising rigid territories, and opening up space for something new to form (Deuchars, 2011). Much new was created from Jenny's housing set up – disruption of heteronormativity, reduced environmental impact through sharing spaces and devices, spontaneous gatherings, affordable housing. Radio interviews ensued, introducing others to new ways of dwelling together. An arts festival held an event at their home involved music (Bock et al., 2020), performances (Yen, 2020), a panel on women's housing affordability – the home creation machine unsettled what a house is for. University students (not ours) got involved and made a documentary (White & Sock, 2020). The war machine has unpredictable affects that disrupt hierarchies of power.

The war machine is a destructive force, as opposed to a violent force, that frees desire and generates new possibilities. For example, a tropical storm (through a Deleuzio-Guattarian lens) is not violent, but can be destructive, often establishing new shorelines and flows of water. Destructive forces are wild and contest the domestication of territories. Violence is the assertion of authority in a way that benefits the authority and limits the expression of the bodies within the machine. Violence limits the desiring production of machines and domesticates it in the normative image of the authority. Violence "separates people from what they are capable of" (Deleuze, 1988). By contrast, the destruction and resistance of the war machine is a creative act, an expression of desire, and an expression of powers of action. Destruction deterritorialises the machine and generates possibility for new lines of flight.

Using social machines was productive in that it provided us a way to think through the flows of power and its affects in the interview. We could trace the pulls and pushes, the assertions and disruptions of power. Yet it also produced other more disquieting unintended affects – the masculinist language – the words "war," "machine," "violence," "despot" caused discomfort amongst the researchers (and reviewers). We attempted, with mixed success, to subvert this with talk of yarn bombing, art, and feminism.

Guerrilla tactics and the war machine

In this initial experimental cartography, we conceptually used guerrilla warfare tactics as the subversive deterritorialising force of the war machine. Like the war machine, guerrillas rely on unconventional and disruptive modes of attack – "guerrilla warfare explicitly aims for the nonbattle" (Deleuze & Guattari, 1987, p. 484). Guerrillas rely on mobility and movement, on hit-and-run tactics that utilise surprise in battle (Beckett, 2001; Boot, 2013). Their irregular, strange, unexpected, and improvisational warfare strategies are often deemed unfair or dirty by those with power – as if they aren't following the rules (Guevara, 1961; Loveman & Davies, 1997; Watkins, 2012). The guerrilla does not wage war as an individual, but as a pack; the guerrilla is one "whose principal weapon is not his [or, we would say, their] rifle or his machete, but his relationship to the community" (Watkins, 2012, p. 58).

Che Guevara (1961) outlined key principles and tactics of guerrilla warfare that form our conceptual use of guerrilla as a metaphor for the deterritorialising forces of the war machine:

- *Mobility* – ongoing movement, changing directions, changing speeds.
- *Hit-and-run* – the disruptive element in hit-and-run is surprise – there is advantage in keeping the opposition off balance. One of the ways to surprise the opposition is through an *ambush*, a chaotic intensive hit, followed by a retreat. The opposition thinks the battle is over and relaxes, but the guerrillas ambush again. This is the hit-and-run.
- *Sabotage* – carefully crafted destruction. The goal is to damage peripheral structures that disrupt and stifle the processes and movement of the opposition. Examples include destroying communication systems, roads, and bridges. In addition, sabotage involves taking control of enemy technologies, such as setting traps, and taking control or disrupting supply lines. Sabotage involves destructive acts aimed at hindering dominant efforts (McGeorge & Ketcham, 1983). Sabotage is covert and nonviolent, but often highly destructive (in terms of scale; McGeorge & Ketcham, 1983). It is useful to use hit-and-run tactics alongside sabotage to exploit the confusion of the opposition.

Subversive guerrilla tactics bring to life the deterritorialising processes of the war machine in the dissident interview. Our cartography dramatises the encounter, playfully juxtaposing language of guerrilla combat and violence onto a human conversation. One could say that we have exaggerated a microresistance; however, the absurdity of our retelling develops a sense of urgency/tension, so that we might illuminate "what was lying in the shadows … things we were hardly aware existed"

(Deleuze, 1995, p. 141). Our aim is to interrogate the interview by theoretically analysing affective relations in the interview machine and to perform the dissident interview as successive subversive guerrilla manoeuvres. In our paper, we retold the interview in the form of a nine-movement guerrilla encounter. We share five of these movements here:

Movement 1: Territorialised interview machine
Movement 2: Emergence of a despotic machine
Movement 3: Destructive event and the weakened authority of the despot
Movement 8: War machine's third guerrilla attack – ambush
Movement 9: Emergence of new territorialised machine

When writing this section, Jenny asked "Tim, can you add something here about what it was like to produce movements rather than, say, themes? How did this feel – what internal conversations went on for you, if anything?" To this point, Tim had never considered these nine movements as an alternative to themes. For Tim, these movements were nothing like themes; they were of a different kind altogether (or were they?). It felt more akin to writing a song. There was a cadence that fluctuated, melodies that strung together, dissonant and harmonic moments, tensions and resolution. The nine movements were one way (among many) to traverse the flows of the interview. Still, Tim was compelled to structure the cartography, give it order, territorialise it. There remained a structural tendency to re-produce the interview as it was. One of the most helpful suggestions from Jenny during the process was when they invited Tim to mix up the interview, reorder it – unsettle the linearity of what happened in search of what might be. Disorganising the linear segmentation helped Tim remain at the edge of possibility.

Movement 1: Territorialised interview machine

In a small meeting room in a local community centre, today's research participant, Elliott, and the research assistant, Heather, sit across from each other, with a small round table between them. Heather organises her notes (including her interview guide) and sets up a recording device in the centre of the table, while Elliott sits holding his tablet – his gaze focused on the screen as he scrolls through a list of podcasts, seemingly indifferent to having a conversation with Heather. Research participants for the study were drawn from a community centre's adult literacy program, particularly, people who expressed interest in using technology as part of their literacy. Elliott was initially uninterested in participating in the interview. However, he decided to participate in exchange for some help with his tablet during the interview. Elliott and Heather negotiated a common ground – Elliott would talk about the research topic if Heather helped him get podcasts set up on his tablet.

Tim had hired Heather as a research assistant for her first paid research job. She had experience doing clinical interviews as a mental health support worker but had never done research interviews. Tim provided an interview guide for Heather to follow – a set of semi-structured interview questions designed to explore the experiences of participants around technology use and connectedness.

Tim is the organising force behind the interview, the hierarchical authority that facilitates relational flows within the interview machine – Tim is the despot. Although not present at the interview, "Tim" in Heather's mind is the tyrant reminding her of the research objectives, research questions, and the predetermined semi-structured interview format. Heather is paid by and accountable to the despot.

The relations and flows in the early moments of the interview are territorialised – there is a shared understanding that the interview is related to technology use and connection. The interview machine follows conventional pathways and linear processes. Heather invites Elliott with the question: "so what would you like some help with?" The machine's production follows the lines of this question. Elliott describes his interest in history and listening to history podcasts on his tablet. The territorial machine navigated podcasts: BBC documentaries, a podcast on the Arab Spring, and other podcasts on natural history and the influence of nature on society. Affective flows in the machine follow a predictable trajectory, finding Elliott's desired podcast series "In Our Time" and a specific podcast titled "The Invention of Photography" that he has listened to in the past. Heather wonders how she might eventually redirect the interview to the study objectives. She strategises – if she permits the territorialised machine, she will be able to gain Elliott's trust and subtly contain the interview, transforming it into a machine that serves the wishes of the despot.

The despot lurks.

Tim would sanction her approach to allow the territorialised machine, to "build rapport" in the early stages of the interview, as a strategy to elicit compliance with the interview objectives and achieve a "successful" interview.

> We notice that the molar despot of systematic qualitative research is entangled here, reminding us that it is important "for the researcher to establish rapport with the interviewee at this 'introduction and small talk' phase that precedes the main interview itself. The intention is to build trust and inform the interviewee about the purpose of the interview in order to get the interviewee talking freely".
>
> (Qu & Dumay, 2011, p. 250)

Movement 2: Emergence of a despotic machine

Heather, having permitted this "rapport-building" territorialised machine long enough, begins to take control of the interview. Heather reterritorialises the interview under the filiation of the despot. Rapport had been sufficiently established, and it is time to recode the interaction as the collection of data. Elliott, having signed a consent form, and Heather, the despot's representative, are both indebted to the despot, paying the despot in the form of data according to the determined interview guide. In an act of reductive violence, Heather guides the machine away from history podcasts, toward a conversation about how Elliott uses technology.

HEATHER: Do you have a computer at home?
ELLIOTT: My mum has a computer that I can use.

The despotic machine truncates the interconnections within the machine, limiting conversation to Elliott's use of technology, in line with the despot's objectives. Yet, Elliott did not directly answer the question – as if not interested in talking about the study from the start. Instead, Elliott opens the door a crack, a small glimpse of his desire for a relational encounter. Heather does not yet have control of the interview.

Severing the lines of conversation in the territorial machine, the despotic machine continues to attempt to funnel the conversation toward the research aims – Elliott's use of technology. There are fewer lines of affective relation in the despotic machine and limited opportunity to explore creative ideas (constrained desire). The despotic machine encircles Elliott with questions related to the study, preventing any deterritorialisation away from the despot's agenda.

> Again, we see the dominating and hierarchical structure of qualitative research surface, highlighting who should and should not have control of the interview. "Traditionally the structure of the in-depth interview dictates that the interviewer maintains control over the interaction with the interviewee's co-operation. Accordingly, the roles assigned by the interview structure pre-empt the roles the interviewer and interviewee have in their social worlds outside the interview event".
>
> *(DiCicco-Bloom & Crabtree, 2006, p. 317)*

Movement 3: Destructive event and the weakened authority of the despot

Counter to the despotic machine's desire for efficient capture of data, there is a slowness to Heather's interview facilitation. Heather is familiar and comfortable making conversation with people who have learning disabilities and diverse ways of thinking/expressing. She is accustomed to non-dominating encounters with people. Despite the despot in her mind pushing a tyrannical agenda, Heather reverts to helping Elliott with his tablet, resisting the urge to hasten the pace. She repositions her chair beside Elliott, both turning their attention to the tablet, interacting with the screen alongside one another. Heather spends the next few moments immersed in Elliott's search for history podcasts – giving way to insurgency. Destruction.

HEATHER: [Noise] Whoops, sorry.
ELLIOTT: I know how to do it.

Heather, helping Elliott download podcasts, made an unexpected error on his tablet – the despotic machine is disrupted, hierarchical forces are unsettled – Elliott's
power to act is enhanced. There is a breaking down of the territories of the despotic
machine. The authority of Heather is now in question as the two of them navigate
the tablet together, both engaging with their fragile digital literacy.

ELLIOTT: See, it's a challenge even for you.
HEATHER: It is because I … I don't use a Samsung.

Heather attempts to recover her expert status, but the destructive machine has
given a foothold for the insurgency. The research hierarchy is disrupted. Heather,
although somewhat unsettled, reverts to a territory of familiarity and maintains a
slowness that is counter to the despot's desire.

> … don't lose control of the interview (this can occur when respondents stray to
> another topic, take so long to answer a question that times [*sic*] begins to run
> out, or even begin asking questions to the interviewer).
>
> *(Turner, 2010, p. 759)*

As the interview continues through Movements 4–7 the despotic machine sputters
to a halt each time it is restarted – its flailing, floundering out of control. Unable to
repair its damaged territories, the despotic machine again and again tries to recode
the interview back to a focus on Elliot's use of information and communication
technology. Heather repeatedly attempts to ask direct questions about Elliot's use of
technology, attempting to suppress the social production of the war machine. These
questions fail to generate any new information, rather, they produce repetitive and
truncated responses …

Movement 8: War machine's third guerrilla attack – ambush

Dropping into the shadows, the guerrilla prepares for an ambush. Having weakened
the territories of the despotic machine using sabotage and unconventional hit-and-
run tactics, the war machine surges with a wild and animalistic machine of destruction. Deterritorialising the domestication of the interview, Elliott regains control
over the weapon of the despot, "the question."

ELLIOTT: Do you know what people are most likely to be very easy to talk to?
HEATHER: Is that a question or are you …
ELLIOTT: A question.

The momentum turns – Heather is unprepared. The despotic machine is sufficiently weakened and vulnerable as Elliott confiscates "the question." Disarmed. Heather reacts. As a trained mental health practitioner, Heather slips into a therapeutic mode of capture. Making a therapeutic recommendation may return Heather to her place as the expert over Elliott as the one "in need."

HEATHER: Yeah, ok um, well it just depends, I think lots of people have different personalities and …
ELLIOTT: Mmmm.
HEATHER: Sometimes it helps to go to groups like this and things that you're interested in because then you find people that have the same interests as you.

But the war machine has scattered, lurking in the shadows, and unaffected by this attempted recapture – the guerrilla destruction of the war machine has already deterritorialised the trajectory of the interview away from the research objectives. The hierarchy has been disrupted.

ELLIOTT: But for me it doesn't work that way unfortunately.
HEATHER: Yeah?
ELLIOTT: Do you know which people I find most int – easy to talk to often?
HEATHER: Who's that?

Attacking again with "the question," Elliott has evaded the violence of the despotic machine, further destroying the territories of the despot.

ELLIOTT: Oh bubbly talkative people, even if I'm not interested in the same thing exactly, their talking minds work more like me … like I find some bubbly talkative women very easy to talk to.
HEATHER: Yeah is that because they talk a lot or they seem warm?
ELLIOTT: It's because their talking minds are more likely to work like mine.

Gently guiding the disarmed Heather, Elliott begins to open up … affective flows intersect, forming a generative dialogue. Where does Elliott feel safe? Among bubbly talkative women, people with "talking minds." The war machine is wilding and dissociating. The chaos of the guerrilla is unravelling the domestication of the interview.
　　Talking minds. Destruction. Ambush.

ELLIOTT: Do you know what I think of when I think of technology?
HEATHER: What?
ELLIOTT: Sci-fi … um would you like um um um um um to be locked up in a sci-fi prison?
HEATHER: I don't want to be in a prison and I think a sci-fi prison would be extra scary.

ELLIOTT: Why do you think it would be scary?
HEATHER: Because sci-fi they usually have aliens and lasers.
ELLIOTT: <Laughter> Would you like to be abducted by aliens?

Elliott looks at Heather in anticipation, anxiously awaiting her response. Heather smiles as her shoulders drop and her body relaxes. Destruction. The war machine swirls amid the despotic machine. Out of the destruction, a creative and whimsical conversation emerges. Elliott and Heather embark on an expedition together; they discuss aliens, intergalactic travel, gender identity, and friendship. They laugh. Heather is affected, by words, humour, absurdity. She doesn't resist these relational affects. Heather is disrupted, but not violated. Elliott invites her on an adventure to new planets, new ways of looking at the unfamiliar. Heather and Elliott travel together.

ELLIOTT: <Laughter> Would you like to be abducted by aliens?
HEATHER: No, would you?
ELLIOTT: If they were friendly and could take me on trips around the galaxy.
HEATHER: <Laughter> Actually that's a good point if they were friendly I just thought that they would be mean.
ELLIOTT: <Laughter> If they could take me around trips around the galaxy to (uninhabited planets).

Elliott's questions disrupt the typical and unsettle the given order. Heather remains uncertain and tentative but has become interconnected with the war machine, Elliott's travel companion in this wild machine. Swarming, Elliott's talking mind takes them places, meeting new friends.

ELLIOTT: How would you like it if you were abducted by aliens and teleported back to earth as a man <laughter>, if they could change it? How do you think I would feel?
HEATHER: If you were teleported and then made into a woman?
ELLIOTT: Yeah.
HEATHER: I don't know.
ELLIOTT: <Laughter>
HEATHER: I'd have to ask you. How would you feel?
ELLIOTT: Oh I could cope ok if that's how it was.

Desiring production. Affects. Lines of flight. Destructive guerrilla tactics have disarmed the violence of the domesticating despotic machine. The destructive war machine generated and affirmed the affective capacity of the research participant. Two bodies ruptured, spilled out, and entangled in an intergalactic journey.

Perhaps THIS is what technology does for Elliott. Is it a vehicle for intergalactic travel? A way to discover new worlds and revisit old ones? A way to explore identity and desire? An otherworldly conduit for connection?

Following the ambush, the space smooths. Affective flows take Elliott and Heather back to earth.

ELLIOTT: <Laughter> I think it's strange men are starting to grow beards more today, do you know why?

HEATHER: Why?

ELLIOTT: Because they're listening to more gentle pop music, that's clean-shaven music, that's not bearded music.

HEATHER: Actually I remember talking about this and we talked about how people with beards should listen to metal music ….

ELLIOTT: But it's not necessarily that simple because hippies have beards and they listen to soft folk music, don't they? Hippies don't listen to heavy stuff, usually listen to soft folk, and they have beards.

HEATHER: Might be a flaw in our theory, oh no.

ELLIOTT: <Laughter> Hippies.

Laughter. Connection. Mutuality. The insurgency is no longer destroying territories, but still wildly generating creative, affective flows. Heather and Elliott intersect with beards, music, hippies, and humour. Territorialisation.

Conceptually, the war machine serves to "carve out space, rather than occupy the space" (Deuchars, 2011, p. 4). We see an example here of how a war machine can create new territories and how the destruction of the war machine is only a relay point, a point of rupture, leading to new affective flows. Thinking back to Bey's (1991) Temporary Autonomous Zones, disruptive guerrilla events are only temporary if we try to extend them they would lose their creative energy.

Movement 9: Emergence of new territorialised machine

Heather and Elliott wrap up their time together by listening to Bon Jovi's "Livin' on a Prayer," forming a new territorialised machine:

> We've got to hold on to what we've got
> It doesn't make a difference if we make it or not
> We've got each other and that's a lot for love
> We'll give it a shot
> Woah, we're halfway there
> Woah, livin' on a prayer
> Take my hand, we'll make it I swear
> Woah, livin' on a prayer.

(Bon Jovi, 1986)

ELLIOTT: Do you know what he sounds like?

HEATHER: What's that?

ELLIOTT: A man that suffered a lot

HEATHER: Does he?

ELLIOTT: He sounds like it ... did he suffer a lot?

HEATHER: I don't know.

ELLIOTT: <Laughter> Oh he probably didn't but he just has that pained ... because there are some people that have very good lives but they just have a pained sound to their voice when they sing.

...

HEATHER: Yeah, so um Tim was having a conversation with you last time about technology, do you remember that conversation?

ELLIOTT: I forget.

HEATHER: Yeah, yeah ok.

End scene.

Conclusion, or

So, where does this leave us? What did this cartography of the interview do? Borrowing from Alexander and Wyatt (2018), we are "wary of endings, resistant to notions of conclusion and finitude" (p. 107). Thinking with theory, we experimentally traversed the peculiar, creating a cartography of the affective production within a dissident interview. Performing the interview as a nine-movement guerrilla encounter, we charted how the war machine (using destructive guerrilla modes of attack) deterritorialised the interview and disrupted the despotic interview machine. These doings have moved us to work differently in the project of this book on freely given relationships and think differently about interviews in our research. In this interview, guerrilla modes of attack generated an array of affective flows, liberated desire from the confinement of the despot, and opened space for the generation of new territories. Seeing these micropolitical processes in action, we took measure to prevent the actions of the despot from taking too much control in our book project on freely given relationships, at times more successfully than others. The cartography in this chapter was a thought and methodological experiment, and in many ways so is *Edge Entanglements* – this is perhaps, the very nature of both Deleuzio-Guattarian cartography and postqualitative research more broadly. By "(pushing) toward the intensive, barely intelligible variation" (St. Pierre, 2017, p. 307), we have re-produced an interview encounter in a way that moves.

Doing analysis differently helped us bravely move to the edge of the forest from the predictability of a tamed environment. Shifting our perspective from the extensive and divisible to the intensive and interconnected, we have drawn attention to the micropolitics of the dissident interview, a peculiar interview that didn't fit in. The shift in our thinking unsettled the domestication in the initial project, unravelling the "taken-for-granted" in our past research practices, and the ways that we had unintentionally privileged the common and recurrent patterns in the "data." What didn't fit into a thematic analysis was opened up by thinking with (guerrilla and Deleuzio-Guattarian) theory. We used this learning in our cartography of freely given relationships discussed in the next chapters. Our experimentation surfaced some of the ways an interview can be despotic, how procedural interview strategies can work to stifle affective production, and how analytic research processes control and reduce. We've seen how researcher and participant are entangled in a research machine, they dance/fight/struggle for territory. In this entanglement, destructive and deterritorialising processes have the potential to produce something new, unleash desire, and create new relational territories. By remaining in the fray, interviews and other research can be intergalactic travel. Or help generate lists of themes. Or.

Note

1 There is much beneath the surface of Tim's "safety." He held a permanent academic position, he had professional qualifications as an occupational therapist to fall back on – he is a white male whose legitimacy and credibility has not been called into question. What if he were precariously employed, racialised, psychiatrised? What if his credibility was already questioned? What if he was considered "impulsive," "irrational," "unstable," or "too emotional"? So, yes, Tim was "safe enough" to experiment in this way, and much of this "safety" is propped up by major social forces. In some contrast to Tim's sense of safety, Jenny was in a different position. Although having physiotherapy qualifications as a back-up career option, as a queer person without tenure, their legitimacy in the academy felt more precarious.

6

AN ENTRY POINT

Here, we turn to our encounter with "data" – our entry point into "what counts as data" and what counts as "appropriate data" (St. Pierre & Jackson, 2014, p. 715) and the beginnings of our micropolitical mapping of ally assemblages. In this chapter, we introduce the four ally assemblages from this project and provide an initial glimpse of what is produced in each assemblage. While introducing ally assemblages in this chapter, we have tried not to essentialise each into a set of key points or divisible patterns that transcend each assemblage. Rather, we aimed to remain amidst each assemblage as we introduce their elements, movements, and processes.

A (postqualitative) cartography is constructed in the in-between, zigzagging between a tracing of what is stable and identifiable and a mapping of rhizomatic ruptures. Tracing is the reproduction and coding of sociomaterial within existing ways of understanding; a tracing is a fixed image of what is or has been. For example, in this chapter, we describe how long participant pairs have known each other and the things they do together. But mapping "is entirely oriented toward an experimentation in contact with the real" (Deleuze & Guattari, 1987, p. 12). Hillevi Lenz Taguchi (2016) refers to the double articulation of tracing and mapping as a "joint expression" rather than "an antagonistic relationship between the two" (p. 221). A cartography[1] is an "entangled action or movement of tracing-and-mapping" (Taguchi, 2016, p. 214, emphasis in original). The introductions in this chapter are tracings in that they extract and re-present extensive characteristics and divisible processes, while simultaneously mapping an entryway to the rhizomatic movements explored in the chapters to follow.

> *Between* things does not designate a localizable relation going from one thing to the other and back again, but a perpendicular direction, a transversal

DOI: 10.4324/9781003286486-6

movement that sweeps one *and* the other away, a stream without beginning or end that undermines its banks and picks up speed in the middle.

(Deleuze & Guattari, 1987, p. 27)

We do not endeavour to tell *the* story as it *was* or as it *is*, but rather construct a point of entry to the middle of these assemblages. "A map is open and connectable in all of its dimensions; it is detachable, reversible, susceptible to constant modification…. A map has multiple entryways" (Deleuze & Guattari, 1987, p. 12). The chapters that follow rhizomatically break open these assemblages, looking at their molecular flux and flows of social production.

Ally assemblage introductions

There were four ally assemblages in our project. Their unfolding in this chapter incorporates theoretical concepts, but our aim is not to intensively work and rework the assemblages using theory (as will be done in later chapters). This chapter presents each assemblage as a separate vignette, whereas in later chapters we consider the assemblages alongside one another, thinking and performing them together using theory. The majority of this chapter is written in first person, where Tim describes his encounters with each assemblage. Table 6.1 presents some basic descriptive information for each ally assemblage.

Krispy and Chips … and Tim

Krispy, Chips, and I (Tim) met every second Friday for a few months over a fish and chips lunch. Sometimes I'd catch the bus to Krispy's unit, and then we'd all drive to the fish and chips shop in Chips' car, while other times I'd meet them at the shop. The two of them would always share a fish-n-chips platter, taking turns paying

TABLE 6.1 Characteristics of ally assemblages

Pseudonym	Age	Gender identity[1]	Length of relationship (years)	Encounters with Tim (n)
Krispy	52	Male	12	6
Chips	74	Male		
Alan	34	Male	2	10 (3 only with Jack)
Jack	56	Male		
Carol	41	Female	8	6
Julie	43	Female		
Batman	49	Male	15	5
Robin	52	Male		

1 Most of the freely given relationships that developed through APTB were same-gender pairs. In discussion with Neil, it was not their intention to foster same-gender relationships; however, there were some context-specific circumstances that contributed to this trend, which are touched on in this chapter.

the bill each week, while I was left with a (huge) platter all to myself. They would always save their lemon for me, which I would religiously consume at the conclusion of my meal – my senses heightened by the citric acid dancing on my tongue. Sometimes we'd talk over our meal and then part ways after lunch, and other times we'd head back to Krispy's place to talk about their relationship in more detail or work through their social maps. While he doesn't eat sweets or drink anything caffeinated, Krispy always had M&Ms and instant coffee on the counter for us. I recall leaning back in my chair, the calming warmth of a mug in my hands – a little machine of hospitality. On our final meeting as we wrapped up our conversation, Krispy said to me with a smile: "at first I didn't know what to make of you, but you turned out to be alright." Krispy selected their pseudonyms for the project – he picked his nickname because he wants to be cremated when he dies, and then thought that "Chips" would be a suitable accompaniment to "Krispy" given their affinity for fish and chips.

Krispy and Chips met when Krispy was in a long-term locked forensic psychiatry unit (male only), a majoritarian apparatus of capture for people who deviate from psychiatric *and* legal norms.[2] Krispy described feeling lonely – he did not receive any visitors while in the unit, no friends or family. Before meeting Chips approximately 12 years before the study, Krispy expressed a desire to have someone to talk with, someone to visit him on the unit. The chaplain at the facility had a connection with Neil, the manager of APTB, and asked him if he knew of anyone who might like to meet and spend time with Krispy on the ward. Neil knew Chips through his work in the community and thought he might be a good fit – Chips was mature, non-judgemental, had experience meeting people in prison-like environments, and was interested in spending time with someone in a tough spot. Neil went with Chips to the forensic institution to introduce him to Krispy. The two of them report "hitting it off" on their first couple of meetings, initially meeting every two weeks and then starting to meet weekly – something they have done consistently for 12 years. Over the years, Krispy and Chips have become a prominent part of each other's lives.

At the time Krispy and Chips met, the treatment team had little hope of Krispy transitioning out of the institution. Nevertheless, that is what Krispy wanted. Every six months, Krispy had to sit before the Mental Health Review Tribunal[3] to review his case. These meetings were particularly stifling for Krispy. The meetings were dominated by professionals and their recurring reminders of the violent things Krispy had done in the past. He recalled not having much say over the decisions affecting him. Chips helped Krispy prepare for these meetings, something that no one else had done before, and started attending the meetings to help advocate for Krispy. With Chips' support, Krispy began to slowly break away from the rigid territories of the institution, at first with visits to the community, then day passes, and eventually to a supported living complex.[4] Over the 12 years preceding the study, Krispy moved from a locked forensic unit to supported living, and most recently to independent living (in a monitored Community Care Unit[5]). Since connecting with Chips, Krispy's assemblage has expanded to include a wide variety of connections (e.g., people, places, interests, activities), many of which are inter-connected with Chips. They have shared friends, shared a love for fish and chips, and Chips' daughter is even Krispy's optometrist. Boundaries are blurred and hier-archies disrupted.

At the time of the project, Krispy was happy with the direction of his life, the changes that he had made and was continuing to make. "I've come a long way, haven't I Chips?" Krispy proudly said in one of our final meetings.

Alan and Jack … and Tim

Alan, Jack, and I met at Alan's apartment every second Friday for a couple of months. We had a predictable and routine rhythm to our meetings. Each Friday, I'd catch the bus from the university around 12:30 pm and then walk the 10 minutes from the bus stop to arrive at Alan's place by 1 pm. Occasionally I'd run into Jack on my walk, as he would also catch the bus to Alan's place. I usually brought along a snack for our meeting, such as muffins, cookies, or doughnuts. My intention was to buy something "local" from a bakery, but on all but one occasion (the time I brought doughnuts), I would buy something from McDonalds on the walk over. I was always a bit embarrassed about this – I felt as though bringing snacks from a (major) mega-corporation contaminated our (minor) encounter. But neither Alan nor Jack seemed to be too bothered by my poor use of purchasing power. Alan, always an impeccable host, would make us each a cup of tea, and we would sit and enjoy our factory-produced baked goods. It was over tea and a snack that we talked about their relationship.

The two of them had met about two years earlier, in 2016. Jack had recently been discharged from in-patient psychiatry at a local Brisbane hospital, and was referred to APTB by one of the hospital social workers. He was referred not as a "client," but to be a tutor in APTB's adult literacy program. Jack has a degree in law and crimi-nology, and is strong academically, so the social worker thought he would make an excellent tutor. APTB pair up individual tutors with literacy students so that they can work one-on-one towards students' literacy goals. At the time they met, Alan was a new student of the adult literacy program and Jack a new tutor. The two of them were matched up as a tutor–student pair. When Alan was a child, he had brain cancer and spent most of his primary school years receiving and recovering from treatment. Due to this childhood illness, Alan never became proficient at reading or writing. Alan and Jack met at the literacy program every Tuesday, worked through their liter-acy lesson together, and also connected and talked over coffee breaks. During these coffee breaks, their relationship assemblage began to deterritorialise the boundaries of a tutor–student relationship. They started to get to know each other, learning that they shared experiences of hearing voices and the diagnosis of schizophrenia. Alan confided in Jack, describing his struggles with substance use and his despair over his living situation in a men's hostel. Alan said that he valued the advice he received from Jack. Alan and Jack's connection reterritorialised around their shared Christian faith, and much of their conversation related to their spiritual beliefs and practices.

About a year and a half after they first met, Alan and Jack decided that they would like to spend time together outside of the literacy program. Both were aware of APTB's approach to community work and that freely given relationships were encouraged. Alan and Jack described to me how they formed a different kind of relationship, how their assemblage broke away from the territories of a "literacy program," and was restratified as an "ally relationship." APTB encourages non-hier-archical community connections, but in this instance I consider APTB an apparatus of capture, coding and labelling Alan and Jack's friendship as a hierarchical (freely given) relationship of support (a hierarchy that is eventually disrupted). Jack was the ally, and Alan the one being supported.

At the time Jack and Alan started meeting outside of the literacy program (six months before I met them), Alan was at a point where he could not handle living in a hostel any longer. The two of them described Alan's most recent hostel as a "very rough place," with people urinating in the halls, frequent fist fights, and substance (mis)use. He never wanted people/friends to meet him there or to come inside – Jack had never been inside. Alan hated it there and wanted out. Alan's hos-tel was a marginal and minor space, the relegation of the minor to the fringes and a by-product of the (human services) apparatus of capture. Alan was territorialised with the minor – stuck.[6] This stuck-ness is illustrative of Deleuze and Guattari's (1986) cramped spaces, minor territories where life flow is limited.[7] But cramped spaces vibrate with intensity and are potential sites for deterritorialisation. Together, Alan and Jack (along with other supportive people in Alan's life, namely his mum) developed a strategy for him to break away from the confines of the hostel – it was Alan's desire[8] to get his own apartment flat. Alan deterritorialised from being stuck in a repetitive cycle of substance use, cut all ties with people he thought were bringing him down (limiting his affective potential), and found an apartment of his own. He had been living on his own for just under six months when we first met. It was at this new apartment that Alan and Jack met every Friday afternoon; they would usually just sit and talk over a cup of tea and sometimes walk over to the local cinema. It was in this apartment that Alan proudly gave me a tour and offered me a cup of tea each time we met.

Alan described how Jack supported him get through a tough time in his life and helped him enjoy the good times afterwards. The ally relationship hierarchy was deterritorialised, giving way to what they referred to as a "brotherly" friend-ship. There was mutual support, each increasing the other's capacity to act (affect). Trace elements of the old hierarchy remained, as Jack was like a "big brother," yet still mutually receiving and offering support.[9] The three of us spent hours talking about their relationship assemblage, mapping out the elements, and just spending time together having tea and eating snacks. Future chapters explore the intricacies of affective relations and social production in their assemblage.

Unfortunately, Alan died at the end of July 2018 from a brain aneurism. Jack and I continued to meet and talk about their relationship for three meetings after Alan's death. Jack said that Alan was in a "really good space" when he passed; he had been developing new connections (lines of flight) and was seeing changes in his life that he wanted. They had both attributed these affirmative developments in Alan's life, these rhizomatic deterritorialisations and lines of flight, to having supportive community relationships and to the (unconventional) work of APTB.

Carol and Julie ... and Tim

Carol, Julie, and I met at Julie's apartment on Sunday mornings every two to three weeks (over a period of four months) for breakfast. The territories of our interaction were predictably unpredictable – the plan was always for me to ring Carol on Sunday morning and then pick her up in my vehicle on the way over to Julie's place. But, without fail, I'd receive a call on Saturday night from Carol to change our meeting time or pickup location, or to reschedule. Then on Sunday morning, things would often change again ... keeping me on my toes. Sometimes I'd drive to Carol's place and wake her up with a knock on the door and help her with her morning coffee (and find her smokes). At other times I would meet her at the grocery store to do some light grocery shopping before heading to Julie's, or I would drive around looking for her (when she was out selling the *Big Issue* magazine).[10] Then once in the car, Carol would routinely ask, "Timothy, how the fuck are ya?! How's the bubs?" (referring to my young children). Our drive to Julie's place usually consisted of me answering Carol's 20 questions about my parenting (e.g., "So what ya do when they don't listen? What if they're a real pain in the ass?" and "Do you tell 'em that you love 'em?"). It was a refreshing encounter that disrupted the researcher–participant hierarchy. Julie typically had a wonderful breakfast prepared for us when we arrived, except for one time when our change of plans did not leave her time to prepare. Nevertheless, there'd always be a delicious homebrewed pot of tea on the table to look forward to. We'd sit around her kitchen table, talking about the food, their lives, and their relationship – with brief intermissions for Carol to have smoke breaks out on the patio.

Carol and Julie first met eight years prior when Julie was on placement as a social work student at APTB, and Carol was a mental health service user in Julie's team. Julie told me about how she had entered this placement with a desire[11] to develop a friendship with someone on the fringes of society. At the time, she had read and believed that natural community connections were important in mental health work and wanted to develop a supportive relationship with someone. She thought that Carol was someone she might be able to connect with. Julie, with the help of Neil at APTB, asked Carol if she would be interested in spending time together outside of a professional capacity. Following the completion of Julie's placement, the two of them started to develop their relationship, their friendship.

From the outset of their relationship, Julie made it very clear that she did not want to play the role of a support worker in Carol's life. Carol accessed numerous formal supports in her life (either with day-to-day activities or acute psychiatric support), and Julie didn't want to be her crisis support. Julie resisted the pull of the major to take on the role of a "support" person (and binary of support/supported); rather, she was drawn to be simply a friend for Carol. Carol was familiar with the type of relationship where professionals (or "mentally well" people) provide the support, as most of Carol's relationships were territorialised within the confines of majoritarian mental health services. Julie did not want to be like the other paid supports. Their relationship assemblage deterritorialised away from how typical "supports" were in Carol's life and reterritorialised as a friendship, with clear boundaries on the nature of their friendship. Julie wanted to be a consistent presence in Carol's life, someone to talk with and spend time with, and when necessary, point her to appropriate crisis supports. Over the years, Carol has developed vast and continually changing networks (explored in depth in future chapters) that she could draw on when in crisis. An instance of their relationship territorialisation occurred during the study – one night Carol called me and said that she needed help, that she was struggling and needed to go to the hospital but didn't have any way to get there (she wanted me to drive her). I rang Julie (as Carol's ally) and asked if she had any recommendations for handling this situation. Julie named several people that would be suitable for Carol to reach out to for this kind of support, and if they were not available, to recommend that she call 000.[12] Julie reiterated to me that she does not offer crisis support but is aware that when Carol is in a tough space, she reaches out to anyone that might be able to help. I'm not sure who she ended up calling, but Carol did go to inpatient psychiatry that night and was back home the next day.

Carol and Julie talk on the phone almost every day at around 5 pm. They noted that Carol feels most vulnerable at this time of day, a time when she does not have formal supports available. They do not usually talk about much significant, they just spend time together over the phone (sometimes Julie puts Carol on speakerphone while she prepares dinner). Their nightly phone calls are the most consistent thing in both of their lives. Carol describes Julie as a "good friend, she's always there when I need her, and even when I don't."

Before getting an apartment in West End,[13] Carol spent a long time living on the street. She recalls meeting with Neil from APTB over ten years ago as a moment when things started to change, when she started to live a life of her choosing. Carol's relationship with Julie is one of many connections that increases Carol's capacity to act and have a life that she is happy with. Carol lives a life that is on the edge; at any moment, she is at risk of capture (e.g., hospitalisation or eviction). Yet the social production of rhizomatic connections in her life supports her life in the community. The assemblages of Carol's life assemblage have helped her resist the apparatus of capture and territorialisation of the major and contributed to ongoing transformative lines of flight.

Carol and Julie both looked forward to our breakfasts together. They lived quite far from each other and rarely got to see each other in person.[14] Each week, Carol would ring me up midweek to check in and ask when our next meeting was. It was during one of these phone calls early in the project where Carol asked me about my dog (a whippet named Latigo), and if he could come to our next breakfast. Carol disrupted the research assemblage, inviting Latigo to join in our Sunday breakfast meetings. And so, after clearing it with Julie, Latigo accompanied us for our last four meetings. Carol loved it – she would ring me on Sunday mornings (before I had a chance to call her to say "on my way") to make sure Latigo was coming along. Having him there brought vitality to our meetings – Carol seemed to be more interactive and willing to share when Latigo was with us. She would sit on the ground, pat him, and give him treats – it felt like half of our conversation was centred around the dog. At the end of our last breakfast together, Carol and I took Latigo for one final walk down the street behind Julie's home. Even months after the project finished, Carol continued to ring me, ask about my family (mainly my kids), and Latigo. (In 2021, my companion of ten years had to be euthanised – as I write I imagine scattering traces of his gentle, loving presence in these pages.)

Batman and Robin ... and Tim

"We're off to the speedway tonight, you're more than welcome," said a text from Robin on a Friday afternoon in mid-2018. I'd commonly receive these spontaneous invitations to hang out with Batman and Robin. Compared with the other three assemblages, my time with Batman and Robin had very little structure or predictable flow. There was no consistent format, activity, or frequency. We'd usually make plans spontaneously, which sometimes made it difficult to connect – I have a young family and want to be home with them in the evenings and most weekends. It was disappointing for me to decline Batman and Robin's invitations, such as getting a call on Friday night to go on a road trip the next day – I'd have loved to respond with: "I'm in!" Batman and Robin get together almost every weekend, but they often don't decide what they're doing until the day before. Their times together are not straightforward coffee catch-ups; they are full-day adventures or evening outings to the speedway. Our research meetings occurred in coffee shops, at their mutual friend's home (watching Rugby League), at a Monster Truck event, and in a community kitchen (booked through APTB). It was in the community kitchen, making homemade pizzas together, that we were able to spend a couple of hours doing social mapping. Batman and Robin's assemblage is an active and fast-paced one; they are always on the move – I had to jump in, hold on, or be left behind.

Batman and Robin met about 15 years prior to the project, when Robin was a street outreach worker with a large NGO. He used to visit Batman at the city botanic gardens, where Batman used to sleep, and bring him dinner. Robin was drawn to Batman and saw him as being quite vulnerable.[15] Robin deterritorialised from his role as a support worker, and they started regularly spending time together, doing things such as having meals or going for drives together. Batman, as Robin's friend, would often come to Robin's workplace to hang out. Robin talked about how it was sometimes difficult for other staff to understand their friendship. One time Batman was in the staff only area of an outreach centre where Robin worked. Batman's soiled high visibility jacket drew the attention of staff, who then tried to usher him out (as if to say, "That jacket and the person inside it do not belong here"). Robin jumped in, saying, "He's family, is it not ok for us to have family back here?" Together, Batman and Robin deterritorialised the cramped spaces of Batman's everyday life and what relationships should look like between them. Robin has helped Batman tap into professional supports when needed, one of those being APTB, but Robin has also been a strong advocate for Batman when there was risk of capture (e.g., when treatment priorities have been imposed on him by service providers, including APTB). During the time we were meeting, Robin was in the process of becoming Batman's guardian. Aware that Batman was getting older, had been having some health issues, and had ongoing issues with accommodation, Robin wanted to have a formal influence in Batman's life. In some ways, pursuing guardianship was a safeguard against the capture and control of Batman, but also a reterritorialisation and alternative stratification.[16] For example, Robin wanted to be able to kick people out of Batman's apartment if they moved in and took advantage of him.

Batman and Robin spend every Saturday together. It is a significant amount of time for Robin to spend away from his partner (and I imagine that it might be a point of tension in their relationship). Batman and Robin are both very active when together – they are biking, kayaking, taking off on road trips to the coast, going swimming, or sometimes just sitting around playing video games. You will not find them sitting in a café having a heart-to-heart; they will only be in the café long enough to consume their food and then hit the trail. When we met for breakfast, Robin and I were able to sit and have a short conversation after the meal only because Batman was making friends with the café staff. Batman's vocabulary and verbal communication is limited, but he is able to playfully communicate with people using gestures and minimal words. In a short time at the café, Batman had the staff joking with him about coming to the back and doing the dishes. Batman's friendly affect was observed to effortlessly produce connections with people, something I have witnessed in this project and when I have seen Batman in the community outside of this project. Never sitting still, Batman was like a rhizome, always moving and in lines of flight. It was difficult for this researcher to capture him. As Robin said, "I've had to stay on my toes to keep up with him." Robin is entangled in the small, everyday aspects of Batman's life. Robin troubleshoots Batman's broken bike, fixes his TV, changes the settings on his phone, arranges for repairs in his apartment, and replaces his video game system. Robin is the first person contacted whenever there is an issue with his health or health services. The two of them even go on holidays together.

I had the pleasure of spending time with Batman and Robin at their mutual friend's home, watching Rugby League. I observed a group of friends rowdily watch "footy" together. Batman and Robin's pseudonyms (picked by Batman) suited the two of them that night. Robin was Batman's sidekick. When watching the game, Batman's cheering would get Robin revved up, and the two of them wound up the whole group. The affective production between the two of them was palpable. They are like other infamous duos: Bert and Ernie, peanut butter and jelly, Hans Solo and Chewbacca, Mario and Luigi – an assemblage that enhances the affective capacity of its constituent parts.[17]

And ...

The next three cartographic chapters explore the flows and social production of these ally assemblages – they explore the movements and lines, not points of significance or stable forms. Mapping the topography of these assemblages, the following chapters respond to the questions: What are ally assemblages (and their territories) like? How do they assemble/disassemble? What do they do? What do they produce? How do transformative processes unfold (if at all)?

Chapter 10 then spills out our cartography into the scholarly landscape of befriending practices and allyship, and theorises a micropolitical form of allyship that has transformative potential in the mental health sector. Our desire from the beginning of this project was to produce something that could be helpful for the mental health sector, for our community partners at APTB, and ultimately for psychiatrised people. Dangling at the threshold of theory/practice, this final chapter outlines a theory-infused approach to encouraging transformative ally assemblages in the community.

Notes

1 The words mapping and map can be problematic in cartographic research given that Deleuze and Guattari (1987) distinguish between tracing and mapping. Still, Deleuze and Guattari maintain, along with more recent scholars such as Mazzei and McCoy (2010) or Taguchi (2016), that the two are inseparable, just as a rhizome has arborescent offshoots. In this book, when using the word map or mapping (such as in Chapters 7–9), we acknowledge the simultaneous movements of tracing-and-mapping when experimentally producing a cartography of ally assemblages.

2 We discuss this territory and the territory of Krispy and Chips' assemblage further in Chapter 7.

3 The Mental Health Review Tribunal "is an independent decision-making body under the Mental Health Act 2016. The Tribunal's main role is to review the appropriateness of treatment authorities, forensic orders and treatment support orders made under the Act" (Queensland Government, 2021, para. 1).

4 We discuss the transformative processes in Krispy's life in Chapter 8.

5 Community Care Units (CCU) "provide medium to long term mental health care and rehabilitation in a supervised residential setting for people aged between 18-65 who are in recovery, but require support to transition to independent living" (Queensland Health, 2018).

6 Slamming against the wall, pushing on all sides – being "stuck" is an intensive vibrating potential in cramped spaces.

7 The concept of cramped spaces was introduced in Chapter 2 and is further explored in relation to ally assemblages in Chapter 7.

8 See Chapter 9, where we explore a Deleuzio-Guattarian notion of desire, a creative and transformative impulse, in ally assemblages.

9 These relational hierarchies are further explored in Chapter 7.

10 The Big Issue is "an independent, not-for-profit organisation dedicated to supporting and creating work opportunities for homeless, marginalised and disadvantaged people." "The *Big Issue* magazine is a fortnightly, independent magazine that's sold on the streets by homeless, marginalised and disadvantaged people" (https://www.thebigissue.org.au/).

11 This is an example of desire that is explored in Chapter 9.

12 "000" is the emergency call number in Australia.

13 West End is an inner-city Brisbane suburb.

14 This has since changed. Julie now has a car and more frequently visits Carol or picks her up.
15 This project is about relationships for people psychiatrised with serious mental illness, but Batman also had a learning/intellectual disability.
16 This is discussed further in Chapter 7.
17 We explore the affirmative qualities of ally assemblages, their ability to enhance the affective capacity of each other and their assemblage in Chapters 7 and 8.

7

CARTOGRAPHY OF TERRITORIES

In this chapter, we speak of territories, the structure (and structuring) of ally assemblages. There are no rules or parameters for how to consider territories – this is our perspective on what the (un)structure seems to be, informed by and imbued with theory. We touch on the lines of segmentarity, the territories that group and segment ally assemblages. Yet, when speaking of territories, we cannot help but also discuss the (dis)assembling processes that generate or soften territories. At times we consider the ruptures that disorganise the territories of ally assemblages and the formation of new territories – becomings. We interweave processes of becoming into this discussion of territories to create a sense of movement and process – assemblages, and specifically these ally assemblages, are not bounded within determined or fixed territories. So, in this chapter, we articulate the shifting territories of ally relationships. As we write we run our hands along the lines and territories. How soft and flexible are they? Or are they rigid and fixed? What are the boundaries like? Where are they most porous or vulnerable to breakdown? What gives the assemblages stability and what destabilises them?

In Chapter 2, we outlined how territories of the major are characterised by striated lines and rigid territories, whereas territories of minor assemblages are characterised by supple lines and flexible territories. While minor assemblages can, at times, have arborescent characteristics and hierarchies, their hierarchies are not fixed and their segmentation is malleable. In this chapter, we examine how porous the territories of ally assemblages are, how they shift and move. While Chapter 8 will scrutinise processes of becoming, affective relations, and transformative lines, this chapter considers the territories of becoming. First, we introduce the concepts of *active* and *reactive force*, along with Erin Manning's (2016) *minor gesture*, and then use these concepts to describe the territories in ally relationships. Second, we explore how territories transform in reactive becomings;

DOI: 10.4324/9781003286486-7

we map out how territories of allies (the major) are unsettled, ally relationship territories soften, and supple hierarchies develop.

Active and reactive

In Chapters 2 and 3, we presented the major and the minor as a way to consider the structure of things in society and the organisation of power hierarchies that have the potential to be oppressive for psychiatrised people. We presented becoming-minor (including processes of deterritorialisation and lines of flight) as a disruptive process that enables the transformation of assemblages. Before moving on to a discussion of territories, we introduce the Deleuze's concepts of active/reactive and becoming-reactive, along with Erin Manning's concept of the minor gesture. We think that these add nuance to the concepts of major, minor, and becoming in a way that is attentive to the micropolitical entanglements of psychiatric systems, the mental health sector, and relationality.

The concepts of active and reactive refer to the quality of differing forces and are useful for considering affective relations (how things affect and are affected) and how power shapes these relations. Deleuze's (2006) formulation of active/reactive extended on the work of 19th-century philosopher Friedrich Nietzsche and his articulation of master/slave[1] relations. All events and relations are the collision of unequal forces – one that commands (active force) and one that obeys (reactive force) (Deleuze, 2006). At first this reads as reductionistic, and it is. But just as there is tension and nuance to the concepts of major and minor, the dynamism of active and reactive force relations will unfold in the pages that follow. At a very basic level, our fingers hitting keys on a keyboard is an example of this active/reactive relationship – my fingers are an active force, dominating the keyboard, and the keyboard is a reactive force, being depressed with each keystroke. Deleuze (2006) takes this further, relating force relations to the development of hierarchy:

> The superior or dominant forces are known as *active* and the inferior or dominated forces are known as *reactive*. Active and reactive are precisely the original qualities which express the relation of force with force. ... This difference between forces qualified according to their quality as active or reactive will be called *hierarchy*.
>
> *(p. 40, original emphasis)*

Active/reactive force relations offer a way to consider an assemblage as a complex entanglement of force relations. The characterisation of force relations brings depth to understanding how arborescent, major assemblages are constructed and proliferate. "Appropriating, possessing, subjugating, dominating – these are the characteristics of active [major] force" (Deleuze, 2006, p. 42). Active forces within an assemblage have less flexibility than reactive forces – active forces exert power and reactive forces respond to power. Deleuze (2006) suggests that active forces are always at the limit of what they can do, whereas there are infinite possibilities for how reactive forces respond. The concepts of active and reactive offer an additional lens to consider the major and minor, which is useful for thinking about lines and processes in ally relationships. In Chapter 2, we characterised dominant assemblages in mental health as major assemblages (e.g., recovery-oriented practice), in which the composition of forces is primarily active and dominating, whereas the minor (individuals or assemblages) are principally reactive forces.

Just as the minor have revolutionary potential, so too do reactive forces. Reactive forces are malleable, they adapt and shift – water, when scooped into a cup, is a reactive force; it sloshes around and fills every crevice of the cup – the cup on the other hand remains static as the active force; it is at the limit of what it can do. We suggested in Chapter 2 that a liberating way forward in mental health research and practice is the pursuit of a machine of dissonance that separates the machine of resonance from what it is capable of. When we spoke of separating a dominating force "from what it is capable of," we were drawing from Deleuze's active/reactive force relation to describe deterritorialising processes. Deleuze and Guattari (1987) describe the minor and minorities as "seeds, crystals of becoming whose value is to trigger uncontrollable movements and deterritorialisations of the mean or majority" (p. 123). Typical major hierarchies are active: dominant/dominated, doctor/patient, male/female, supporter/supported force relations. However, active hierarchies have the potential to be destabilised by reactive forces. Deleuze states that "everything which separates a force is reactive as is the state of a force separated from what it can do. Every force which goes to the limit of its power is, on the contrary, active" (Deleuze, 2006, p. 59). When reactive forces separate power from what it can do, there is a "triumph of reactive forces ... where the weak have conquered, where the strong are contaminated" (Deleuze, 2006, pp. 60–61). This is not to say that the reactive force has transformed into an active force – a reactive force has the potential to disrupt an active force, not dominate it. "(W)hen the weak triumph it is not by forming a greater force but by separating force from what it can do" (Deleuze, 2006, p. 59). Immanent to this dissonant moment of displacement is what Manning (2016) refers to as a minor gesture, a "gestural force that opens experience to its potential variation" (p. 1). Minor gestures are vibrating potential within each moment, each encounter – potential for re-ordering and producing unknown rhythms yet to come.

Becoming-reactive (or a reactive becoming) is when reactive forces (and minor gestures) create a fissure or crack in active forces that separate an active force from what they are capable of. Becoming-reactive is the process of a reactive force or forces demonstrating the "power of splitting up, dividing and separating" (Deleuze, 2006, p. 64) and an active force "being separated and turning against itself" (p. 64). Rather than being at their limit, reactive becomings creatively produce unknowable lines of escape. In ally relationships, there is a becoming-reactive that flexes territories and revises the hierarchy between an ally (someone typically in the active position of "supporter") and a person psychiatrised with "mental illness" (someone typically in the reactive position of "supported"). We want to bring Deleuze's becoming-reactive into conversation with how becoming is conceptualised by Deleuze and Guattari in their work together, such as becoming-woman, becoming-animal (1987), or becoming-minor (1986, 1987). In these forms of becoming, subjects do not become a woman or an animal or a minority, but rather they enter into a "zone of proximity" (Deleuze & Guattari, 1987, p. 273) with women or animal or minor. Becomings travel in the in-between, the intermezzo – between what was and what will be. The zone of proximity, the intermezzo, is a responsive and smooth space where (often unrecognisable) minor gestures vibrates with potential.

Thinking with theory, the concepts of active/reactive are useful for mapping relationality and affect in ally assemblages in this book. Turning our attention to force relations, we map the minor gestures within ally relationships and the affects that weave new territories. The concepts of major and minor are effective for drawing attention to the micropolitical elements and positionality in hierarchical relations, but less effective for the analysis of affect. Becoming-reactive brings nuance to this and future chapters. Considering an ally assemblage as one that is always in a process of becoming-reactive invites explorations of the transformative processes amidst the relationship.

In this chapter, we map (with words) the territories (created by force relations), the structure (and structuring) of ally assemblages. We sketch the entanglement of rigid active territories with soft and flexible reactive territories. We trace the suppleness of reactive lines in these relationships that continually reorient force relations, and how rigid territories are nurtured into malleable territories.

Active/reactive territories in ally assemblages

Ally relationships find themselves moving within/among major assemblages, primarily mental health assemblages, dominated by active forces. Reactive forces tend to find themselves in what Deleuze and Guattari refer to as cramped spaces, territories produced by dominant power relations and active hierarchies. While the major and minor are useful concepts for describing cramped spaces (see Chapters 2 and 3), Deleuze's active/reactive relations offer an additional way to consider the production of cramped spaces, such as in the lives of psychiatrised people in *Edge Entanglements*. We recognise that not all active/reactive relations produce oppressive constraint, but active forces (always at their limit) either attempt to capture and contain or disperse reactive forces to the margins. Cramped spaces in society could be considered minor, reactive spaces, which are socially produced through hierarchical force relations. Major assemblages, with their rigid segmentation and swirling active forces, are a machine of resonance that attempts to capture and contain the minor. Turning to the experience of Krispy and Chips vividly illustrates these force relations and the production of cramped space.

Krispy, having spent several years (in the late 2000s) living in a secure forensic mental health unit, was familiar with the cramped spaces. "It's a place for the criminally insane, that's where I was," said Krispy. Every six months a mental health review tribunal meets to review Krispy's progress and his "mental health," and to determine the course of treatment (and the degree to which he is confined) for the following six months. Krispy has attended these tribunal hearings for the last 12 years. "They [tribunal] make you look really bad, don't they?" Krispy said to Chips, talking about what it is like to be "on trial" every six months. There is no escaping the territory of the tribunal. Krispy will attend these hearings every six months, potentially for the rest of his life. The decisions of the tribunal are binding – once a ruling is handed down, there is no revisiting the decision until the next meeting six months later. Krispy's ally, Chips, reflected that Krispy's future was, and is, "very much controlled by the [tribunal] … to be honest, it's very daunting, it's totally de-personalised." Before Chips started attending tribunal meetings with Krispy nine years ago, Krispy was unable to share his wishes and opinions at these meetings, both feeling like he couldn't speak up and not given the space to. And, there were no processes to encourage his participation. Krispy has a vivid memory of one tribunal meeting – unannounced and unexplained, the chair of the tribunal called unknown "others on the phone." These unknown experts were put on speaker-phone for all to hear, talking about Krispy's situation and offering a judgement. Faceless, nameless authority. "It's very daunting because the person at the other end, you can't see what they're doing and you're unaware of their agenda," Chips chimed in while Krispy recounted the story to me. In another recent tribunal meeting, the chair was replaced unexpectedly by someone they had never met before, and she spent most of the hearing interrogating Krispy about events 12 years prior, the unsettling events that had landed him in the institution. They were "increasingly confrontational, but we coped fairly well," remembered Chips. The territories of the tribunal are rigid and their force active and dominating – Krispy (and eventually Chips) were reactive.

Our fish and chips lunch is interrupted with a phone call from the community housing unit that Krispy lives in – "I'm just out with Chips right now … yes, I'll come to the office when I return." Krispy hangs up the phone, "they're just checking in."

Before Chips was on the scene, Krispy was not reliably allowed to attend the tribunal meetings: "they said I was too unwell to go to the tribunals." Krispy said that the tribunal panel was "frightened" of him and were of the opinion that he would never return to the community. I (Tim) found this quite striking at the time – someone that was once considered too dangerous to attend a tribunal meeting is now sitting across from me at a fish and chips shop. "And if I became unwell again, I used to have ECT treatments, didn't I? … 44 ECT treatments I think." Later in this conversation with the pair, Krispy says, "I can't remember much … [the] electronic convulsion treatments has made my memory a bit fuzzy." Active forces have dominated Krispy's life, leaving an imprint on his body. Recalling visiting Krispy on the forensic unit, Chips said, "It's tougher … than in jail."

Krispy doesn't appear to resent the tribunal, nor the institutionalised life that he has lived for most of his adulthood. "They want to make sure I never hurt anyone again, so I'm quite happy about that … I don't want to hurt anyone again either." There is a tension – simultaneously feeling violated and helped by the mental health system. Krispy describes himself as a "good patient" that "always take[s] my meds. I'm happy with taking medication because I don't want to hurt anyone ever again." Krispy is a reactive force. The machine of resonance keeps him in line, for better or worse. He currently lives in an independent community support unit, it's an apartment complex with a front gate and a main office occupied by a psychiatrist, psychologist, and numerous support workers and staff. Krispy has a nice unit on the second floor, with an inviting open plan kitchen and living area – he keeps it pristine. Krispy is hoping to transition to an independent living arrangement in the next six months but has to prove his cooking and independent living skills first. Krispy described needing to be able to cook meals from scratch to be allowed to transition – he has enjoyed developing his cooking skills. On one of the days we met, he made a lovely potato bake that he was proud of: "It turned out beautiful, bubbling away there and the cheese was melted on top. Got spinach as well in there. It's yummy." The machine of resonance has very specific requirements – apparently being a good cook is one of them. The territories shift over time; Krispy remains caught up in this machine with its active dominating forces. On the surface, he has been a submissive force, but he and Chips have strategically and slowly carved space for him to move. Despite the progress that has been made, if Krispy is permitted to live independently, he will have limited choice over where he will live (social housing), limited income (welfare recipient), or control over his finances (public trustee), and will be faced with the ongoing risk of re-institutionalisation.

> "I better let them know I'm back," Krispy says, as we return to the unit after lunch.

In contrast to most of his relationships, Krispy's relationship with Chips is by choice:

CHIPS: That's all mandated, see? He has to go through that, whereas with me he could ring me up tomorrow afternoon and say he doesn't want to see me anymore.
KRISPY: I wouldn't do that.
CHIPS: … but you can.
KRISPY: I wouldn't do that.
CHIPS: I know you wouldn't, but you could …

Krispy became a little concerned at the thought of not being in a relationship with Chips. Out of all the relationships in Krispy's life, the one with Chips is the most important to him.

All of the psychiatrised people discussed in *Edge Entanglements* have had relations with active forces; however, the qualities of their reactive force varied. A characteristic of reactive forces is that they are not predictable like active forces. In Chapter 5, we mapped out a dissident interview where a minor gesture opened the interview to unpredictable variation – we could not have predicted that the conversation would turn to aliens, space travel, gender, and bearded hippies. To further illustrate, we turn to an example from the relationship of Carol and Julie. The two of them recalled a time, about eight years ago, when Carol had an encounter with city police while selling the *Big Issue* on a street corner in Brisbane. It is not entirely clear why the police approached her, but Julie remembers watching from across the street. She saw Carol sitting down on a bench and the two officers standing in front of her – Carol kept reaching out and touching them, each time the officers becoming more aggressive in their communication and posture. Carol, as an embodied reactive force, is responding by agitating and testing the active force of the police officers. Julie recalls, "… eventually I saw him [one of the officers] grab her arm and turn it behind her back. I ran through traffic to get there and help." Active forces do one thing, they assert power, they extend to the limit of what they can do. In this example, the police officer asserted authority and dominance over Carol, and when challenged by Carol's touch, he aggressively stepped closer. The officer, as an embodied active force, was inflexible and only capable of further extending to the limit of his domination. Here, we see Carol being forced into submission – but we also see Julie being affected, becoming-reactive, and running through traffic to get to Carol.

"You know they don't like being touched," jests Julie.
"I know," laughs Carol.
"And you called them 'cunts,'" added Julie.
"Of course they're cunts, all of them," Carol replies.

Further mapping the varied (reactive) force of people in this project, I turn to Batman, who had been under a forensic treatment order over 15 years ago and spent some time in a psychiatric unit. "I escaped," proclaims Batman at one of our meetings. His ally, Robin, fills in more detail: "Yeah, he escaped and ran away, he had some run ins with the police … the story goes, he got released into boarding houses." "Shitholes," Batman mutters, referring to the boarding houses he lived in. "You were running wild back then, weren't you?" Robin responded. It was not my sense that Robin was scolding Batman or describing him as "wild" in a pejorative sense; rather, Robin observes that Batman is not to be contained. Reactivity "runs wild" – it is unpredictable. Major, active forces assert power; it's what they do. But the undomesticated and "wild" reactive force can separate power from what it is capable of. Cramped, reactive territories spill to the edges. This plays out time after time in the cartographies of ally assemblages. The collision of active and reactive forces demonstrates the ways cramped spaces are produced (be it in a forensic institution, psychiatric institution, community living complex, hostel/boarding houses, or the street) and also the unpredictable quality of reactive force.

Supple territories and the becoming-reactive of allies

Considering how reactive forces can separate active forces from what they are capable of, we turn to a discussion of ally relationships as reactive becomings – but, focusing on territories, we consider how these relationships temper the boundaries of everyday assemblages. At the end of Chapter 2, we offered several examples as to how deterritorialising processes might disrupt the territories in the mental health sector. Here, we outline some of the deterritorialising processes that supple major territories in these relationships and the characteristics of their in-process territories. The lines of flight and transformative flows that burst through the cracks are covered more directly in Chapter 8. We want to start by discussing the minoring of the ally in these relationships, that is, how reactive forces destabilise the ally, and then move on to discuss the soft and flexible lines that develop in ally relationships. Following this discussion, we move on to our final point in relation to territories, the territory of the intermezzo. The becoming-reactive of ally relationships produces a territory that oscillates around an ally/friend relation that evades capture and resists being reoriented as a typical active/reactive hierarchy.

In all of the relations Tim observed, allies had qualities of an active force, but at some point were tripped up/destabilised by reactive forces, although Jack (an ally) had qualities of a reactive force in his encounters with psychiatric systems, as someone who identifies as "schizophrenic." However, he has multiple university degrees, is a property-owner, and is a tutor in the adult literacy program – Jack has status and power in relation to Alan. Regardless, in all cases there was a flexing of the ally's status or the lines of connection in their life, notably in the early days of these relationships. We interpreted there to be movement of the ally to the margins – into proximity with the cramped spaces. Reactivity, with its potential to separate power, disrupted allies, tripped them up for a moment so that the margins captured their gaze. The territories of ally assemblages are differential, diverging from rigid and hierarchical lines of segmentation of major assemblages. As will follow, ally relationships are becoming-minor, with rhizomatic connections and supple territories. Hierarchies are not absent in ally relationships, but they are flexible hierarchies – they flatten – invert – return. These relationships are tainted with reactivity.

Batman and Robin met in the city botanical gardens in Brisbane about 15 years ago. Robin was an outreach worker with the Salvation Army, providing support for street-involved people in inner-city Brisbane. "We'd go around and do two food vans, and Batman was one of the people we'd come across," Robin recalls. Batman linked up with a woman nicknamed "Kit" on the street. "We'd often ring Kit … and come around at night and check on them … we'd bring them a bit of food and help them out." As I listen to Robin talk about these early encounters with Batman, I find myself wondering, "Is this what typical outreach is like?" There was a supple characteristic to those early encounters, a blurring of professional role and personal desire. Robin continues, "I'd always know where to find him … used to come around with a BBQ chicken. What time did we wake you up?" "About 1 o'clock," replied Batman.

We used to go around the spots late at night, and go and see if everyone was safe and we'd always pull in and see these guys. At 1 or 2 in the morning, we'd wake them up and say, "do you want a cup of coffee?"

Robin chuckled (Batman shook his head), "That's a good memory." When we read back over this exchange we feel conflicted as to whether this is an expression of care (becoming-reactive) or the fulfillment of Robin's role as an outreach worker (active force) or in-between. We suspect sleeping in the botanic gardens isn't the most restful to begin with, not to mention being woken up at 1 am by an outreach worker.

> I (Jenny) recall sleeping in the botanical gardens in another city a few times in my punk days. I was staying in abandoned buildings, in parks or on people's couches. Parks are not very restful at night, my experience was that there was a fair amount of light, frequent disturbances, and a sense of a lack of safety that made sleeping difficult. And that was on top of all the other elements of sleeping outside – exposure to the elements, bugs, etc. I was "sleeping rough" by choice though, which likely made the experience considerably more enjoyable and exciting than it would be if it wasn't.

There was something that drew Robin to Batman. As an outreach worker, he didn't bring meals to others living on the street, but he did to Batman. There was something about Batman, a man "running wild," that disrupted the boundary between them. Robin was aware that he was going outside of his outreach role, an active hierarchy of support worker/support recipient. "My boss at the time wasn't so hard on with professional roles." As an outreach worker, there was frequent contact with the cramped spaces of the street – and thinking with theory, Robin had frequent brushes with reactive forces, minor gestural forces that can disrupt and soften territories.

> I'm (Tim) having a flashback to riding in an outreach van in 2001 in city in western Canada. I was a student at the time doing an eight-week fieldwork for my diploma in Child and Youth Care – our shift would start at 8 pm and run until about 2 am. I was riding with a guy I'll call Will; he was an Indigenous guy from a local Nation. He had a long ponytail, and always wore a black hoodie, jeans, and black sneakers. He made me laugh … and he loved shawarma. I think we stopped for shawarma every night we rode in the van together. But I also remember Will taking the van off the typical route, into some of the back areas of the city that outreach workers don't usually go at night. He used to personally buy food and bring it to people he knew out there. Will would jump out of the van to give a group of three or four people hugs and give them a meal. He'd motion to me in the van, making it seem like he couldn't stop and talk because he had a student with him. Will would tell me, "You'll get to know people over the years in this work," and that was it.

Robin was an outreach worker but was offering food as an initial gesture of friendship to Batman, a "client." At night, darkness shrouded the gardens, shadows wrapped themselves around Batman and protected him while he slept. Yet, Robin "always (knew) where to find him." Robin became entangled within a machine of dissonance on the street, harmonising with the minor melody of reactive forces. "We (himself and Batman) know a whole lot of people on the street, so we'd do things together" and eventually started "going for drives" together. Affected by the cramped spaces and affected by Batman, Robin moved towards the minor. Robin welcomed Batman into his car – an extension of his personal space, a vehicle that brings him from home to work each day, the place keeps his personal items safe while he is at work as he locks the doors. Yet, when Batman steps inside there is a fracturing of the professional/client division. This is something that we have seen in all these relationships, allies flexing the territories and moving towards the minor – allies being disrupted from their active force and becoming-reactive.

Turning now to the relationship between Carol and Julie, on Julie's first days as a social work student at APTB, her supervisor simply asked her "to have a relation-ship with Carol" – no other agenda apart from having a "relationship." And so they spent time together. Carol remembers, "We used to meet on a regular basis just to talk and muck around." Julie remembers, "When I was a student, I used to go to Coles [grocery store] in the morning and pick up one of these packs of pancakes and just bring them over." From the outset, the territories of their relationship were flexible. Like Robin above, Julie would purchase food to bring to Carol's apartment – the sweetness and nourishment of pancakes elevating their mood and filling the bellies. (Over eight years later, their relationship is still entangled with pancakes and other meals prepared by Julie.) While she was comparatively a person of greater status than Carol (e.g., university educated, mentally "well"), Julie also had a minor experience. "My health has been bad for like 20 years … I just have a different kind of lifestyle to what I thought I could have," said Julie, reflecting on how her priorities have changed over the years. Having her own brush with cramped spaces, as someone with chronic health challenges and income limita-tions, Julie was already in proximity with the minor and at times displaced from her position of relative power. At the end of her placement, Julie said to her super-visor, "I'd like to have a relationship with Carol after I finish the course … so we sat down with [Neil] and Carol and talked about it. Talked about how I wanted to spend time with her." Movement towards the minor – Julie was drawn by the minor gesture of Carol.

Supple territories of the intermezzo

Becomings are always in process: they are neither what they were nor what they will be; they are *intermezzo* (in-between; Deleuze & Guattari, 1987). The territory of change processes is the space of the *and*, the territory between two relay points, between what was and what will be. This intermezzo is a threshold. What follows considers the territories of the intermezzo in ally relationships.

Suppleness was a prominent characteristic of the ally relationship assemblages in the project. We entered this project thinking that the transformative value of these relationships was their reciprocity, that these were non-hierarchical friendships. However, we have come to see that the value of these relationships is also their supple hierarchies and the in-betweenness of their territories. The territories of these relationships are the intermezzo. Yes, there is evidence of reciprocity, but it is not the transactive or balanced reciprocity that we anticipated. In many instances, it is this very nonreciprocity and unbalanced reactivity that bursts into lines of flight (see Chapter 8). Here, we outline the supple territories of ally relationships and how they oscillate between relationships of support (active/reactive relation) and friendship, leaving them somewhere in-between – an ally/friend relation.

Ally relationship. Freely given relationship. Both of these language codes denote a hierarchy, with the ally as the active force and psychiatrised person as the reactive recipient of support. The one who *freely gives* at the top, and the gift recipient at the bottom. But, as we have already discussed, the ally relationship hierarchy cannot be coded as a typical active/reactive relation. This is not (simply) a supporter/supported force relation – if it were, it wouldn't have transformative potential (by Deleuzio-Guattarian standards). A supporter/supported relationship would reproduce the dominant/dominated relationship that drives major/arborescent assemblages, a binary that we want to dismantle in the field of "mental health" (see Chapter 3). As disruptive processes of becoming shake up this relationship (reactive forces deterritorialising active forces – separating power from what it can do), the force relations continually shift. What we present is an in-between territory that oscillates around an ally/friend relation that is at the intermezzo of supporter/supported relation and a friend/friend relation. The ally/friend assemblage swings back and forth, never remaining still – it swings towards the major segmentation of active/reactive relations, then back towards the smoothing reciprocity of friendship. Never fully one or the other, always in-between. The ally/friend is also a body itself, an assemblage acting as a force together. The revolutionary potential of ally relationships is not the elimination of hierarchy, but the continual unsettling of hierarchy and production of a supple hierarchy. In what follows, we breakdown the suppleness of these assemblages, looking primarily at their slowness and their softness/flexibility, and conclude with a discussion of their supple hierarchy.

Slowness

The ally relationships in *Edge Entanglements* disregarded convention for efficiency or the rapid pace that we've become used to in our social relations – for example, one hour get-togethers, busy schedules. Allies were generous with time and energy, not in a structured way (e.g., schedule meetings for two hours instead of one hour) but in a way that had disregard for structure. Here, this disregard for structure in the intermezzo is characterised as a slowness.

The most telling example of slowness was in the relationship of Carol and Julie and their evening phone calls.

I try to stay on the phone with Carol as long as she wants to, especially if she is not feeling that well. Sometimes for hours. Sometimes we don't even talk for a while. We just stay on the phone you know? I'm tired and yawning, she's tired and yawning.

Julie describes having no agenda when they're together "except to spend time with Carol." The reason for connecting was connection itself. Across all of these relationships there is very little to justify why these relationships exist; it is not because they have x-y-z in common. When asked, Julie and Carol struggled to find common interests. Was it movies? Well, they both like movies, but Carol likes horror and Julie drama and action. Eventually Julie resolved, "I really don't feel like, Carol, that we don't need to have much in common to be friends."

Ally/friend assemblages carelessly meander. Batman and Robin, in their feverish pace (as noted in Chapter 6), carelessly connect – the demands of life usually take a backseat to their time together.

"Remember when (your) Uncle Bob died?" asked Robin.
"Yeah," Batman nodded, stopping to look at Robin.
"Do you remember what we did?"
"Go drive."
"Yeah, we went for a long drive."

I (Tim) feel myself slow as I listen to them talk about grieving together. While they are an energetic pair that are up to some sort of adventure each weekend; their movements are on a smooth and slow plane. I remember being out at the monster trucks with them, or out with them watching a rugby league match, and not really knowing how long they were going to spend together – no agenda. The monster truck event didn't quite turn out as we expected – there was a big crash with the crowd that sidelined the entire event. But Batman and Robin carelessly meandered around the site, checking out a local market, goofing around in the park.

Slowness continues with Jack and Alan – let's look back on my second meeting with them. It's one o'clock in the afternoon, or more like 1:15 as I'm a little late. "Come on up mate," says Alan, buzzing me in to his apartment. I apologise for making them wait. "It's ok, would you like a tea?" I sit down, place my backpack beside my chair, ready to get talking with these guys. I lean forward, I breathe in – one of those breaths that you take before starting to speak. Jack is looking at his mug, sunken deep into his chair with his hips well below his knees. Alan is in the kitchen pouring some boiling water over a tea bag for me. I pause. Neither of them appear that interested with me at that moment – I'm sitting there leaning forward, tripoding my elbows on my knees, which now feels quite strange. I slowly lean back and wait. Alan brings me a mug of tea and sits down. I hesitate, but fill the void with my voice, "So how are things going?" "Good, yeah," Jack says. "Really good," rattles off Alan. I wait again, but can't help but speak again, commenting on the tea, which was actually quite nice. I wait some more, this time a little more comfortable with the silence. After some time, Jack jumps in, "Alan's been telling me about the importance of nutrition when bodybuilding." Our conversation slowly meanders for a few minutes, and I eventually ask, "If I wasn't coming today, what would the two of you be doing?" Jack, still mainly looking at this mug, responds, "We'd be having tea and talking just like this." No doubt my presence has affected their interaction in some way, but they do seem quite comfortable at this pace. I had this impression of slowness for most of our conversations.

One of the things that struck with me was the slowness that Jack demonstrated when encountering unexpected things in Alan's story. One meeting over a cup of tea, Alan describes his "encounters with God," and a number of spiritual experiences that I find quite unsettling as I listen. "Satan says stuff like, 'I'm going to slit your throat or gonna hunt you down and kill you' and all that shit ... he's full of shit, he's just a bully." Alan continues, "God let me experience that so that I would trust him." He talks at length about how "God revealed himself" through spiritual visions. "Not many people believe me," he says.

> This is difficult for me (Tim). I consider myself quite open to understanding how different people experience their life and their senses, open to hearing how people make sense of these experiences and the value their experiences have within the context of their life. But I can't help but say to myself in that moment, "No, no, no, that's bullshit, what sort of 'God' would reveal themselves that way? Why would you ever want to trust something that exposes you to trauma?!"
>
> My (internal) response is charged with echoes from the past, growing up attending a conservative Christian church, where fear was often used as a coercive tool. I feel an uneasiness as Alan speaks, but I don't think they can tell.

"I believe that God revealed himself to Alan," said Jack, matter of fact. I'm a bit taken aback by Jack's response ... it comes at the moment that I struggle with Alan's interpretation of his sensory experience. I invite Jack to share more about what he thinks of Alan's spiritual experiences. Rather than directly responding, Jack describes his process for when someone says something that he's not quite sure about:

> just put it on the back burner. Let it simmer. A metaphor of the kitchen. Just let it simmer, don't take it off the burner. Let it simmer until you have a better idea of it. Just sit and think about it, don't reject it.

Jack is conveying not simply a slowness in pace, but a slowness of listening and responding – a slowness of interpretation and coming to conclusions. In this interaction, I was an active force, directing the flow of conversation – but then unsettled by the minor gesture within Jack's response, I was invited to new ways of responding and listening.

Softness and flexibility

On our second last meeting together, Jack asks me, "What's the rhizome?" He had overheard me talk about a Deleuzio-Guattarian rhizome with a support worker at APTB about a year previous. Jack and I spend a good 10 minutes talking about the rhizome, leading him to ask if he could read one of my papers[2] before our final meeting together. In that final meeting, we talk about the differences between rhizomatic and arborescent assemblages, drawing connections to ally relationships. He describes how he thinks that ally relationships are rhizomatic assemblages. "All these wonderful connections. Makes life fulfilled, even though we're not in the hierarchy," Jack says, discussing how ally relationships are outside or in parallel to the mainstream and how psychiatrised people are positioned within major assemblages. Jack continues, "[Ally relationships] take the hard edge off capitalism." This is a reference to an earlier conversation we had, where Jack described himself as "politically conservative" but also influenced by socialist values from his father. He had said that "socialism takes the hard edge off capitalism." Jack identified that ally relationships soften the harsh, dominating, individualistic and at times violent, edge off the mental health sector and the production of cramped spaces in Western society. Reflecting on Alan's relegation to the cramped spaces of a men's hotel, Jack stated: "Well, that's what happens when you've got a mental illness in Queensland. You have to go to sub-standard accommodation."

There are several examples in my encounters with the ally relationships that illustrate the softening of the "hard edge" of the mental health system. Here is an example of a common conversation between Batman and Robin – the lightness of their discussion brings a softness to the exchange:

ROBIN: You've got a free transit pass, haven't you?
BATMAN: Yeah.
ROBIN: Where is it?
BATMAN: There (pointing down).
ROBIN: No, that's your belly mate.
BATMAN: Oh shut up.
ROBIN: Show Tim your pass, see, this criminal-looking fella.
BOTH: <laughter>

Then, a couple weeks later, while watching State of Origin[3] together at a friend's place:

BATMAN: Send me in there [onto the footy field to play].
ROBIN: Get in there, Batman! Do you wear clean underwear?
BATMAN: Yeah.
ROBIN: Well, get in there mate!
EVERYONE: <laughter>

Both of the examples above give us pause – upon re-reading these quotes, Robin's humour undermines Batman as a "criminal-looking fella" who may not "wear clean underwear." We might say that this is typical of Australian male humour – playfully degrading someone else is common. However, we imagine that there is a fair bit going on under the surface (consciously or not) of this type of humour – how far can jokes that "punch down" go without causing harm?

I'm laughing, big belly laughs as I listen to their banter. Batman and Robin are relaxed around each other, their banter flows; these are very casual and soft spaces. Chips put words to this sentiment when speaking about his relationship with Krispy, "I'd like to think the sort of casualness with which we operate is helpful." Chips reflects on the lack of rigid segmentation in their relationship, "It's not regimented, you know what I mean?" The casualness in these two relationships contributes to the softening of territories, a generative casualness.

There was also the blending of lives and flexibility in the territories that separate them, particularly in the relationships of Krispy and Chips and Batman and Robin, a deterritorialisation of boundaries and relationships. Their friendship circles have begun to overlap – for example, both pairs watched the State of Origin match together with their mutual friends. However, the entanglement of lives is most prominent in Batman and Robin's relationship. Many of Robin's friends are through his relationship with Batman; as the years go by, important people to Batman have become important to Robin as well. They have started going on holidays together, at times travelling down to Sydney to spend time with Robin's family. Batman stays with Robin at his sister's home – "My sister shouted us tickets to [the speedway]." "We had water fights and things like that too," recalled Robin. "I got [your sister] good [in the water fight]," laughed Batman.

TIM: How many of your own personal fond memories are ones that involve Batman?
ROBIN: Recently, there'd be quite a few. Like I tell everyone, he's a friend …
    we're with each other nowadays nearly every Saturday.

These are not (only) relationships between a voluntary support and someone who needs support, but genuine relationships in which they become entangled in each other's lives.

Ally relationships, in particular the allies themselves, enter into a "zone of proximity" (Deleuze & Guattari, 1987, p. 273) with psychiatrisation and the cramped spaces. They take on reactive qualities and are affected by minor gestures. Rosi Braidotti (2011) describes "powers of affirmation" as a force of another kind, a disrupted active force. An affirmative force is one that creatively "contributes to conditions of becoming" rather than one that is predetermined, justified, and seeks compensation (Braidotti, 2011, p. 293). Powers of affirmation do not require a reason, as "reason has nothing to do with it" (Braidotti, 2011, p. 292). The becoming-reactive of ally relationships produces an affirmative force that does not require compensation – it is a tainted active force that contributes to becoming. Ally relationships vibrate with potential to transform and dissonate; they become an affirmative force that can trigger enumerable becomings. Ally/friend relationships are at/in the intermezzo, where reactive forces can be wild and active forces unhinged.

Consideration for reactive becomings can help to re-imagine change processes in the field of mental health as creating conditions that permit reactive forces to separate active forces from what they are capable of, and to nurture powers of affirmation. However, we caution against the impulse to generate a program: "Let's scale this up! Let's produce ally relationships! Come, join the program, we'll tell you what to do!" The apparatus of capture can swiftly entrap our thoughts and good intentions, returning us to our prior dominating position and active force relation. As an ally with a man referred to as Stanley, Tim recalls being contacted by a team member at APTB to provide a tally of his volunteer hours. The request for hours was to support their documentation of true service hours provided to Stanley. Tim declined to provide the hours, as he didn't see himself as a volunteer and felt uncomfortable "reporting" on their friendship. The machine of resonance is a ruthless and cunning predator, the apparatus of capture can be quick to rein in the ally.

We think that those who work in the mental health sector can cultivate reactive becomings by transversally bringing different people together, by welcoming encounters that might trip up the dominance of active forces and dispel the myth that people become (negatively) tainted by reactivity. We can ask people like Julie to spend time with people like Carol, invite people like Chips to visit people like Krispy in psychiatric institutions, support people like Robin to check up on people like Batman in the park, have people like Jack tutor people like Alan. We can experiment with relationships just to see what happens. Ally relationships are one way for dissonance to occur, one of multiple – reactivity can burst in any direction.

A supple hierarchy

"Alan is a mate of mine, a friend … I want to help him make wise choices in his life."

Jack's words nicely diagram the in-betweenness of ally/friend relationships. This is not a typical active/reactive hierarchy; this is a destabilised hierarchy that can change at any moment, a soft hierarchy that doesn't dominate. There is simultaneous allyship/friendship.

It was clear that one person in each of these relationships was a support and the other was often supported. Whether it was Julie being available for a phone call with Carol every evening, or Alan receiving advice from Jack on how to break away from harmful relationships, one of the roles for the ally was to be a supportive person, a (destabilised) active force or an affirmative force. When asked what they would talk about if I wasn't there, Krispy and Chips responded:

KRISPY: How I'm doing.

CHIPS: How he's going, what he's done that week ... It's mostly just sort of a general yack.

The focus is on Krispy, and the same could be said for the other ally relationships. Robin keeps track of Batman when they are out in the community, such as watching his interaction with a police officer at the monster trucks. He monitors how generous Batman is with others in his life. He keeps an eye on Batman's relationships to make sure others don't take advantage of him. Batman has a desire to help people who are houseless and regularly invites people to stay at his flat, but Robin notes that sometimes people take advantage of him – they might stay too long or take his money. During the study, Robin was in the process of becoming Batman's guardian.

ROBIN: Guardianship has been on the table for a number of years and I've been resistant to it. I'm still resistant ... but it's becoming more necessary ... they exploit him. Batman gets in these relationships where he gets quite attached and wants to help, but they end up freeloading off him.

But there is a tension for Robin, an awareness that this step of guardianship was a very formal move that makes him more of an authority in their relationship. However, guardianship also further entangles their lives – where Batman's struggles become Robin's struggles. They become more a part of each other, operating as one force, an affirmative force.

ROBIN: I try not to have a lot of influence with [the mental health support organisation]. I just kind of mind my business and make sure things are going right for him. But they know that I come running when some things are not right. So, you know, I will roar. And there's been times I've had to roar.

An ally "will roar." As a major/active force in society, Robin has the power to influence Batman's experience in life when things are not going right for him. Robin described how about eight years ago he helped make necessary institutional connections for Batman to stay afloat during a housing crisis. This is an example of Robin operating as an affirmative force, one that potentiates becoming rather than constraint. The affirmative force of allies does not serve or compensate the ally but enhances the powers of action of their friend. This force manifests in Chips attending the mental health tribunal with Krispy, in Jack suggesting Alan "break the connections with toxic connections" in his life, in Julie standing up for Carol when she is being robbed, and in Robin standing up for Batman when things aren't right. Ally relationships can swing towards a more hierarchical relation in order to have their friend's back, but these are not hierarchies of dominance.

There are moments where the hierarchy flattens and the ally/friend relationship becomes a friend/friend assemblage, such as in the following exchange.

KRISPY: Today is Chips' shout so I came along [Chips' turn to buy fish n chips]
CHIPS: When it's my shout, he never misses.
KRISPY: When it's my shout I never miss either.
CHIPS: Well, that's true.

Robin recalled his speech at Batman's 50th birthday party, where he said, "Next to my wife, Batman is my best friend." These are relationships of friendship – an ally supports their friend. On the night when Batman and Robin invited me to come over to their mutual friend's home to watch rugby, I had the pleasure of watching friends spend time together. Batman and Robin were going back and forth all game – joking, yelling, cheering, and jesting with each other.

BATMAN: Blues come to my place to party [after winning the match].

There is an intensity in the room. The match is almost over and we are all vibrating with energy (and caffeine). Both Batman and Robin are bouncing behind the sofa as the final moments wind down:

ROBIN: Well, do you have food?
BATMAN: Yeah.
ROBIN: What you got?
BATMAN: Cornflakes.
EVERYONE: <laughter>

We all get a kick out of imagining the after-game party featuring cornflakes.

STEVE (ANOTHER FRIEND OF BATMAN AND ROBIN'S): I can give you some
    strawberries.
ROBIN: Cornflakes and strawberries!
EVERYONE: <laughter>

I witness the force relations fluctuate all over the place that night – their relationship swings at the intermezzo. Robin seems to feed off Batman, the two of them affecting and being affected by each other all night. They are like two reactive forces swirling and bouncing off one another. At one point towards the end of the night, Batman takes a phone call in another room – the energy leaves with him. It is a call from a mutual friend mentioned earlier, Kit. Robin stands at the back of the room, keeping an ear out for the phone conversation, waiting to see if he should jump in or not. But Robin also stands expectant, as if waiting for Batman to come back so that he could release his energy – electric energy birthed from their relationship. This night, Robin was Batman's sidekick.

While being careless, the ally relationship was not without care. Allies were usually quite aware of the challenges their friend experiences and kept an eye on the complexity of their everyday life – there is intentionality and care in being an ally.

They are looking out for their friend even in basic everyday interactions. For Krispy and Chips, this involved Chips planning for an upcoming doctor's appointment with Krispy, discussing the side effects of his medications and what they needed to do to prepare, or preparing for an upcoming tribunal meeting. Julie would follow-up with Carol during our breakfast meetings, check on whether she brought her tablets along to the meeting and what time her next dosage would be.

Jack and Alan's relationship was a little different. There was a hierarchy in that Jack was the advice giver, Jack's life was more stable, and Jack was the one offering support to Alan. However, the hierarchical swings were not of the same magnitude as in the other pairs. Jack was someone who was there to listen, to offer friendship and advice – perhaps like a mentor. But Jack wasn't actively advocating for/with Alan. Perhaps this was (in part) because they were in a peer relationship, as Jack would say, "fellow schizophrenics." Peer allyship (a relation between people with a shared minor experience) may produce different affects compared to non-peer allyship (such as the other ally relationships in this book). Nonetheless, ally assemblages are characterised by non-dominating hierarchies that potentiate becomings rather than generate cramped spaces.

★★★

In this chapter, we have traversed the territories of ally assemblages, exploring how they are assembled and also disassembled. Beginning first with an introduction of active/reactive force relations, we examined how hierarchical force relations have produced cramped spaces in the lives of psychiatrised people. However, while active forces are predictable and dominating, reactive forces are unpredictable and have the potential to disrupt/trip up active forces. In the ally relationships in this book, one of the early movements in these assemblages was that of allies towards the minor/cramped spaces. The active force of allies was disrupted by a minor gesture, leading to the development of an atypical ally/friend relationship. This ally/friend relationship, where allies enter into a zone of proximity with a minor/reactive force, inhabit an intermezzo/in-between space that vibrates with potential. In this intermezzo territory of ally assemblages, there is slowness, soft/flexible lines, and supple hierarchies. Ally assemblages at the intermezzo produce a force of another kind, an *affirmative* force that has the potential to generate ongoing transformative processes of becoming.

Notes

1 We do want to casually and conceptually use the language of slavery given the ongoing sociohistorical affects in much of the world, and have intentionally avoided using the master/slave dualism in this book. While Deleuze and Guattari used these terms in a similar way to using their concepts of major and minor, we think that Deleuze's active/reactive is a clearer articulation of affective relations and elements of becoming.

2 The paper shared with Jack was Barlott et al. (2017), which also forms the majority of Chapter 3 of this book.

3 State of Origin is an annual rugby league series between the Australian states of New South Wales (Blues) and Queensland (Maroons).

8

CARTOGRAPHY OF BECOMING

Becoming, when the structure breaks down and transforms into something else.

Becoming, when power separates from what it can do – active forces become entangled with reactive forces – forming a force of another type, an affirmative force of radical non-reciprocity.

Becoming, when a crack makes room for something imperceptible to burst/ooze out of it as a line of flight, escaping the cramped spaces and forming something new.

★★★

ROBIN: I'd always know where to find [Batman]. After finishing my shifts, I'd take him some food or we'd go for a drive in the morning – we became friends.
TIM: How'd that all happen?
ROBIN: It just did. We had a connection – I saw his situation.
TIM: Why'd you start spending time together and bringing him food?
ROBIN: I dunno, I guess just to see where it goes.

The conversation above between Robin and Tim illustrates the process of becoming in Batman and Robin's relationship. The structure is breaking down – an active force is separated from its power, a crack makes room for something to burst/ooze. The boundary between an outreach worker and client blurred – Robin went to Batman after his shift, he *saw* Batman's situation and was stirred. The assemblage between Batman and Robin transformed into something else – active and reactive forces become entangled, forming an affirmative force and a differential a line of flight out of the cramped spaces. Robin brought Batman meals, took him out for

DOI: 10.4324/9781003286486-8

drives, formed a connection with him ... they became friends. But why? "Just to see where it goes." Imperceptible.

Having traversed the territories of becoming in ally assemblages (Chapter 7), we turn our attention in this chapter to mapping processes of becoming. We have mapped out how allies were tripped up by reactive forces, entering into a zone of proximity with the minor and reactive forces. Ally/friend assemblages, with their flexible lines and supple hierarchies, form an affirmative force that can catalyse imperceptible becomings. We now interrogate these processes of becoming by, first, considering the surging affirmative force that propagates becoming. We surface the vitality of immanent and haunting affirmative forces that swirl amidst the assemblage, and use Deleuze and Guattari's notion of a sorcerer to express how affirmative forces catalyse becoming. We outline how these affirmative forces are produced through the entanglement of ally/friend, a collective force. Second, we map the processes of becoming that unravel and transform ally assemblages, notably the deterritorialising movements and lines of flight, and conclude with an overview of their reterritorialisations.

Affirmative force and the sorcerer

Let us re-turn to the formation of an affirmative force (see Chapter 7), but, this time, by considering the formation of an affirmative force as the affect of proximity, contagion, and infection. We are re-turning to the formation of affirmative forces so that it is clear that affirmative forces are not inherited or passed down ... there is no lineage of affirmative force as with active or reactive force. Affirmative force is not learned, taught, or imbued through social positions or structures. To aid in this discussion, we draw from Deleuze and Guattari's (1987) conceptualisation of becoming-animal (one of the many forms of becoming discussed in their work). We suggest that a destabilised affirmative force is also an infection, a mutation of force that occurs in becoming-animal. In the case of allies, as they enter into a zone of proximity with the minor, the reactivity of their friends trips them up. Allies and ally/friend assemblages become *infected* with reactivity.

Proximity

Contagion-Infection

Becoming

Becoming

Becoming

Becoming

Becoming

We borrow from Deleuze and Guattari's (1987) conceptual personae of the sorcerer[1] to convey the affirmative force of ally assemblages. In their account, sorcerers enter into an alliance with the wild, an alliance with the unpredictable or reactive nature of an animal (Deleuze & Guattari, 1987). Becoming-animal is to enter into a zone of proximity with what is considered wild in society. Mapping this onto ally assemblages, the sorcerer is not an individual; the sorcerer is the incorporeal force generated by the alliance of ally and friend. The ally, tainted by wild reactive forces, become entangled with their minor friends, and together enter the intermezzo – the place of sorcery and magic. "Sorcerers have always held the anomalous[2] position, at the edge of the fields or woods. They haunt the fringes. They are at the borderline of the village, or between villages. The important thing is their affinity with alliance" (Deleuze & Guattari, 1987, p. 287). The sorcerer's affinity with alliance is interrelated with becoming as a collective enunciation, something that we touch on throughout this chapter.

I (Tim) facilitated a workshop in the mental health sector on this project in late 2020 – there was a word I stumbled over again and again: *magic.* "The magic of these relationships, I mean the significance of these relationships …," I fumbled. "What was most magical, I mean notable …," I clarified.

Why not embrace the idea of magic? Could not the affirmative force of ally relationships be a form of sorcery of the intermezzo, whose spell generates the conditions of becoming? There is an underlying assumption in my mind that sorcery is bad, dangerous, and fictitious (see Afterword).

The sorcerer's magic is produced through proximity with the wild. At the edge of the forest, the intermezzo. Powers of affirmation are not inherited or learned; they are produced through alliance – "witchcraft is contagious" (Deleuze & Guattari, 1987, p. 288). Allies are wilded through proximity and connection with the minor. Infected. Displaced. The becoming-reactive of ally assemblages produced an affirmative force, the force of a sorcerer. Wielding their magic at the edge of the forest, the sorcerer is at "the cutting edge of deterritorialisation" (Deleuze & Guattari, 1987, p. 284). We re-turn to the notion of being at the edge of the forest again in Chapter 9.

The affirmative force of the sorcerer is a collective force, always a rhizomatic force of alliance. Assemblages of sorcery are difficult to categorise; they are "always on the fringe of recognised institutions … anomic." They are tainted but powerful – not the power to dominate, but power to creatively produce new assemblages and becomings. Affirmative forces nudge and propel assemblages through ongoing movements of becoming – "The affirmative cut of the minor gesture catalyzes a reordering" (Manning, 2016, p. 201). In what follows, we demonstrate how the affirmative sorcery of ally assemblages is that of radical non-reciprocity: careless generosity and care-full generosity.

Careless/care-full generosity

It was mid-2020 when I (Tim) first wrote this section, I was attempting to get back into my research after a challenging year away – I had major surgery in the latter half of 2019 and, well, there was COVID. I was remembering a time in 2018 and the feeling of meeting with people for the project. Back then I had a sense of immersion, or of sinking into the project. I felt an alliance or a with-ness, as though I were amidst the swirling forces of the project assemblage. I was comfortably in-between – thinking with theory, living with theory. Proximity, contagion. But in 2020, nothing.

I carefully walk the trail back to forest – the foliage looks different, but the path is familiar. As I approach the tree line I see familiar stumps and logs. This is it!

"I'm back," I whisper, my eyes darting side to side looking for the sorcerer.

"Hello?" I speak louder. "Are you still here? I've missed you."

Standing alone, destitute, I make one final plea: "Can we pick up where we left off?

[Silence]

I hit my head against a pile of transcripts day after day, wondering, "Where did that affect go?" Where is the desire that was bubbling before? For a period of time in 2018 I was in the intermezzo with ally assemblages, but reterritorialised back to the rigours of academia. I reverted to old modes of analysis, rather than following flows of affect I began coding the data with theory. "This looks like a becoming" (places post-it note). I categorically ordered the data – there were no impulses of desire in my analysis. There is no formula for generating desire. Deflated. I was no longer thinking *with* theory; theory was no longer my companion. I stopped my categorical use of theory. I paused, walked, wandered, drank coffee. I put away my post-it notes and decided to just read and read and read … waiting for an encounter that I could follow (see Chapter 5).

Go first to your old plant and watch carefully the watercourse made by the rain. By now the rain must have carried the seeds far away. Watch the crevices made by the runoff, and from them determine the direction of the flow. Then find the plant that is growing …

(Deleuze & Guattari, 1987, p. 11)

It happens as I follow the watercourse. I read and reread transcripts, I read and reread theory, over and over, day after day – then, I hit Jack's transcript from the 16 August 2018. This was our first meeting after Alan died, about a week after his funeral. I remember the meeting fondly; it was a solemn and reflective coffee time with Jack. I recall ordering an almond milk flat white (they were out of soy milk) and Jack had the same. I forget if it was Jack's shout or mine (Jack – knowing I'm Canadian – explains that calling it a "shout" was very Australian). We were talking about the things Jack appreciated about Alan. As I read the transcript, the sorcerer swirls and whispers to me: *come.*

"Well, I had a friend," Jack said slowly.

Jack did not talk about any qualities at this point. He had a friend. There is something in these words that starts to pull me. Time shifts – Jack had a friend and he lost a friend. Jack continued:

I gave him all the friendship he could possibly want.

The words grab me by the trachea – they grip – they pull. I feel an uncomfortable tightness in my neck and jawline, like a cramp. I can't swallow, my eyes fill with tears. I'm pulled in for the first time in months ... maybe years. I read his words over and over again. Jack's words give the impression of excess, careless excess – friendship that drips and oozes through every crack and crevice. Jack's words speak to a generosity that brings me back to a Rosi Braidotti (2011) book I have not picked up since 2017, where she speaks of "a deep and *careless generosity*" (p. 298, emphasis added). This is the affirmative force of ally assemblages, the displaced force of the intermezzo, the sorcerer's magic, an "ethics of non-profit at an ontological level" (Braidotti, 2011, p. 298).

Jack's allyship was an act of careless generosity. As mentioned in previous chapters, I have been thinking about these relationships as reciprocal for years, perhaps even from day one of this project. I have persistently discussed the mutually beneficial characteristics of these relationships as one of their transformative affects. And, indeed, these relationships were mutually beneficial, there is a deep sense of fulfilment for both people in these relationships. But is there not also a sense of fulfilment in being a formal volunteer or a paid support worker? Is there not mutual benefit? A support worker receives pay and (hopefully) feels some satisfaction for their work. A volunteer worker would (hopefully) feel some satisfaction, maybe similar to that of an ally. The revolutionary potential of ally relationships is different though. It is the stirring of a desire for careless generosity – "I gave him all the friendship he could possibly want." It is as if I am hearing Jack say, "Want more friendship? Here, have more. Don't worry if you don't have much to give in return, here." Perhaps an ally desires to give friendship (and), without expectation of anything in return.[3]

Careless generosity is for posterity's sake – for the future of another. "Given that posterity per definition can never pay us back, this gesture is perfectly gratuitous" (Braidotti, 2011, p. 298). Careless generosity is flippant, excessive, with disregard for convention or social expectation.

But the generosity of allies is also care-*full* – generosity that is full of care, that is full of intention to bring benefit to a friend. Generosity that is full of care is vigilant and cautious generosity. Manning (2016) refers to this cautious vigilance as "experimental prudence, a prudence patient enough to engage with that which experimentation unsettles, a prudence attuned to the force of the in-act" (p. 7). While cautious, experimental prudence is not passive – in the fullness of care, the experimenter "jumps at the chance to discover what else the event can do" (Manning, 2016, p. 7). Posthumanist scholars have explored the idea of "care-full" care as being imbued with relational vitality that can activate becomings (Fullagar et al., 2017; Gibson et al., 2020). Care-full care, care that is attentive to the micropolitical entanglements, can create breakthroughs where rules or procedural pursuit of human rights cannot (see Deleuze, 1988). We do not (only) need predetermined procedures, we need micropolitical, situation-specific responses. A care-full generosity is not one that responds to expectation or convention, but one that deeply cares for the surviving and thriving of the other (see Eales & Peers, 2021).[4] This is Robin becoming Batman's guardian – it is careless in that it disregards convention or what might be expected, but care-full in that it is full of intention to "make sure things are right with [Batman]." In crafting the words "care-full generosity," we were inspired by Eales and Peers (2020) and their entanglements with queer crip Mad care, and Mazzei's (2013) use of the words "meaning-full" and "purpose-full" to emphasise the "fullness" in meaning and purpose. In this way, care-full generosity is filled with care – at the limit, perhaps in excess. Yet paradoxically also full with elements of being careful: consideration, caution, vigilance. We posit that the revolutionary force of ally relationships is simultaneously careless and care-full generosity.

Turning briefly to Derrida, we want to consider the possibility that completely gratuitous generosity is impossible. Derrida (1992) considers the paradox of generosity and hospitality, as a possible-impossible paradox. He argues that all gifts bear the obligation of a counter-gift. "In short, the gift is not neutral, it is the paradoxical creator of obligations, a cause with overabundant effects. Being a free act, it produces constraint in the recipient" (Champetier, 2001, p. 17).

When I (Tim) initially wrote parts of this section in 2020 I paused to think about generosity in my own life. My family and I had moved out of our house in Brisbane, in anticipation of moving back to Canada in the next few months. Our neighbours generously invited us to store some of our belongings in their garage until we have a solid relocation plan. Soon, their garage became full of our stuff.

I felt terrible taking up so much space in their garage. "How about we arrange for a storage unit, it could be months before we're ready to ship this stuff" I told them. "Don't be silly, we don't use the garage anyways, just leave it here until you have a plan," my neighbour replied. "Ok" I said, "but *I owe you big time.*"

Endless cycles of gift and counter-gift. This is a major generosity, generosity as an active force where the giver is simultaneously a taker – taking back a "thank you," claiming some social capital, taking credit for a good deed. Derrida (1992) wonders whether it would be possible to dissociate giving from the cycle of reciprocity (receiving/taking). Generosity as an affirmative force is a deterritorialised generosity, a becoming. Ally relationships seem to destabilise the association of gift and counter-gift, or at least soften the lines so that the generosity doesn't generate constraint. The force at the intermezzo is careless; it has disregard for required response/counter-gift.

Keep moving. The sorcerer chases pure generosity. "I gave him all the friendship he could possibly want." Disrupt. Destabilise. Keep moving. Ally assemblages produce friendship of another kind, not one (solely) based on mutual benefit or reciprocity. Ally relationships generate relations of non-reciprocity, gratuitous generosity. This is a destructive generosity that destabilises territories and potentiates becoming.

ROBIN: For me it was "oh here's someone in a rough spot, maybe I can do a little bit more."

Tripped up, Robin "saw [Batman's] situation" and started to bring him food. This was a generosity at the intermezzo, without expectation of receiving anything in return – generosity that was produced through the becoming of force. Robin became infected with reactivity when in proximity to the cramped spaces of Batman's life. Disregarding professional roles, disregarding relationship conventions – careless generosity. The two of them spend every Saturday together, be it at the speedway, canoeing, riding bumper cars/dodge-em cars, cycling along the Gold Coast, road trips to the countryside, and, and, and. Robin covers the costs. Over the last couple of years, they have started going on holidays together, travelling down to Sydney to visit Robin's sister, visiting Kit in Canberra.

BATMAN: A high rise.
ROBIN: You like high rises, don't you, when we go on holidays?
BATMAN: Yeah, yeah.
ROBIN: So, he likes to holiday in some of the ritzier places. <laughs>

While careless, Robin's generosity …

> Hold on – have we sneakily made this all about the generosity of some do-gooders? Is this just about allies being charitable? Are the psychiatrised people in this project not also "generous" with their time/energy in these relationships? Have we deemed the time/resources of allies as more valuable?
> *We hold this in tension – it is not what it seems.*

… is also care-full. Mindful that Batman hasn't had many opportunities to travel, Robin intentionally works in holidays together. In becoming Batman's guardian, a huge responsibility, Robin has formally and generously taken on Batman's struggle as his own.

In the early days of Chips' relationship with Krispy, Chips said he used to think to himself, "Mate, what's going to happen with all this?" Continuing, he said,

"There was nothing I could do, except stand by, which is what I did." Chips just gave. No (overt) expectation for receiving anything or for a particular outcome. Still, Chips hoped to make a difference in Krispy's life – there is a tension between generosity and reciprocation. Chips spent time with Krispy on a weekly basis, slowly supporting him to transition out of the forensic institution.

CHIPS: I make myself pretty available – Krispy rings me quite a few times, even if it's only for two minutes or something, and I'm happy with that … if he rang me at night, I'd answer it … I say, "If something happens, give me a call and I'll come and get you."

An affirmative force, a careless generosity – but also care-full, a force that is full of concern for seeing things go well for Krispy. I asked Chips for more detail about the sense of fulfilment that he gets from their relationship, Chips responds, "I can enjoy it to the extent that I hope it'll make a difference to Krispy. That was my main motive for doing it. There was no other motive [than to see Krispy do well]." Krispy recalls the early years of their friendship, when Chips would come to the mental health review tribunal and "[help] me along when I didn't know what to say." Speaking up for a friend when they could not speak up for themselves – "he's always there for me," reflects Krispy.

Generosity, a collective force of becoming

To this point in the chapter, we have articulated the affirmative force of ally assemblages as if it were an individual expression, which is not the case. Becoming is a collective enunciation, a transformative process produced within and by assemblages. Even individual actions are infused with the intensity of entangled multiplicities. When Deleuze and Guattari (1987) refer to becoming as collective, they are not necessarily referring to people and other sociomaterial acting directly together, such as protesting alongside one another. Rather, a collective enunciation could be in the form of disparate parts flowing in a similar trajectory. For example, in Chapter 2, we discussed how diverse disruptive movements can work together to unsettle the mental health sector. Ally relationships are a part of these ongoing, collective revolutionary processes.

The affirmative force of ally assemblages is a collective force. Forces of generosity come out of the entanglement of lives, where allies take on the struggle of their friends as their own. The liberating potential of these relationships eludes us if we reduce these ally relationships to "the generosity of allies" – acts of kindness by a bunch of do-gooders. That path arborifies the assemblage, reifying the pair as "the charitable ally" and "the supported." Rather, the relationship is a rhizomatic assemblage of generosity – an encounter between the major and the minor – a collision of forces – the stumbling of major/active force into the life of someone who experiences struggle. The *assemblage* produces and reproduces careless and care-full generosity. The encounter produces an electro-magnetic impulse in allies, a desire to connect and give. The entanglement produces a careless non-reciprocity that is without need for personal gain or benefit (though they receive it). Across all ally relationships, there was a sense of: *I do it for Krispy – I do it for Alan – I do it for Batman – I do it for Carol*.

However, taking the collective nature of ally assemblages a step further, we would like to pause for a moment to deterritorialise generosity. Generosity could be thought of as an active force, the force of giving – to give. This is at the heart of Derrida's paradox, the gift (active) generates the counter-gift response (reactive). Generosity puts someone in a position of power. But generosity as an affirmative force is a destabilised generosity, a force separated from what it can do – separated from its power to give.

Generosity as an affirmative force is not a dominating individual force, but one that enhances the assemblage. As allies take on the struggles of their friends – it is not simply *I do it for Krispy/Alan/Batman/Carol*, it is *I do it for us*. An affirmative generosity deterritorialises the gift/counter-gift relationship – there is generosity (i.e., abundance, plenty, amplitude), but without an expectation of reciprocity. The careless and care-full generosity of ally assemblages is a minor generosity that enhances the expression of an assemblage rather than serving an individual (e.g., an ally's need to feel good about themselves). The example below from Batman and Robin illustrates a minor generosity that enhances the assemblage:

ROBIN: There's been some mourning periods … someone will let me know [when a person in Batman's life has died] and we would meet up and go for a drive, do something in *our own way* [to grieve].

Here, generosity is not a gift given by Robin to Batman. When there is loss in Batman's life, Batman and Robin grieve together, in their "own way." There is abundance – they don't go for a drive around the block, they go for a drive to the countryside or to the beach. Careless (they just drive) and care-full (intentionally grieving in a particular way) generosity enables them to grieve together, in their own (unconventional) way. As Robin takes on the role of Batman's guardian, their lives become further (carelessly and care-fully) entangled – Robin formally takes on Batman's struggles as his own.

Speaking further to the affirmative force of generosity as a collective force, we turn back to Krispy and Chips:

CHIPS: Krispy has gone through a lot of rough times in our time together, but you know, we sort of managed to get through it.

We. Slowly, year after year, Krispy and Chips "managed to get through it," *together*. The belief among Krispy's mental health team in the early days of his forensic order was that he would never live on his own again, and it was difficult for him to imagine anything otherwise. How could he transition out of the institution if he wasn't even permitted to attend the tribunal meetings and advocate for himself? But once Chips became a part of Krispy's life, they were able to patiently work towards Krispy's desire to live on his own. "It was all very slow," said Chips, but they were able to do it together. When Krispy and Chips told me about a recent tribunal meeting where the chair called unknown experts on the phone (see Chapter 7), I (Tim) responded by saying, "That must have rattled you." Chips replied, "Oh, it rattled us!" It didn't only rattle Krispy, it rattled *"us"* ... they are in this fight together.[5]

Kinship and the production of (un)real family

The entanglement of these assemblages could also be considered a kinship – a closeness and sense of mutual obligation that is often reserved for conventional family. During one of our meetings, Alan talked about how he used to stick up for his little brother when he used to get picked on in grade school – this is what I envision when Robin says "I will roar" when "things are not right [for Batman]" (see Chapter 7). Alan/Jack and Krispy/Chips all referred to each other as "like brothers," and Carol/Julie as "like sisters." Yet, in the same breath, when asked if she would be comfortable talking about her family of origin, Carol replied: "No thank you, not my *real* family. Mum's a bitch and I don't care where dad is." Carol is dismissive and uninterested in talking about her "real" family and continues by saying, "You make your own family." The kinship of Carol and Julie's assemblage is the rhizomatic production of a family of choice, an (un)family.

At the start of this chapter, we noted that becoming is "when the structure breaks down and transforms into something else." In ally assemblages, the structure of "real" family is fractured and an (un)family bursts through the cracks, an ongoing process of becoming-family. "Chips is the only family I've got," said Krispy as the two of them shared a plate of fish and chips. While talking about family was a source of pain and turmoil for Krispy, his "brotherly" relationship with Chips was a source of joy.[6] Like Chips, Batman no longer had any ties with his family and the only positive familial relationship was with an Uncle who died in 2012. Batman and his uncle used to frequent the speedway together, something that Batman and Robin now do on a regular basis. "I never used to be into that sort of thing," reflects Robin, "but Batman loves it. We've been going ever since his uncle died." The kinship of ally assemblages is a collective and unconventional union of (un)family that is produced rather than inherited.

There have been times of tension and conflict across these relationships as might be expected in close connections. Whether it be Robin and Batman disagreeing about who should live in Batman's apartment or Julie being firm with Carol about the boundaries of their friendship (as discussed in Chapter 6). These moments of tension were not explored in-depth in our project, but it seemed as though there was a willingness to have difficult conversations with each other or at least a sense of care and respect in challenging times. Carol and Julie reflected:

CAROL: If she doesn't like something I say, she'll tell me. That sort of thing. We are both honest; we are both straight forward with each other. If she says something that I don't like, I'll tell her. If she doesn't like something I say, she'll tell me, and we both apologise and think of other ways to talk about it and make up.

JULIE: Although, we don't really have arguments or disagreements.

Likening this back to the kinship of ally assemblages noted above, Krispy and Chips described how the "brotherly" nature of their relationship extended to how they approach disagreement. When I asked what it means to be brothers, one of the things Krispy mentioned was "He pulls me in line, sometimes; I get a bit cheeky, don't I?" To which Chips responded: "Yeah, that's sort of a brother thing." In this exchange there are traces of a (paternalistic) familial hierarchy where the big brother pulls the little brother "in line," an active/reactive relation. There was no indication of the reverse occurring, where Krispy pulls Chips in line. However, as noted in Chapter 7, the territories and hierarchies of ally assemblages are flexible and non-dominating.

★★★

The forming of an affirmative and collective generosity is a becoming as well as an ongoing disruptive force that catalyses, bursts, and ruptures of innumerable becomings. Forces of affirmation swirl amidst these assemblages as they shift and shape over time. The sorcerer wields her reactive magic in the depths, as becomings bubble to the surface. So, as we move on to a discussion of lines of flight and transformative reterritorialisation, we are mindful of the immanent force that transversally cuts across these assemblages.

Lines of flight

Lines of flight are inseparable from deterritorialisations – together, these concepts comprise the process of rupturing and breaking away from the rigid territories of the major (or resistance to the apparatus of capture). A line of flight (also conceptualised as a line of escape) is where the territories of an assemblage break down or become unsettled, transforming into something else (Deleuze & Guattari, 1987); it "manifests as something distinctly different, an 'intensity' that defies representation and categorization" (Potts, 2004, p. 20). Brian Massumi (1987), in his "Notes on the Translation and Acknowledgments" for Deleuze and Guattari's *A Thousand Plateaus*, notes that the French word *fuite* (commonly translated as *flight*) has multiple meanings. "*Fuite* covers not only the act of fleeing or eluding but also flowing, leaking, and disappearing in the distance (the vanishing point in a painting is a *point de fuite*). It has no relation to flying." (p. xv). Deterritorialisation creates a crack or a rupture that releases into a line of flight where intensive forces ooze, drip, burst, escape, or flee. Processes of transformation occur when there is a rupture from the stratification of the major, forming a line of flight that evades the apparatus of capture, and reterritorialises away from the major (Deleuze & Guattari, 1987). In this section, we point out a number of the lines of flight in ally assemblages.

Now retired, Chips often reflected on his career during our research meetings. In the early days of his relationship with Krispy, over ten years ago, he was still working full-time. Krispy said that Chips' phone would often ring during their get-togethers. Chips was in a position of status as an engineer and manager of a major building company, but while holding a major identity, he described the active forces of the economy and building sector as controlling him. "I was basically Shanghaied [*sic*] away from humanity," Chips reflected, but getting involved in his community and meeting Krispy was "a real release into life for me." Encounters with reactive forces "released" him. Unsettled by reactivity, a fissure opened up for something to escape. "It's been great, I've loved it, and it's got me doing a few other things with other people" – and and and. Rhizomatically generating new connections.

Even though Krispy transitioned into the community a few years ago, he had not felt safe attending social events or being out on his own in the neighbourhood. But in the last year, Krispy started to do grocery shopping, go to major shopping centres, and go to the bank on his own. During the time we met together, Chips had invited Krispy into one of his friendship circles, inviting him to watch State of Origin with them (also watched by Batman and Robin with their mutual friends). Krispy was not able to do something like that in the past, but agreed to this time.

CHIPS: You liked that, didn't you?
KRISPY: I liked it, yeah.
CHIP: It was all guys. Just blokes over, about eight or nine blokes.
KRISPY: All eating pizzas and m&ms, cheering on …

Krispy is smiling, proud of himself, rupturing from the limits of the cramped spaces and feeling safe – once sentenced to the confined spaces of a forensic psychiatric institution, now breaking into a line of flight in the community. Chips generously welcomed Krispy into his circle of friends, setting off a cascade of rhizomatic connections:

CHIPS: And what happens now too is, even with just going to watch the State of Origin at someone else's place gives him another circle to operate in just out of the normal circle, which he found really positive.

Stretch, expand, connect – assemblages, connecting with other assemblages. One of the most common lines of flight across ally assemblages was this cascade of relationships and connections. Batman has an expanding network of friends and supports, "his network has really expanded over the years," reflects Robin. Much of these connections have "evolved from our relationship, probably from Kit, Batman and me." These relationships have generated a multitude of flows and relations – not just between people, but also the development of new interests and activities. Similarly, Carol has had an opportunity to be an educator (in the community development and community mental health sector) and to do things like develop computer skills. When mapping out Carol's interests and connections in one of our meetings, she chimes in, "You're running out of room sport," as I struggle to fit everything on the map.

I (Tim) repeat this in my head, "You're running out of room sport."

I slow my thoughts for a moment – I liked that she called me "sport." I felt the smoothing of hierarchies. I felt like a chum. It was a similar feeling to the one I got when Carol calls me "Timothy." There aren't many people who call me that.

Carol is getting a kick out of making her social map.

CAROL: "I've got more than you, Julie!"
JULIE: "It's not a competition, Carol."

Carol's broad assemblage (of which her relationship with Julie is a part) is full of atypical connections/lines of flight. She's friends with her chemist/pharmacist, the owners of a bookstore, the tobacconist, and and and. She has an informal relationship with the newsagents, where she drops off a few coins each time she passes by, and they hold it for her under the counter. Then, whenever she would like to pick up a newspaper, they have money saved up for her.

> The sorcerer's powers "[inspire] illicit unions and abominable loves."
> *(Deleuze & Guattari, 1987, p. 287)*

And the bookstore has a copy of her apartment key stored behind the counter in the event that she locks herself out. The territories of Carol's everyday life are soft and flexible, generosity seeps into all the cracks and crevasses … generating a multitude of lines of flight, further producing connections with others. People whose lives were once highly confined to the cramped spaces have rhizomatically taken flight.

Simply having someone to talk with catalysed lines of flight for psychiatrised people in the project. Carol, when asked about the value of these types of relationships, said, "If you're lonely or you're going through tension or you're just frightened, all you need to do is call someone like Julie and you'll be ok." While a phone call may seem like a small thing to many, we do not want to overlook the micropolitical significance of a phone call. The mental health sector typically discourages professionals/volunteers from sharing their phone numbers with people who have a "mental health diagnosis" as part of maintaining "healthy boundaries" (see Cassidy et al., 2019). As discussed in Chapter 2, boundaries and risk management protocols are an example of restrictive and arborescent processes in the mental health sector – whereas the Carol-Julie-phone assemblage ruptured into a liberating line of flight.

Alan described his experience of having someone he could casually talk with:

ALAN: [Talking with Jack] helped me get things off my chest. When I'm having a bad day, when I'm not feeling so good, if I got someone to talk to, it really helps. In the past I didn't have people to talk to, that's when I would blow up or get pissed off and go drink a bottle … I would bottle it up.

Through sharing his struggles with Jack, one of the lines of escape for Alan was from the cramped spaces of a men's hostel. Let loose by affirmative forces of generosity, ally assemblages break into rhizomatic lines of flight. Yet the flight is not an endpoint. Assemblages are continually assembling, disassembling, and reassembling – continually transforming into something else.

Reterritorialisation – transformation

Assemblages are not understood by breaking them down into their parts, assemblages are understood by what they produce. One of our guiding questions has been: What do ally assemblages do? Since Chapter 6 we have attempted to articulate what ally assemblages produce: disrupted territories, flexible lines, and supple hierarchies – careless and care-full generosity, lines of escape, and lines of connection – the force of a sorcerer at the intermezzo. However, an analysis of becoming is incomplete without considering the reterritorialisation, the new assemblages that are produced. So, we bring this chapter to a close by looking at each ally assemblage, considering: What has changed in these assemblages?

Krispy and Chips

Over the last 12 years, Krispy has slowly transitioned from being considered very dangerous and on a forensic treatment order to living a life of his choosing in the community – becoming. He still has several constraints and is closely monitored by major health and legal authorities, but the constraints are softening.

CHIPS: It was a gradual process, it took quite a while. At first it was just short trips out, first it was only into the canteen at the institution … then gradually it was out to a shopping centre [not far from the institution] … it was little steps at a time.

Small, care-full disruptions, small zigzag cracks, lines of flight, new territories. Speaking with pride about Krispy, Chips says:

[Krispy] is becoming less and less timid … understanding that he is allowed to have a voice, he is allowed to tell [someone], "You can't have my money," and he is allowed to go to the bank and say, "There's a mistake here, can we fix it?" It's very difficult to articulate it even, how well [he is] now compared to 10 to 12 years ago.

Chips has become the most important person in Krispy's life, and Krispy one of the most consistent people in Chips' life. After Tim shared some of the ideas presented in this book with Chips, he said, "I know you think I've been generous and all, but I've gotten more out of this than I have ever put in – it's been incredible." The collective force of careless and care-full generosity has enhanced their lives together/apart. They do not know what will come next, but they'll take it as it comes, together.

Alan and Jack

Six months before Alan died, he transitioned from living in a hostel, a living situation that he detested, to having his own apartment – a line of flight from a cramped space. When Jack and Tim caught up for coffee a couple of weeks after Alan's death, Jack reflected on a conversation he had with Alan just before he left the hostel:

> [Alan] asked me, "Jack, how do I change? How do I change?" I said, "One of the ways to change is you break those associations with people who have bad habits … you got to break those connections and never go back to them." … He needed to get his own place … so I was just waiting, biding my time, waiting for the best opportunity to be a good example and to offer wise advice. He went out and did it! Within two weeks!

Jack was swelling with pride for his friend. Alan described Jack as a "great friend" that generously "helped me make progress over the years" and "struggle with my demons." When he died, he had his own place that he loved and took immaculate care of, and an expanding assemblage of allies and friends. And on top of that, with Jack's tutoring, Alan was able to pick up a book and read. "I'm a lot happier," he said, transformed.

In our final meeting, Jack thought back on his time with Alan. "I think it's not all loss. I think it's mission accomplished. We helped him have a good life." Although Jack frames this as "mission accomplished," their transformation was not necessarily finished. Their assemblage would likely have continued to shift/crack/break open into ongoing lines of flight.

Carol and Julie

Julie is a part of Carol's ever-expanding assemblage. Julie is the most consistent person in Carol's life and a long-term ally. Carol, with the (careless and care-full) generosity and friendship of allies like Julie, has gone from someone running away from psychiatric institutions and living on the street to having a consistent residence and a life she enjoys.

JULIE: A lot has changed in the time I've known Carol. I think she definitely has less crises generally. Carol's life can be erratic and it can be hard ... that telephone call in the afternoon is stability for both of us. [Pause] I know she values the relationship and I do too.

CAROL: She helps me when I think I'm gonna have a turn [in my mental health]. Sometimes I forget what she says ... but she helps me from staying in mental wards ... She's a good friend.

Carol has become a valued educator (in community mental health) and prominent member of her community. Despite having an "erratic" life, at the threshold of cramped spaces, Carol regularly delivers workshops and lectures at university and mental health training events, about her life and the importance of community connections.

Batman and Robin

Batman has gone from living on the street to having a consistent and stable residence, an expanding network of connections (including other allies) and a deter-ritorialised reliance on formal health services. "His network is really expanding ... We've moved away from some formal organisations over the years, mental health services, and the Department of Health," says Robin. Batman and Robin are having a blast together every weekend, doing things that Batman was never able to do before: going to the speedway, dodge-em cars, laser games, visiting theme parks, bike riding down the coast, caving, rappelling, canoeing, camping, wall climbing. Story after story. But, not only has Batman's life transformed, together they have been a destabilising force, in Robin's words, a "reality check" for others:

ROBIN: I reckon the funniest [story] was when we went to this charismatic church [with a friend]. So, we went to the church and [the preacher] said, "This is what we're going to do," blah-blah-blah, and then they said, "Anyone who needs healing come up to the front" and they're going to lay hands on people and you know you get pushed. Not pushed, the "energy of the Lord" throws you down or whatever. And Batman said, "I want to go up." I said, "you're not sick. You've got to be sick to go up." He said, "I want to go up."

BATMAN: I said, "I'm going up."

ROBIN: And the preacher came to you and laid hands on you and all the people were falling around you, and you just stood there. You didn't get the script. [The preacher] would come, he looked at you, then he thought he'd come back for a second try and you were just standing there waiting for something to happen. And [the preacher] leaves and comes back again, nothing! Good times like that when you've been a reality check for some people.

EVERYONE: <laughter>

Batman has a long-term ally in his corner, now a formal guardian. And Robin has a best friend. Their assemblages are entangled – their memories and friendships are bound up with one another.

Becomings – sorcerers – lines in all directions

Ally assemblages are not all transformative in the same way, there is no replicable pattern, there are just lines. Affirmative forces of careless and care-full generosity saturate the depths, giving rise to fissures and escapes – there is a suppling of boundaries and a multiplicity of affects. But an affirmative force of generosity is not an individual act of kindness by an ally; it is a collective force of taking on the struggle of another as your own. It is the generosity of an assemblage that is in this together rather – producing a multitude of transformative becomings. Zigzagging back and forth across the production of radical generosity in ally assemblages, Chapter 9 delves into the underlying creative impulses of desire at the threshold of transformative processes.

Notes

1 We do not want to conceptually fetishise or appropriate sorcery or witchcraft, nor do we want to ignore that sorcery has led to the marginalisation, harm, and death of racialised people and ethnic minorities, psychiatrised people, and women and diverse gendered people. Sorcery and witchcraft are perceived as threats. But also, those perceived to be a threat (differential others and minorities) have been labelled as sorcerers or witches, justifying harmful practices (e.g., death, racial discrimination, psychiatric diagnosis, and confinement). See Dein (2003), Federici (2004), Uromi (2014), Coțofană (2017), Gibson (2012), Hill (2000), Bullough (1976), and Roxburgh (2019). Our conceptual use of sorcery is charged with echoes from the past. If you are interested, we suggest turning to the Afterword where we pause to discuss sorcery and some of our entangled affects.
2 Anomalous: to deviate from convention in a way that is peculiar and difficult to classify (Deleuze & Guattari, 1987).
3 We do not mean to conflate allyship with friendship in this statement. We discuss the distinctions further in Chapter 10.
4 In Chapter 4 we turned to Fisher and Tronto's (1990) definition of care as "everything that we do to maintain, continue, and repair our 'world' so that we can live in it as well as possible. That world includes our bodies, our selves, and our environment, all of which we seek to interweave in a complex, life-sustaining web" (p. 40).
5 We question this notion of being "in this fight together" in Chapter 10 – can they really?
6 See Chapter 9 where we discuss joyful affects in ally assemblages more fully.

9

CARTOGRAPHY OF DESIRE

At the edge of the forest the sorcerer paces. A snarling pack of wolves froth within her, like fire, burning in her chest, crawling up her throat and to the tip of her tongue. An uncontrollable impulse takes over her as she throws back her head and howls an enchanting and shrill melody.

A wanderer passing close to the forest's edge hears the wild and animalistic sound. Terrified. Mesmerised. Lured. "What was that sound? Am I in danger?" they wonder, but can't help but stumble towards the sound.

The wanderer catches the gaze of a thousand glowing eyes in the forest – yet in the blink of an eye, the people are missing (or are they yet to come?). They sense an imperceptible spectre – around them, above them, below them, through them.

The sorcerer sings a minoring spell of confusion on the wanderer who gazes at the forest's edge. The wander's mind becomes twisted – beginning to forget where they are (without forgetting where they are), they forget the way home (without forgetting the way home).

At first, the wanderer feels ashamed for being lured to the woods – but calms as they follow the sorcerer's enchanting impulse. A thousand eyes, a pack of wolves inside.

Desire.

★★★

Deleuzio-Guattarian conceptualisation of *desire* is not (only) a human need or want but an(y) vital force, human or non-human, that propels creativity. In this chapter, we introduce a Deleuzio-Guattarian conceptualisation of desire to explore how generative/creative impulses cut across ally assemblages. We have previously mapped out the territories of these relationships and how reactivity trips up major/

DOI: 10.4324/9781003286486-9

active forces, generating an affirmative force of the intermezzo (Chapter 7) and how the becoming of ally assemblages produces an affirmative force of careless/care-full generosity, a sorcerer that cascades processes of becoming (Chapter 8). In this chapter, we consider how the affirmative force of ally relationships is produced through creative impulses of desire. We suggest that desire in ally assemblages is at the threshold of becoming – it triggers/catalyses transformative flows in these relationships.

At the moment differing forces come together near the edge of the forest, the sorcerer swirls and whispers: *desire – create*.

Throughout this chapter, we revisit quotes from Chapters 7 and 8, re-presenting the underlying incorporeal impulses within these situations. We begin with an overview of Deleuze and Guattari's (1984) concepts of desiring-machines and desire in relation to ally assemblages – we explore how desire constructs an assemblage and how desire is socially produced in ally assemblages. We conclude by exploring how ally assemblages produce a particular form of Deleuzio-Guattarian desire.

Desiring-machines

Assemblages, also referred to as machines by Deleuze and Guattari (1987), are continually changing – they are continually assembling and disassembling. As they change, they take on a variety of forms, one of which is a *desiring-machine* (or a machine that desires). A desiring-machine is not a sustained assemblage, but one that takes shape at the moment of deterritorialisation. The assemblage becomes charged with creative energy (desire) and then dissipates:

> Desire as the ontological drive to become (*potentia*) seduces us into going on living. If sustained long enough, life becomes a habit. If the habit becomes self-fulfilling, life becomes addictive.... [desire] runs on entropic energy: it reaches its aim and then dissolves, like a salmon swimming upstream to procreate and then die.
>
> *(Braidotti, 2011, p. 134)*

Deleuze and Guattari (1984) identify that "desiring-machines work only when they break down, and by continually breaking down" (p. 18). Desire is produced through deterritorialisation, when assemblages break down and when there is the possibility of transforming into something else. A desiring-machine takes shape when there is a disruption – when dominant forces are unsettled, when territories become soft, when cracks start to form. The product of a desiring-machine is "always an offshoot" (Deleuze & Guattari, 1984, p. 45), a creative line of flight produced through desire. Below, we outline a Deleuzio-Guattarian notion of desire and discuss how it manifests in ally assemblages.

Desire – a creative impulse

What does desire do? It assembles, this is the core function of desire. Desire is the impulse to create or act within an assemblage (Deleuze & Guattari, 1987).

Highlighting the relational quality of desire, Fox and Alldred (2017) describe it as "the creative capacity of a body to act, feel or otherwise engage with other bodies and the physical and social world" (p. 101). This understanding differs from common usages of the word, where desire is understood as fulfilling a need. The idea of an object of desire might come to mind: one might desire a romantic partner, or a new job, for example. Deleuze and Guattari (1984) refer to this as "desire as lack," where someone has a desire for something that they want to possess/consume, something they perceive to be missing. Conceptualising desire as lack limits what desire can do, as it "presents a linear and terminal picture of the desiring process, a constrained version of desire" (Barlott & Turpin, 2022, p. 134). Desire as lack also creates possibilities for marginalisation: of mastering, appropriating, or excluding. As anti-colonialist scholar Simone Bignall argues, Deleuze and Guattari conceptualise desire differently — as "a productive, transformative and ethical agency, which is also potentially postcolonial because it is grounded in a non-imperial ontology of selfhood, no longer defined by the desire to master, appropriate or exclude the Other." (Bignall, 2008, p. 130). Deleuze and Guattari, building on the work of Baruch Spinoza and Friedrich Nietzsche, conceptualised desire as a creative force, an impulse to experiment and produce (Barlott & Turpin, 2022; Widder, 2010). "Desire does not lack anything; it does not lack its object.... Desire and its object are one and the same thing: the machine as a machine of a machine" (Deleuze & Guattari, 1984, p. 39). In this conceptualisation "desire *produces* reality rather than being *caused* by a perceived lack" (Bignall, 2008, p. 138, original emphasis).

It is by desire that people, and their entangled social assemblages, creatively move and joyfully transform. Further, this desire is unique to the assemblage it is a part of — it flows "along the lines afforded by a particular assemblage" (Barlott & Turpin, 2022, p. 135). For example, in their work using Deleuze and Guattari in disability studies, Abrams et al. (2019) reflexively consider research to be a product of desire: "all research, ours included, is applied desire" (p. 41). Our desire to pursue this book could be understood as a socially infused impulse to create. We continue to unravel the complexity of desire throughout this chapter.

As allies moved into proximity with the cramped spaces of the minor, a desire was stirred in them. Not a desire to *have* anything, but to *create* something. For Julie, this desire had been festering for some time, but came to the surface when she met Carol:

> Before I met Carol, I wanted to have, you know, this kind of relationship with somebody because I knew that a long-term relationship was important in terms of mental health.... it doesn't matter what happens along the way in a relationship, the best thing [is] a long-term relationship.

Julie's was a desire for a "long-term relationship" where "it doesn't matter what happens along the way," not a predetermined picture of a friendship. The desire is not one of lack, Julie was not seeking to capture something for herself; it was not a desire for more friends or to "fix" Carol. When Julie met Carol, the desire came to life. Looking back on those early days of connecting with Carol when she was a social work student, Julie remembers that feeling of excitement and anticipation: "I just thought it was a huge opportunity, like this is what I was looking for before I met Carol and I was going to jump on it." Before Julie met Carol she didn't have an image in her mind of what the relationship would be like or motivated by that image (desire as lack), she simply followed her impulse to connect.

TIM: Is this the relationship you were hoping to have way back, eight, nine years ago?

I (Tim) asked this question with an expected response in mind. While I wasn't consciously aware of it in the moment, this is the script:

ME: *Is this relationship all you had ever hoped for?*
JULIE: *Yes, it has been all I ever dreamed it would be. It is exactly what Carol needed.*

This would have been a charity model, a hierarchical active/reactive force relation. The relationship would have fulfilled Julie's desire (as lack) rather than creating an opening for creative and rhizomatic processes.

How about I start that one over again:

TIM: Is this the relationship you were hoping to have way back, eight, nine years ago?
JULIE: I think so, I think just the fact that Carol tolerates me ...
CAROL [interrupting and playfully jesting with julie]: Yeah tolerates
JULIE [chuckling at carol]: ... is evidence of that. I think so, this is – I mean just the fact that a friendship exists is enough. The connection was initially there, I just hoped for it to continue and see if it worked out.

The sorcerer wields a spell that generates openings and impulses, not fixed outcomes, mastering or appropriation. Julie's response is tentative: "I think so." She resists Tim's arborescent prompt. There was no rigid schema for their relationship – she was merely happy that Carol "tolerates" her, she merely "hoped for it to continue and see if it worked out." Julie desired a connection with Carol, a desire at the intermezzo that could rupture in any direction. Their relationship, as a becoming, is continually folding and unfolding, assembling, and reassembling.

> That is how we sorcerers operate. Not following a logical order, but following alogical consistencies or compatibilities.... no one, not even God, can say in advance whether two borderlines will string together or form a fibre ... [or be] susceptible to transformation. No one can say where the line of flight will pass.
>
> (Deleuze & Guattari, 1987, p. 292)

The magic of these relationships is in their unpredictable unfolding, their compatibilities are unknown or "alogical" (Julie: "we don't need to have much in common to be friends"). Desire needs neither logic nor reason for its creative energy. Like Julie's response, Robin also problematised my need for a "reason" as I searched for the compatibilities between him and Batman: "If you're looking at synergies and all that, I guess we discovered that along the way. We didn't know that at the beginning."

When thinking through (and in) these encounters, we continually re-turn to the advice provided by St. Pierre et al. (2016) for doing postqualitative research: "Our best advice is to read and read and read and attend to the encounters in our experiences that demand our attention" (p. 106). Their advice is to follow the flows of desire. Our sense was that allies, in their pursuit of a relationship with people in cramped spaces, followed the flows of desire and the encounters that grab/lure/attract/enchant them. Allies embraced uncertainty as they were carried by desire, never quite knowing how things would turn out. Chips recalled the early days of his relationship with Krispy: "I thought, 'shit, where's this all going to go?' and I thought, 'oh we'll just wait and see.'" There was a willingness to follow the impulse, not knowing what comes next. There was an openness to what *might* be, not knowing the outcome or where/when the lines of flight might break through.

Desire is produced in moments of uncertainty, when the machine breaks down. An example of such a breakdown was introduced in Chapter 6 in the relationship of Batman and Robin:

ROBIN: I try not to have a lot of influence with [Batman's support services]. I just kind of mind my business and make sure things are going right for him. But they know that I come running *when something is not right*. So, you know, I will roar. And there's been times I've had to roar. (emphasis added)

Using Deleuze and Guattari's conceptualisation of desire, there is the formation of a desiring-machine in the ally/friend relationship. At the moment when "something is not right" (the machinic structure breaks down), a protective impulse/desire surges to the surface for Robin to "roar." The desire that manifests in Batman and Robin's assemblage protects Batman from restrictive arborescent forces. When asked what made him "roar," Robin described examples of when Batman's support services failed to accommodate his unique challenges. One example was when a support agency continually gave Batman (unhelpful) verbal instructions on how to clean his apartment without adapting or adjusting, such as demonstrating the steps *with* Batman. Robin described Batman's apartment as very unkempt: "I understand that their job isn't to be cleaners, but I just wanted them to help [Batman] learn by cleaning the apartment with him. Maybe they'd pick up on some useful strategies along the way." Robin continued, "My biggest thing is that they acted like Batman doesn't have a disability, like he could follow instructions like everyone else." Desire propelled Robin to care-fully advocate for more responsive and situation-specific support services.

> Upon reviewing this part of Tim's PhD thesis, one of his supervisors (not Jenny) interjects: *At what point does friendship slip into something more paternal? There is a very protective quality here – which you could argue is part of friendship, but could equally be interpreted as control.*
>
> Yes! Let's hold onto this point, we'll come back to it in Chapter 10. One of the risks of allyship is crossing the threshold back into an active/reactive force relation – at one moment the relationship can be an affirmative force where "this is our fight," but it can easily slip into an active force where "this is MY fight."

Desire constructs an assemblage

Desire is not for a discrete object, but for an assemblage: "to desire is to construct an assemblage" (Deleuze, 1996, p. 16). Discussing desire in an interview with Claire Parnett, Deleuze (1996) offered an example: "I don't desire a woman, I also desire a landscape that is enveloped in this woman" (p. 16). When someone desires a romantic partner, their desire is not only for the body or presence of a partner. Elsewhere we have elaborated:

> They desire an assemblage of that partner, which might include things like physical closeness, intimate conversations, mundane coffee encounters, grocery shopping on weekends, feelings of safety and security, the approval of their peers, etc. When we desire something, we desire the assembling of affects and arrangements of socio-material.
>
> *(Barlott & Turpin, 2022, p. 135)*

The creative impulse of ally relationships constructs an ally assemblage. Rather than a fixed image of a friendship, it is a flexible desire to loosen the cramped spaces of psychiatrised people (see Chapter 2). Thinking back to what initially drew him to desiring an atypical relationship with Batman, Robin says, "I was probably seeking something more than just doing social work you know? The belief about community." Robin's desire was the construction of "community" in the life of someone in the cramped spaces. As Robin transitions to becoming Batman's guardian, his desire is not for guardianship but for an assemblage where Batman is not taken advantage of, where he has stable housing, and where he has someone looking out for his health. Robin isn't desiring an arborescent assemblage with fixed expectations, but one where Batman is free from the constraints of his past.[1] This could be said for all ally assemblages in this project – there was a common desire among allies for an assemblage where their friends rhizomatically flourish. It was these flows of desire that gave rise to affirmative forces of generosity in ally assemblages. Braidotti (2011) speaks of desire as a "propelling and compelling force.... This is a desire not to preserve, but to change: it is a deep yearning for transformation" (p. 154). The following section expands beyond what desire produces to consider how desire itself is produced, the social production of desire.

Social production of desire – drawn/released at the intermezzo

While desire constructs an assemblage, it too is constructed within the assemblages of our everyday lives. The micropolitical, affective relations within an assemblage produce desire and shape what desire can produce. In Chapter 7, we outlined how force relations can produce different kinds of assemblages, which give rise to particular desires. In a major assemblage, desire serves the dominant sociomaterial bodies and is throttled in the cramped spaces. But in a rhizomatic assemblage, desire is unrestrained and can catalyse innumerable offshoots of transformation.

The sorcerer – at the edge of the woods, the intermezzo – releases desire from its self-serving and arborescent confines. As active forces are disrupted, desire cascades into a multiplicity of becomings. Desire oozes with intensity – it generates an affective burst of energy that has the potential to transform assemblages.

Over 20 years ago, when Carol was living on the street, her desire was limited. She slept on the same shopfront every night. The shop owners didn't kick her off their step – instead, they slowly developed a relationship with her. *Active force disrupted – the sorcerer swirls into the intermezzo of their relationship.* One day, Carol asked these shop owners for help – desire – they spent time with Carol and helped her make connections with people at APTB. Not able to fully articulate her desire, when asked what she would like her life to be like, Carol simply pointed at people using an ATM and said, "I want to do what those people do." Desire has cascaded in the assemblages of her life – in our time meeting together, Carol relished in the freedom to earn and access her own money. "I like buying clothes, like dresses and shorts and stuff like that."

One pancake breakfast together, I (Tim) invited Carol and Julie to talk about the things they like to do in their life. Most of the things were along the lines of swimming, listening to music, and socialising, but there was a notable exception:

CAROL: I like sorting out my own situations … if I'm in a difficult situation or I don't know what to do or I don't know how to handle a phone call or something like that, you know, I like sorting them out.

This comment seems to catch Julie off guard, I notice her pause for a moment before our conversation moves on. Years ago, professionals in the mental health sector didn't think Carol was capable of complex problem solving – and there were times when she was not able to manage the challenges of everyday life. But, now, the assemblages of her everyday life have produced a desire to "[sort] out my own situations." Carol comes back to this point again a few minutes later: "I like finding situations where I'm not used to them, steps that I'm not used to … figuring out how to do stuff." Again, Julie pauses, but this time speaks up: "I actually didn't know you loved problem solving so much Carol." As the constellation of her assemblages transforms over time, Carol's desire (and affective capacity) to problem-solve continues to surprise people.

As I (Tim) write about desire and how desire is produced by the assemblages of everyday life, I find myself more attentive to the ways a research assemblage can affect desire. When I'd meet with Carol and Julie, every time I took out my phone to start recording our conversations, Carol would say something to the effect of "do you have to turn that bloody thing on, bloody hell, Timothy." The minutes that followed were usually filled with silence, or me trying to start up conversation again.

To further explore the notion of the social production of desire, we turn to the assemblage of Alan and Jack. On their very first meeting together, Alan told Tim about his motivation to participate in the project: "I want to help. That's one thing I want to do in life, is, now that I'm better and getting my shit together and getting life together, one thing I want to do in life is help people." Before moving on, we want to break this down into two parts, the initial desire ("getting my shit together") and the cascading desires that follow (e.g., "now that I'm better [I want to help people]"). Six months prior to this conversation, Alan sought advice from Jack about how to break free from the cramped spaces of the men's hostel (see Chapter 7). In the intermezzo of their relationship, Alan expressed the desire to "get my shit together." This was a collective desire, a social production, where others came alongside Alan, producing an affirmative force out of the cramped spaces.

Simultaneous/parallel (entangled) desires were produced in Jack: "What I want to do is help Alan make wise choices in his life, because that's what's going to make him happy. I've wanted him to be happy and this is all coming together to facilitate that. His happiness." Alan's desire to "get his shit together" was not an individualistic desire, it was a collective desire.

Alan's desire was for an assemblage. "I want to be there for my family, be there for my mum, my brother, my family … I don't want to bottle things up."

> *The sorcerer carefully and magically weaves the threads of desire together – catalysing into an explosive rupture.*

Riding the flows of desire, Alan experienced transformation in his life and ongoing rhizomatic outgrowths: "now that I'm better and getting my shit together … one thing I want to do in life is help people."

This breaks me (Tim) up a bit knowing that Alan died just a couple months later.

There were times when we met together and Alan would agonise over his desire for more connections in his life and the underlying disappointment with how things turned out. He described wanting more friends, wanting a girlfriend, wanting to go camping. There were times in our meetings where we diverged from the topic of the project and brainstormed together about how Alan might be able to do things like camping. "I've never really thought about asking anyone to go camping before," he responded to one of my suggestions.

I'm holding on to Alan's desire to "help people" – his force lives on in the assemblages of his life and in this thesis.

Take good care, Alan.

Desire for a people to come

> "The people are missing!" panic comes over the major.

> "And?" calmly responds the sorcerer.

> "But we carefully categorised them and contained their madness. Where have they gone?" cries the major.

> "Slippery buggers, aren't they?!" exclaims the sorcerer with a smirk, "they are a people to come."

> "Eh?"

> "They are becoming, always a people to come," the sorcerer sings in a haunting harmonic tone.

Transformative and revolutionary desire is for an unknown people to come. It is not for a particular person or for a specific outcome, desire splinters away from rigid territories and systems of categorisation. When speaking of the people who occupy cramped spaces in society, Deleuze (1989) refers to the "missing people" (p. 217). This phrase speaks to the elusive and asignifying quality of the minor, reactive force, and a non-unitary and in-process view of sociomaterial (Deleuze & Guattari, 1987). Major, arborescent forces seek to establish discrete identities, to categorise, to colonise, whereas minoring forces are non-unitary and difficult to classify. However, the people are also missing because the major apparatus has deemed them insignificant and other. Speaking to this notion of the missing people as a by-product of the major apparatus of capture, Luce Irigaray (1985) begins her book *Speculum of Other Woman* by critiquing Freud's depiction of "femininity":

> So it would be a case of you men speaking among yourselves about woman … woman will therefore constitute the *target*, the *object*, the *stake* of a masculine

discourse, of a debate among men, which would not consult her, would not concern her. Which, ultimately, she is not supposed to know anything about.

(p. 13)

The people are missing, they are reactive and rhizomatically spilling to the edges. Despite major forces of capture and control, minor desiring-machines vibrate with creative potential. "The moment the master, or the colonizer, proclaims 'There have never been people here,' the missing people are a becoming" (Deleuze, 1989, p. 217). Desire and transformative becomings are "like the seeds of the people to come, and whose political impact is immediate and inescapable" (Deleuze, 1989, p. 221). To desire a people to come is to desire an unknown future that has not yet arrived, one where active forces are disrupted and cease their domination – and reactive forces are freed from constraint, which is liberating for people in the cramped spaces of society. This is a desire that constructs an assemblage, an invention of a people yet to come.

What can an ally assemblage do? Desire a people to come.

There is always potential becoming in every present, always a people yet to come in each moment. Becoming is always immanent, it is always right here – and in that moment, always to come. Desire. The sorcerer wields magic of the people to come, stirring a desire for what could be. Minor assemblages have "diabolic powers to come or as revolutionary forces to be constructed" (Deleuze & Guattari, 1986, p. 18). Assemblages are never fully formed, they are always forming – always escaping, shooting, constructing the *to come*.

The affirmative force of generosity in ally assemblages is birthed in a desire for a people to come. In all ally/friend relationships in this project, there was a desire for an unknown and imperceptible future, but one where things were well for the friend. In the early days of their relationship, Carol was not very trusting of Julie.

CAROL: I didn't used to leave my bag near Julie when she come to see me … you got to have that trust.

JULIE: I don't blame you. I was aware that you had every reason not to trust me initially, so I just tried to continue until you did, just exist, maintain the connection until you did trust me.

The people in the cramped spaces are shifty and reactive, and in Carol's case, not quick to trust people. Julie desired an assemblage where there was trust, a Carol to come. Earlier, we mention that the desire of ally relationships is a desire for what *might be*. Julie slowly and patiently stands by for a relationship to come, a relationship of unknown type, simply one where there is trust.

In one of their final meetings together, unprompted, Chips described the motivation/compulsion behind his relationship with Krispy. "I can enjoy it to the extent that I hope it'll make a difference to Krispy. That was my main motive for doing it. There was no other motive." Although any act is likely to be underpinned by a multiplicity of motives, Chips' desire was to see Krispy flourish, to see his life transform, however that may look. There is desire here for a Krispy to come. But it was what

Chips said at the end of this sentence that intrigues us the most: "it was something I was led to do, I suppose." We cannot be certain of the meanings and desires within these words – is he speaking of a religious or spiritual "higher calling"? Still, Chips' words speak to the impulsive characteristic of desire, a creative surge. And, in this case, an impulse for a people to come.

There is a joyful quality to the affirmative movements of careless and care-full generosity in these assemblages. Baruch Spinoza, who influenced Deleuze's thinking about desire and affect, described the creative passion of desire as a joyful affect, where joy is "any passion involving an increase in my power of acting" (Deleuze, 1978, para. 20). Further still, joyful affect is produced through alliance – it is the enchanting sorcery of bodies colliding in such a way that their powers enmesh with one another (Deleuze, 1978). In contrast, Spinoza describes sad affects as those which inhibit a body's power of action and constricts what is possible within an assemblage. Blackman (2011) refers to these as "unhappy affects," where experiences of trauma, shame, lone-liness, and isolation constrict the lives of people who have been psychiatrised (p. 183). "The affects of joy are like a springboard, they make us pass through something that we would never have been able to pass if there had only been sadnesses" (Deleuze, 1978, para. 54). Drawing on Spinoza's ethics Bignall (2008) adds that:

> every body should be disposed to act in relation to others according to a type of desire that will bring about joy. The experience of joy is necessarily mutual, since joy is simply the creation of enhanced power of being, through the development of a more complex and richer community. Where the asso-ciation detracts from one of the participating bodies, it will not bring about a richer unity, and therefore is not joyful. The creation and experience of joyful associations benefits every body; every body ought to organise their associa-tions according to a desire that will produce a joyful satisfaction.
>
> *(p. 141)*

While the cramped spaces and arborescence of the (major) mental health sector discussed throughout this thesis are imbued with sad and constricted affects, ally assemblages are dripping with joyful and collective affection for a people to come.[2]

The impulse to create a people to come was common across each ally assemblage – none more evident than in the relationship between Batman and Robin. Robin "saw" Batman's situation and was moved to act: "here's someone in a rough spot, maybe I can do a little bit more." Robin's desire was an impulse to con-struct an assemblage where "someone in a rough spot" could experience something different. Robin's desire was an impulse to "do a little bit more" for posterity's sake, for a people to come. To desire a people to come is to joyfully construct an assem-blage that carelessly and care-fully swings at the intermezzo, pursuing what might be.

Generating desiring-machines – desire for ally assemblages

To this point, we have sketched a cartography of ally assemblages that highlights their transformative potential. These are relationships with non-dominating hier-archies/territories. They generate an affirmative force of generosity, whereby allies take on the burdens of their friend as their own and generate ongoing becomings and lines of flight. And in this chapter, we have explored how the construction of ally assemblages can be traced back to creative impulses of desire – the affirmative force of ally relationship assemblages is created by a desire for a people to come. Most of this has been a theory-driven exploration of the cartographies of ally assemblages, their structure, composition, and social production. What do they do? How do they work? What do they produce? But we have not yet covered what this learning might suggest as possibilities for practices in (and out of) the mental health sector. As we conclude this chapter, and as a prelude to Chapter 10, we wonder: How might we generate allyship? How might we cultivate desiring-machines between people?

> Your drives have been constructed, assembled, and arranged in such a manner that your desire is positively invested in the system that allows you to have a particular interest.
>
> *(Smith, 2011, p. 136)*

Desire is always affirmative. *Always?* Yes, we mean *always*. Although Deleuze and Guattari critique universals and rigid representations, they are very specific on the nature and quality of desire. "There is no desire that does not flow – I mean this precisely – flow within an assemblage" (Deleuze, 1996, p. 16). As Smith (2011) has said above, desire is constructed within an assemblage such that it serves to open up offshoots within a given assemblage. Take Carol's impulse to jump out of the window of a psychiatric institution over 20 years ago – this was a desire for an assemblage free from psychiatric control. This is not the valuing of desire as "good" or "bad"; it has nothing to do with being contextually good or bad; desire flows. Carol's body plunging to the ground from an open window of a psychiatric ward may be considered good and/or bad, but regardless, it is an affirmative impulse of change. So, a possible step in the generation of a desiring-machine is the production of assemblages where desire can flow, conjuring the sorcerer to swirl at the edge of the forest. This is not the formation of an organisation or a program based on a model of allyship (as discussed in Chapter 7) to replicate a desiring-machine and reproduce desire. Liberating desire is not produced by arborescent assemblages.

Locating the desiring-machine at the edge of the forest is important, the place of (dis)organisation, the "threshold between the major apparatus and the confined minor, carefully wearing down and softening restrictive boundaries" (Barlott, Shevellar, et al., 2020a, p. 1340). Our community research partner in this project, APTB, is an example of an institution at the threshold of major and minor. They dangled and zigzagged at the edge of the major mental health apparatus and the cramped spaces of the inner-city, supporting psychiatrised people to develop a sense of connection in the community. APTB had a desire for freely given relationships. "'A place to belong' is anywhere and everywhere – connectedness can occur through 'amateurs' getting alongside others and through seemingly small and insignificant and ordinary process" (Barringham & Barringham, 2002, p. 56).

This quote comes from a booklet titled *Finding People to Be There* published by the organisation soon after it was established. APTB's desire for assemblages ("connections") sparked relational offshoots in all directions. Whenever possible, APTB encouraged relationships to develop with little interference from the organisation (e.g., not use occupational health and safety or risk management practices disrupt relationships). At the edge of the forest, APTB created space for desiring-machines to creatively take flight.

> It's not a matter of designing programs but of creating visions; not of following protocols but fulfilling dreams. And believing in those dreams: believing that a woman who has been isolated could still have friends, or that a man whose life has been controlled could still escape and be free. … This work is also not about "fixing" people so they fit into society. You need to come at the question from another side: finding the place, or the way, that people *do* fit.
>
> *(O'Connell, 1988, p. 18, emphasis in original)*

APTB routinely invited members of the community to an old inner-city house, where its office was located, for learning circles, workshops, and other community events. People of diverse social positionings were brought together to learn from and with each other (e.g., services users, service providers, friends, family, and general members of the community). At one of these community events, a Sunday Workshop, a desiring-machine was formed that produced a collective writing group. Together, mental health service users, mental health professionals, peer workers, support workers, and academics formed a writing assemblage. Meeting over a two-year period, the group wrote a collective narrative about the experience of being a psychiatric patient (see Wyder et al., 2018). Multiple offshoots were produced, not simply a publication: friendship, writing skills, appreciation for creative writing, confidence, research innovations, ongoing writing projects, and and and. Desires produced at the edge of the forest produce affirmative forces that catalyse innumerable becomings.

> For societies … have always appropriated these becomings in order to break them…. States have always appropriated the war machine in the form of national armies that strictly limit the becomings of the warrior. The Church has always burned sorcerers…. Families have always warded off the demonic Alliance gnawing at them…. We have seen sorcerers serve as leaders, rally to the case of despotism, create the countersorcery of exorcism, pass over to the side of the family and decent. But this spells the death of the sorcerer, and also the death of becoming.
>
> *(Deleuze & Guattari, 1987, p. 289)*

For years, APTB offered a unique community-based approach to mental health work that was applauded by their administering organisation, Anglicare. In 2019,

Anglicare featured the community inclusion of APTB in their *Our Better Selves – State of the Family* report. The article, titled "The Ripple Effect," beautifully depicts how community connections rhizomatically develop in their work (Anglicare Australia, 2019). Unfortunately, in mid-2020, in the middle of a global pandemic, Anglicare swiftly and violently restructured APTB. Once paraded by Anglicare for its approach to community mental health, the small community inclusion organisation struggled to make ends meet in Australia's new market-driven funding model. The apparatus of capture imposed strict new measures, rigidly structuring APTB as a service delivery organisation, and significantly limited their community inclusion work and approach. But desire spills to the edges. While becomings may cease within the confines of the restructured arborescent institution, the spirit of community inclusion still wanders at the edge of the forest as people outside of the organisational structure continue to meet.

Generating a desiring-machine begins with disruption, when the system breaks down. This might come in the form of disrupting boundaries and binaries (such as the disruption of active forces discussed in Chapter 7), or even emerge from the despotic restructuring of a community organisation.

In this chapter, we have traversed the flows of desire in ally assemblages, sketching how creative surges of desire played out in these relationships, how cascades of desire shaped the ongoing production of relational ally assemblages. Revolutionary and asignifying desire in ally relationships is the desire for a people to come. Allyship, taking on another's struggle as your own, an affirmative force of generosity, is energised by a desiring-machine. Desire propels ally assemblages forward/backward/in/out – imagining and reimagining an unknown revolutionary future to come. In the next chapter (Chapter 10), we pragmatically consider how the mental health sector can embrace the value of allyship without appropriation. We suggest a collective commitment to ongoing movement towards allyship, towards an allyship to come.

Notes

1 We are curious about what affects guardianship will produce: will it produce arborescent lines in Batman and Robin's relationship?
2 In writing this paragraph, we acknowledge the complexity of joy/sadness in Spinoza's (as well as Deleuze's) work, for example the ways that sadness can invoke violent affects (desire to hurt that which hurts me) but also spur joyful expression (kindness towards those who have been hurt). This relates to the transformational potential of the minor and cramped spaces in Deleuze and Guattari's work.

10
(DIS)ORGANISING ALLYSHIP, BECOMING-COMPLICIT

As we weave the final threads of this book, we think that the edge entanglements with allyship in this book offer a dissonant contribution to the practice and scholarship in the mental health sector. Over the last nine chapters we have not offered a definition of what allyship *is*, rather we have mapped out what it *does*. And in this chapter, we wonder, are the freely given relationships in this book an enactment of allyship? Throughout *Edge Entanglements*, we have re-presented ally assemblages as those of the intermezzo, assemblages that swing between major/minor, active/ reactive, and striated/smooth. And now, as we consider these entanglements in relation to the literature, the in-betweenness continues; ally assemblages unsteadily sit at the juncture of allyship and befriending approaches in mental health research and practice. There is resemblance, *and*. There is similarity, *but*. Here, we fold the cartographies we have written into the scholarly landscape of allyship and befriending practices. We begin by exploring the befriending (or intentional friendship) literature and then turn to the literature on allyship (both in/out of "mental health"), including a consideration for *accompliceship* as an alternative concept. We consider how the ally assemblages explored in *Edge Entanglements* fit within the befriending and allyship scholarship, as if putting a tracing (the literature) onto our maps and palpating for points of divergence, and and and. Then, we re-turn to the concept of transversality (introduced in Chapter 3) to sketch an approach to producing transformative encounters between people. Transversality offers a way to summon the sorcerer, to conjure magic at the edge of the forest and potentiate becomings. We conclude the chapter by imagining an allyship to come – an allyship not yet materialised, *becoming-complicit*. We (tentatively) present a transverse way forward, situating micropolitical allyship as ongoing collective movement towards becoming-complicit in the life of someone in the cramped spaces.

DOI: 10.4324/9781003286486-10

Befriending practices

Ally/friend assemblages have characteristics of friendship (as noted in Chapter 7). Friendship has not been well explored in relation to people who have been psychiatrised with serious mental illness (Boydell et al., 2002). Most of the literature focuses on the friendship "deficits" of "difficulties" of psychiatrised people, such as "problems in establishing and maintaining relationships" (Ørtenblad et al., 2019, p. 271). While friendship itself has not been the focus of this book, there are some common elements between the ally assemblages explored in our project and scholarship that discusses the therapeutic use of friendship in the mental health sector. It is in the scholarship on "befriending" practices that ally assemblages find both their closest counterpart and their antithesis. On the surface they appear similar, but, as we discuss in this section, befriending practices in the mental health sector are an arborescent form of friendship. We draw comparisons between the two and present ally assemblages as befriending practices of the underworld. The befriending literature might be seen as a cautionary tale to ally assemblages: "don't stray too far from the forest."

We're having visceral reactions to reading the befriending literature. Randomised control trials – systematic reviews. We want to put it away, it kills desire in us.

But, at the same time, befriending is considered an "alternative" approach. Shouldn't we applaud it as an edge approach within the sector?

In their systematic review of befriending practices, Thompson et al. (2016) define friendship as:

> voluntary, private, relationships in which people choose to spend time together and will make an effort to do so. Friends are external to the immediate family. People may have lots in common with friends with respect to attitudes or interests and enjoy their company. The friendship relationship is said to involve respect and reciprocation, mutual obligation, be symmetrical and have some level of equality.
>
> *(p. 72)*

Given this definition, we would suggest ally assemblages could be categorised as friendship. And. The ally/friend relationship *is* a friendship, but it is simultaneously something other (as described in Chapter 7). Ally assemblages drift in an in-between place, distinctly intermezzo. The aim of befriending practices is to construct friendship between two people (Priebe et al., 2020), yet we argue that this approach has been captured by the major apparatus and is a part of the major machine of resonance. For example, while Thompson et al. (2016) present befriending practices along a continuum, "ranging from a relationship that is very similar to professional therapeutic relations, to one that is very similar to a natural friendship" (p. 77), they are entrenched in the major mental health apparatus. The language used (i.e., "similar to a natural friendship") suggests that these are *not* friendships, more akin to counterfeit relationships (see McKnight, 1995) described in Chapter 2. The distinction between volunteer and friend was highlighted by APTB in the early days of their work: "A volunteer is not a friend – although they may become a friend. Further, we cannot fabricate or manufacture '*friends*'" (Barringham & Barringham, 2002, p. 10). Befriending practices, a programmatic practice in mental health work, are not primed for rhizomatic outgrowths or sensitivity to minor gestures – not to say that lines of flight and transformation are not possible; ruptures are always possible. As discussed below, befriending practices sit within a controlled and structured assemblage. Desire constrained.

Befriending is becoming a more common approach in Western mental health practice contexts (see Cassidy et al., 2019; McCorkle et al., 2009; Ørtenblad et al., 2019; Priebe et al., 2020; Thompson et al., 2016). Befriending programs are structured and involve the commitment of volunteers to spend a minimum amount of time each month with their friend (e.g., 4 hrs), typically involve a commitment of one year, and include ongoing monitoring and reporting (Mitchell & Pistrang, 2011; Priebe et al., 2020). Most programs begin with training, such as the following topics found in Compeer training (a common befriending program):

> mental illness, stigma, major diagnoses and symptoms, the role of Compeer volunteers, expectations and responsibilities of volunteers, how to get started with new clients, boundaries, reciprocity of Compeer friendships, conflict management, crisis situations, and the procedure for terminating matches if necessary.
>
> *(McCorkle et al., 2009, p. 293)*

Despite their seemingly arborescent structure, Thompson et al. (2016) consider Compeer friendships to be one of the more authentic befriending approaches.

In contrast to the rhizomatic processes that produced the ally assemblages in *Edge Entanglements*, befriending practices are arborescent and begin with an organisation that systematically matches people. Rather than having people find their own synergies, the organisation determines the best match. However, many of these matches are unsuccessful, with McCorkle (2009) explaining that "before their current successful match, several participants were in previous unsuccessful matches that were terminated due to various problems" (p. 301). Befriending relationships are engineered, cooked, and often programmatically time-limited to one year (Cassidy et al., 2019; Thompson et al., 2016). There is very little evidence of people "having their friend's back" (a characteristic of allyship discussed below). These relationships are primarily about the companionship of a helper to a helpee – an active/reactive force relation. Mitchell and Pistrang (2011) identify the following role description of befrienders in their study: "to listen and provide companionship, take part in social activities and link befriendees with community resources" (p. 153). In some instances, volunteers adhere to rigid boundaries (e.g., not sharing phone numbers) and terminate the relationship after the prescribed time or "when the befriendee no longer 'needed the support of a befriender'" (Cassidy et al., 2019, p. 8). Yet, in other instances there was more flexibility and suppleness to the structured nature of the relationship. When speaking to whether they set boundaries or ground rules in their befriending relationship, one participant stated: "No. Didn't bother, because I thought that would be too restrictive. [...] What grounds do you set in a relationship? Do you set grounds? They evolve, don't they?" (Cassidy et al., 2019, p. 8).

The befriending literature grapples with some of the tensions at play when programmatically constructing relationships (see Cassidy et al., 2019; Thompson et al., 2016). When boundaries are less rigid and there was less structure to the relationship, some volunteers felt uneasy or uncertain, but there was a greater likelihood of a friendship developing. And when boundaries are more rigid and there is more oversight and structure from the organisation, the relationship was more likely to be procedural and hierarchical. McCorkle et al. (2009) noted that some volunteers were disappointed that there was limited transformation in their (engineered) friend's life, that their friend did not "succeed" as much as they hoped. However, Deleuze & Guattari (1987) provide a useful explanation:

> once underscored or over-coded, [assemblages] seem to lose their ability to bud, they seem to lose their dynamic relation to segmentations-in-progress, or in the act of coming together or coming apart.
>
> *(p. 247)*

Taking a Deleuzio-Guattarian perspective, these structured and regulated assemblages are unlikely to produce transformative outcomes. In comparison, ally assemblages in *Edge Entanglements* were long term, unregulated, and unstructured relationships. Had they been "terminated" after one-year, temporary companionship may have been all that was achieved.

Let this be a cautionary tale: resist the pull of the major, disrupt the apparatus of capture, stay close to the edge of the forest – or risk killing the sorcerer. Tucker (2010), using a Deleuzio-Guattarian approach, warns that non-traditional approaches on the fringe of mainstream services are inevitably at risk of becoming a "stepping stone" to capture by the normative and arborescent mental health apparatus (p. 447). Experimental prudence (see Chapter 8) is needed whenever transformative approaches are developed in alliance with the major.

> For societies ... have always appropriated these becomings in order to break them.... States have always appropriated the war machine in the form of national armies that strictly limit the becomings of the warrior. The Church has always burned sorcerers.... Families have always warded off the demonic Alliance gnawing at them.... We have seen sorcerers serve as leaders, rally to

the case of despotism, create the countersorcery of exorcism, pass over to the side of the family and decent. But this spells the death of the sorcerer, and also the death of becoming.

(Deleuze & Guattari, 1987, p. 289)

While befriending practices offer an alternative approach within mainstream mental health services, these practices are in resonance with major/active forces and may have limited potential for becoming. Given that befriending practices feature safeguards to prevent relationships from going rogue (e.g., boundaries, contractual obligations, and termination guidelines), lines of flight and deterritorialising ruptures are programmatically constrained. Major befriending practices are designed to prevent rhizomatic becoming.

Allyship

Turning to the notion of allyship (both inside and outside "mental health"), let's discuss our book project in relation to the scholarship on allyship and consider the unique characteristics of ally assemblages. Allyship is often used as a term to describe the everyday *activism* and/or *solidarity* of people who are not marginalised alongside those who are (Bishop, 2015; Carlson et al., 2020). The literature commonly outlines allyship as an action-oriented process rather than an identity (Anti-Oppression Network, n.d.; Kutlaca et al., 2020; Lamont, 2020), consistent with the ally assemblages in this book. Allyship (and being an ally) is something that a person does or enacts.

Definitions of allyship and related literature are commonly situated in critical race scholarship, and a structuralist view of human oppression and activism – this view of allyship is akin to what critical physiotherapist Nixon (2019) refers to as critical allyship. The Anti-Oppression Network (n.d.) describes allyship as "an active, consistent, and arduous practice of unlearning and re-evaluating, in which a person in a position of privilege and power seeks to operate in solidarity with a marginalised group." The influence of critical race theory is pronounced in Bishop's (2015) definition, where she states that an ally is "a member of an oppressor group who works to end a form of oppression which gives [them] privilege" (p. 152). Much of the current allyship literature takes a macropolitical perspective on alliances between privileged and oppressed.[1] The scholarship tends to (but does not always) dichotomise people into homogenous categorical identities (privileged/oppressed) where allies are often considered to be people who are members of the privileged group who act in solidarity with oppressed groups. For example, men's allyship of women's rights (Carlson et al., 2020), heterosexual and cis-gendered people's allyship of the LGBTIQ+ community (Russell & Bohan, 2016), or white people's allyship of people of colour in the #BlackLivesMatter movement (Kutlaca et al., 2020). The literature tends to generalise that only people with categorical privilege (e.g., men, white, heteronormative) can be allies and those without privilege are the allied, with minimal recognition for the ways that people with a lived experience of oppression are allied with one another (see Bettencourt, 2020). And, while this literature demonstrates the value of macropolitical and activist-oriented allyship, the micropolitical entanglements are not given as much attention. Intersections of power and privilege fluctuate, at least to some degree, from one encounter to another, such that peers can also be allies as in the relationship of Jack and Alan, for example. This book sheds light on micropolitical forms of allyship – small-scale (force) relations between people. As Deleuze and Guattari (1987) state, "everything is political, but every politics is simultaneously a *macropolitics* and a *micropolitics*" (p. 249) – *Edge Entanglements* tells a micropolitical story of allyship of the intermezzo, allyship at the edge of the forest.

There is sparse literature on allyship with psychiatrised people or in the field of mental health, with most allyship literature being focussed on anti-racism (see Bishop, 2015; Max, 2005; McKenzie, 2014) and efforts against homo/transphobia (see Russell & Bohan, 2016). No doubt, those that championed mental health community inclusion, psychiatric survivor, and Mad movements (discussed in Chapter 3) demonstrated characteristics of allyship, but only recently has allyship become a focus in mental health research (see Happell et al., 2018; Juntanamalaga et al., 2019; Lambley, 2020; Liegghio, 2020; Moss et al., 2020). Liegghio (2020) recommends the pursuit of allyship in (child and youth) mental health practice, stating that "our roles as adults needs to shift away from being 'agents,' as therapists or researchers trying to change the child and their experiences of distress, to that of 'allies' working in solidarity with, not for, young people" (pp. 86–87). Still, Juntanamalaga et al. (2019) suggest researchers and practitioners remain vigilant and not assume that allyship is always positive. They identify several limitations to allyship, including that allies at times have a hidden agenda (e.g., doing it for their resume), and that allies can be dominating or take control, paternalistically assuming that psychiatrised people and those accessing mental health services need their help (Juntanamalaga et al., 2019). Allyship, paradoxically, has the potential to be "both beneficial and harmful to social movements" and can reinforce power structures (Blatt, 2022, p. 4). For example, allies of psychiatrised people in anti-psychiatry and critical psychiatry have advocated for the abolition of oppressive psychiatric practices and simultaneously centred their own authority (Reaume, 2022).[2] Some of these tensions came to the surface in our book (see Chapter 9), and we see value in conceptualising allyship as an ongoing and collective process of becoming that includes deterritorialisation of the major apparatus. Considering the macropolitical focus of most allyship literature, *Edge Entanglements* sheds some light on individual, micropolitical relationships between allies and psychiatrised people.

Acknowledging the two poles of allyship (macro and micropolitical), Kutlaca et al. (2020) define allies as: "individuals outside of the disadvantaged group who are informed about and engage in actions that challenge existing systems of inequity, endorse egalitarian values and norms, and provide support to affirm the experiences of the disadvantaged group" (p. 1249). This quote highlights the potential for allyship to be both macropolitical (challenging systems of inequity) and micropolitical (supporting and affirming the experiences of people). Still, the literature is sparse on the micropolitical and relational work of allies to affirm the experiences of the marginalised, such as psychiatrised people. *Edge Entanglements* maps some of the micropolitical movements of power and resistance and what these relational processes do. The affirmative force of ally assemblages is produced through the alliance of major and minor, and the unsettling of force relations – a micropolitical entanglement.

Accompliceship is a relatively new and emerging term that is being used in race activism circles (Bourke, 2020; Carlson et al., 2020; Jackson et al., 2020; White Accomplices, 2020) and is useful to the discussion of micropolitical allyship. We argue that accompliceship effectively incorporates the ways ally assemblages operate and are entangled at the edge of the forest and may be a useful concept for conceptualising ally assemblages to come (discussed further below). The term "accomplice" is subversive and suggestive of being complicit in a crime (Jackson et al., 2020). The major is deterritorialised and then reterritorialised into a collaborator or conspirer with the minor – in the case of the relationships in *Edge Entanglements*, allies could be considered accomplices in the liberation of their friends. An accomplice is someone who works "side-by-side" with people who are marginalised (Carlson et al., 2020), "an accomplice is in the thick of things" with people (Bourke, 2020, p. 12). We suggest that, while allyship may be an effective macropolitical expression, accompliceship may be more suitable to the micropolitical expression of lives bound up with one another as in ally assemblages. It seems to us that the field of Mad Studies is oriented in such a way to invite accompliceship. Allies are invited to work "in harmony" with Mad activists and scholars, but not to lead this work (Reaume, 2022, p. 100). The invitation of Mad Studies is akin to what Blatt (2022) refers to as *allied labour*, which is "the work of both cultivating and resisting allies" (pp. 2–3). Mad allies are called to first learn and unlearn from psychiatrised people, do their own work to unsettle the fascism within, and then work to loosen the cramped spaces *with* psychiatrised people (see MacPhee & Wilson Norrad, 2022).

Contributing to the scholarship in accompliceship, we have presented the becoming of ally assemblages as a collective enunciation. The desire and transformative force of ally assemblages is produced through collective rhizomatic processes rather than through any individual actions of allies/accomplices. Allyship/accompliceship in *Edge Entanglements* is a *becoming-complicit* where allies become entrenched/entangled in the lives of friends such that they are "in this together," and. We turn back to this notion of becoming-complicit after revisiting the concept of transversality.

Transversality

Desiring a social imaginary that is conducive to the formation of ally assemblages, this section revisits the concept of transversality (see Chapter 3) as a practical and non-arborescent approach to bringing people to the edge of the forest and into edge entanglements. In Chapter 7, we invited the possibility of transverse, reactive becomings – the creation of opportunities for active forces to be destabilised by reactive forces, which catalyses something yet to come. Becomings dangle at the threshold that we have come back to over and over, the intermezzo. On one side is the rigid striation of befriending practices and engineered (sometimes hierarchical) friendships. And on the other side is an allyship to come. Here, we outline how the concept of transversality might be a way to think about the production of ally assemblages and movement towards accompliceship in mental health research and practice, a becoming-complicit of ally/friends and movement towards an allyship of the intermezzo.

Transversality is the praxis of cutting across rigid relational lines and producing creative zones of tension between things that are typically discrete and separate (Guattari, 2015). When there is limited transversality, identities are fixed, hierarchical relations dominate and the major apparatus continues to produce cramped spaces. Looking at the befriending literature, there is sparse evidence of transversality and it is unlikely that creative impulses of desire will stir in those relationships unless something cuts across the lines of hierarchy. But, when there is high degree of transversality, where hierarchies are flexible and differing forces can become entangled, there is potential for creative expressions of desire. Transversality offers a way to think about and create an edge encounter and producing yet to be seen affects. And, as an entanglement of theory/practice, transversality is a playful concept that enables zigzag movements across and between territories.

Edge Entanglements contributes to the allyship literature by drawing attention to the gestural forces of intersecting assemblages and the role of the social landscape in the production of ally assemblages. The pursuit of transverse movements in the mental health sector not only involves individual relationships, but also considers the level of transversality of entangled social institutions. In 2020, Tim called Julie, one of the allies from this project, to ask a couple of follow-up questions, one of which was "What things make this sort of relationship possible?" Julie responded, "The context of A Place to Belong matters. Had I been in a typical organisation [with hierarchical leadership] I never would have entered into this relationship." Despite Julie having latent transversality ("I've always wanted this kind of relationship"), it was the institutional transversality and transversality of her supervisor that (in part) released her desire. APTB has played a vital role in establishing an institutional environment with a high coefficient of transversality – bringing together people of different social locations (service users, peer workers, support workers, social workers, health professionals, community members, academics, policy makers) and with differential experiences with psychiatric and mental health systems. Transversality is inviting Chips to come to a secure forensic psychiatry unit to get to know Krispy. Transversality is providing Julie, a social work student, with a simple role description, "spend time with Carol." Transversality is Robin's boss "not being hard on boundaries" and Robin casually becoming friends with people living on the street. Transversality is tutors (like Jack) and students (like Alan) having coffee together at an adult literacy program, and a program manager that encourages people to develop relationships outside of the program.

As mentioned in Chapter 3, transversality is not anarchy or the elimination of hierarchies. It is intentionally cutting across lines of segmentation and softening hierarchical relations. We are reminded of Guattari's (2015) warning, not to "(founder) in the besotting mythology of 'togetherness'" (p. 118). Ally assemblages are a (disrupted) active/reactive force relation and maintain a (supple) hierarchy. While the becoming of ally assemblages discussed in this book was a collective enunciation, these relationships remain a continually assembling entanglement of active/reactive force relations. We are cautious not to give in to the myth that the people in this project are completely "in this together." Transversality is the formation of alliances that are outside of typical relational structures (Colman, 2005, p. 361). Taking a postqualitative, cartographic approach enabled us to attend to the micropolitical movements and surface these elements. The fluidity of these approaches allowed for us to explore the transversality of allyship, as we were not bounded by divisive analytical practices or set procedures.

As a participatory researcher who takes pride in flattening research hierarchies, I (Tim) pause to consider Guattari's "mythology of togetherness" in my research practices. How might my presence affect these research assemblages? How might my entanglement with ally assemblages influence what was sayable or noticeable?

After a few weeks of meeting up with each pair, I routinely (read: systemically) asked the question: "What would it be like if I wasn't out with you? What would you talk about or do differently?" And without fail, each pair would respond with something to the effect of "it would be about the same." Chips response continued with: "[we'd talk about] how (Chips) is going, what we've done the last week." Yet, it was this type of chit chat between them that was missing from most of my research encounters with these assemblages (with the exception of Carol and Julie, who spent much of our time together catching up). I brought a form of arborescence into these assemblages that constricted what was possible. My affect on each assemblage fluctuated and shifted over time; still, I remained a structuring force. So now, I ask myself, what would it have been like I wasn't there? If I wasn't steering the conversation? If I wasn't a white, cis-gendered, heterosexual man? If I was there as a friend rather than a researcher? I would like to think that I established a trusting relationship with research participants so that our conversation could flow naturally, and that each pair could be open and honest (giving in to the mythology of togetherness). But my presence cannot help but redirect/shift/unsettle the flows of affect in these assemblages. It is likely that there were topics that participants did not feel safe discussing with/around me, such as the topic of Krispy's family. There was also a sense that there were things about Chips' meetings with the Mental Health Review Tribunal that they didn't want to talk about when

I was there. In one meeting, as I walked up to their table with my plate of fish and chips, I recall Krispy whispering something and Chips responding, "that's alright, I'll give you a call about it later." With Batman and Robin, I am acutely aware that I interrupted the flow of their assemblage and encouraged (or forced?) them talk a lot more than they typically would. On a Saturday afternoon, when Batman wanted to be out riding bikes or going for a swim, we were sitting around a table doing social mapping (although the pizza and storytelling seemed to stir their enthusiasm). When we were out at the Monster Trucks together, there were times when Robin and I hung back to talk while Batman stood at the front fence in the middle of the action. In those moments, my presence lured Robin away from the forest's edge and redirected the flows of affect towards the collection of data. It could be said that I decreased the coefficient of transversality of their assemblage in those moments.

Thinking about Carol and Julie, as the only pair of women, I wonder, what might have been unsayable around me, a man? I have replayed our meetings over and over in my mind, searching for something I might have passed over. What strikes me is not what I did or didn't find, but that I had to *search* for it. The affect of my gender on this pair of women was not at the forefront of my mind and was difficult for me to see. I consider myself sensitive to issues of sexism and patriarchy and have worked mostly with women and diverse gendered people as colleagues for over 20 years, yet I am often blind to my gender and its impact – the mythology of togetherness with other genders. Undoubtedly there were things that Carol and Julie could not talk about around me and being a man may be one of the reasons why.

Transversality is not a model, it is an experimental (temporary) movement or alignment. When we produce spaces with a high coefficient of transversality, we have the potential to prime bodies for impulses of desire and potentiate the formation of affirmative and revolutionary forces. At the beginning of *Edge Entanglements*, we surfaced the dominating tendencies of those who seek to "help" (looking squarely at ourselves). As a part of the major mental health apparatus, practitioners and researchers have the propensity to constrict the desiring-production of "other(ed)" bodies. Using a postqualitative, cartographic approach (and giving up the comfort of method), we have been able to transversally enter the assemblages of research participants and be affected by their micropolitical movements. Transversality offers a process for analysing and acting in a non-authoritative way, bringing together differing sociomaterial bodies in hopes of conjuring the magic of sorcery. There is no method, simply movement towards the "other" for connection's sake. Practitioners and researchers could consider, *how might I carelessly and care-fully meet others in the community, have an encounter with the cramped spaces, and hold my professional agenda loosely?* This might involve stretching the boundaries of helper/helped or researcher/participant where you can – give someone a lift to the grocery store, accept an invitation to attend their birthday party (and make them a card), attend a community event or protest that they told you about (and bring your friends/ family), and/or. Edge encounters can unsettle arborescent assemblages and open a path for little desiring-machines to break through. Perhaps an incredible research project will develop or perhaps you will develop a friendship.

Tim spoke with Robin on the phone in 2019 to clarify some of the details in his relationship with Batman. They ended up talking about the value of (transversally) bringing people together of different backgrounds, not engineering a relationship but giving space for it to develop. Robin told Tim a story from his work in the human services sector where he supervises a driver training program for folks who are marginalised or have difficulty achieving the required log hours to get their licence. A couple of years ago, Robin matched up a 19-year-old street-involved woman with a 65-year-old man. We do not know the specifics of the situation, but the gist of the story is … they didn't like each other, seeing each other as a cranky old man and an edgy ignorant teenager. But, in time they started to develop a kinship, where the man has become a "grandfather-like figure in her life." Transversality opens up (unknown) relational possibilities.

Becoming-complicit

In this penultimate section, we outline the micropolitics of ally assemblages and accompliceship, and what this suggests as possibilities for practice and research in/ out of the mental health sector: pursuit of an allyship to come. Here, we present accompliceship with psychiatrised people as a becoming-complicit. The orchestration of transverse movements is an act of sorcery. We invite people entangled with the mental health sector who are interested in producing liberating lines of flight to intentionally bring transversality into their workplace, their community, their family. This is an invitation to witchcraft, an invitation to form an alliance with the wild, an invitation to sorcery – in the hope that something magical might burst at the edges and produce some liberation for people in the cramped spaces. While the (macropolitical) allyship literature has limited consideration for how to generate micropolitical ally encounters, *Edge Entanglements* maps the molecular flows and processes of ally assemblages. We have explored how disruptive and transverse movements at the edge of the forest can create a canvas or landscape conducive to ally becomings.

Ally assemblages in our book were a micropolitical form of allyship – two people transversally brought together, and through a process of becoming-reactive became entangled in each other's lives. Through intentionally transversing lines of stratification (e.g., major and minor), opportunities open for territories to flex and for the major to get tripped up. Transversality is the production of the edge of the forest; it is the bringing together of two planes. Transversality is sorcery. At the transverse edge there is potential to produce accomplices that entangle with the minor and conjure of a machine of dissonance. Considering that all power relations are "simultaneously a macropolitics and a micropolitics" (Deleuze & Guattari, 1987, p. 249), transversality and the production of intersecting machines of dissonance has the potential to reformulate macropolitical structures of oppression and marginalisation. Micropolitical allyship can produce zigzag cracks in the major mental health apparatus and create room to manoeuvre for people in the cramped spaces. Molecular entanglements of assemblages with other assemblages (such as rhizomatic webs of ally assemblages and organisations like APTB) can "(make) it difficult for [oppressive macropolitical forces] to keep their own segments in line" (Deleuze & Guattari, 1987, p. 252).

Bearing in mind Guattari's (2015) myth of togetherness, allies can never fully be an accomplice or take on the struggle of another. Becoming-complicit is an ongoing process *towards* taking on the struggle of another as your own. Accompliceship and being complicit is the limit – it is forever on the horizon. The becoming-complicit of ally assemblages is an example of an ongoing revolutionary process in the mental health sector that can bring transformational change in the lives of psychiatrised people. In the face of ongoing risks of housing insecurity, discrimination, poverty, and (re)institutionalisation, ally assemblages engage in ongoing transverse movements of becoming-complicit. "There is no longer any ultimate goal or direction, but merely a wandering along a multiplicity of lines of flight that lead away from centres of power" (Goodchild, 1996, p. 12) in pursuit of a people to come.

As we bring this book to a close, we end with a series of provocations that are entangled with becoming-complicit and may serve as a starting point for conversations (to come) about allyship in the mental health sector.

Do

- Create opportunities for (careless) encounters to develop – increase the coefficient of transversality in your home, community, and workplace.
- Go to the edge of the forest and invite others there, in the hope that the people who are missing catch your gaze. Go close, get infected, and be guided by a desire for a people to come.
- Care-fully and transversally (un)train allies – develop new approaches for disrupting dominance through transversality. For example, ensure all (un)training is informed by people with a lived experience with psychiatric systems and psychiatrisation, as suggested by Carlson et al. (2020) and Jackson et al. (2020) in the accompliceship literature. Mad Studies, for example, is an instructive area of scholarship to draw from in the (un)training of allies and to unsettle entrenched ways of thinking in mental health research and practice (see Beresford, 2020; Faulkner, 2017; LeFrançois et al., 2013).
- Experiment and follow the encounters that demand your attention. When Tim presented some of the ideas from this book to a group of people at a community mental health workshop (including psychiatrised people, peer workers, support workers, practitioners, and academics), they suggested ideas for how to generate lines of flight and ally assemblages:
  - "do this through community art events"
  - "talk about this with employers so that some might give permission for staff to form more authentic relations with people"

- "talk about this with mental health workers so they know it's ok to break the rules sometimes."
- Do all of that, and and and.
- Generate a network of ally assemblages – little assemblages connected with other little assemblages. Enter a journey of becoming together. Reflexively and collectively guard against the appropriation of ally assemblages and the pull of the major.
- Generate zigzag cracks in macropolitical issues of oppression and marginalisation through ongoing micropolitical movements – operating as a continually changing constellation, a pack of wolves.
- Try to be an accomplice (knowing this is forever on the horizon), becoming-complicit.

Don't

- Arborify ally assemblages – don't turn micropolitical becomings into a program.
- Be an authority (active force) in someone's life.

Tim's affectionate goodbye

It is almost time to say "goodbye" to this project and book, to move along a series to another encounter – and – or – but still. Thinking with theory, I find myself at the intermezzo, zigzagging across relationships, theory, transcripts, conversations, emotions, and. I have formed an alliance with this project, folding my encounters with participants and the production of research texts into myself – producing a pack of wolves inside me. I carry this project, and all the encounters that vibrate within it, as a pack of wolves in my chest that continues to charm me.

> What does it mean to love somebody? It is always to seize that person in a mass, extract [them] from a group, however small, in which [they participate] … then to find that person's own packs, the multiplicities [they enclose within themselves] which may be of an entirely different nature. To join them to mine, to make them penetrate mine, and for me to penetrate the other person's.
>
> *(Deleuze & Guattari, 1987, p. 40)*

In the final weeks of this project, I spoke with Jenny about the love and affection I have for (parts of) this work. My fondness was produced in those moments when I entered ally assemblages and they entered me, when I entered theory and theory entered me, where my writing was a loving expression. "Love is the encounter with another person that opens us up to a possible world" (Colebrook, 2002, p. 17). In 2018, I transversally spent time with pairs of people, and for a brief point in time, I was a part of their relationships. I found myself enjoying their presence, the tone of their voices, the creases in their faces, the stories they told with their mouths (but also with their faces, glances, movements, and). My fondness grew as I turned and re-turned to my encounters with them over the course of writing.

> What is involved, here, is a plurality of worlds; the pluralism of love does not concern only the multiplicity of loved beings, but the multiplicity of souls or worlds in each of them. *To love is to try to explicate, to develop these unknown worlds that remain enveloped within the beloved.*
>
> (*Deleuze, 2000, p. 7, emphasis added*)

With growing affection, Jenny and I have mapped and remapped the "unknown worlds that remain enveloped within" ally assemblages. A cartographic approach offered a way for us to explore creative possibilities in *Edge Entanglements* and chart micropolitical movements, but also to guard against paternalistic academic tendencies as we pursued an "acentred, non-hierarchical, non-signifying system without a General" (Deleuze & Guattari, 1987, p. 22). We, and the multiple others involved, affectionately created harmonies between theory and empirical data, sketching ally assemblages in ways that move. We produced fresh perspectives on Deleuze and Guattari's work and generative possibilities for research and practice in/out of the mental health sector (to come). It is our hope that we have created a little desiring-machine, a micropolitical book that produces impulses of desire in others.

And and and

Notes

1 We hesitantly label solidarity with marginalised people groups and activist-oriented allyship as *macropolitical* given the interrelated micropolitical elements. For example, allying with Indigenous peoples broadly and seeking structural change (macropolitical) may also involve micropolitical movements such as learning and observing protocols when inviting an Elder to speak at an event.

2 To a certain extent, this paradox is evident in this book. Although we have tried to centre the experience of psychiatrised people and their allies, and have drawn from Mad Studies, postcolonial, and feminist scholars, we still precariously elevate our own authority and expertise. With some reservation, we assert our (incomplete) expertise in postqualitative thinking-with-theory, but our expertise in disrupting the major mental health apparatus is likely more incomplete given our lack of lived experience of psychiatrisation.

KNOTS–SORCERY–BELONGING, AN AFTERWORD

By Lynda Shevellar, Tim Barlott, and Jenny Setchell

Knots, knotting, knotted

Tim and Jenny have written much about entanglements. More-than-human entanglements traverse space and time and culture – although their qualities shift from affirmative and romantic, to oppressive and sinister. Weaving and knotting things together is one of our oldest and important technologies. We have used them in nets and baskets, fundamental to our survival. They have bound fate, held warriors in battle, tied lovers together, created weapons, cast spells, woven protections, condemned, repressed, and released. The handman's noose, the gordian knot, the triquerta, zhongguo jie, maedeup, and macrame – they are woven into the fabric of our (human) being. We speak of being tangled up in something when we can't get free, tying ourselves in knots when we can't think clearly, and feel knotted up when we are tense.

I (Lynda) am honoured to be invited to contribute to this Afterword, having been entangled in much of this work and its threads in various ways. I first met Neil Barringham at a community development class. Disillusioned by my experience as a counsellor, I was searching for less individualised, less pathologising, and potentially less violent ways of responding to social issues. As I learned about Neil's work, I recall asking him how I might support people who were struggling. His simple yet profound advice was to stand in their corner. Being in someone's corner meant walking alongside someone, through their life, and getting to know them deeply. I didn't realise it at the time, but Neil was inviting me to be an ally. Much like the community development approaches Neil and I were engaging with in the class, I began to discover that it is through walking alongside someone that change can occur. Tim's PhD and broader research excited me with its potential to interrogate this space, but also to honour the informal, often unseen, everyday experiences that can have profound impacts on people's lives.

★★★

A couple of days ago Tim's daughter brought him a tangled mess of yarn and ribbon. "Papa, can you get this apart for me?" She had attempted to untangle the threads on her own, one of her strategies appears to have been pulling at the threads as hard as she could. Tim replied "These knots are too tight, I don't think we can salvage it. Plus, I don't have time for this right now." "But you *can*, *please, try*." Her face became red, urgency in her voice – her knots were a part of her at that moment. Tim swung between saying "no" (and risk a five-year-old's meltdown) and trying with the risk of failing. "How about we cut the knot," his hands reaching for the drawer that contained the scissors, "at least then you can use some of the threads." "NO!!!" she screamed. Tim sighed, his force displaced, and for a moment he felt her sorrow – her knots became his. He used his teeth to grind and soften the knots, a pin as an extension of his fingers to pry and pick at the spaces (or where he hoped there were spaces). "I can't get it." "Yes, you can." And in time they did. The threads were somewhat frayed, stretched, and wet with his saliva. "Yay!" she exclaimed, scooping them from Tim's hand and zipping off to craft a craft yet to come.

The edge entanglements with allyship in this book are a relational knotting and unknotting, unknotting and knotting. The edge of things is a place of wonder, mystery, of relational knots yet to come and worlds yet to be crafted. But there are some tight knots – some so tight they are difficult to re-entangle in different ways. Had Tim not had a transverse encounter with his daughter he would have tossed that ball of yarn and ribbon in the waste bin, or cut it into salvageable parts. Within the context of systematic exclusion, this example of a knotted ball of yarn and ribbon might seem trite or simplistic, and it is. Knots of marginalisation and oppression are, of course, usually considerably more difficult to dis/re-entangle – but this is precisely the invitation of the edge of things, the in-between. At the edge of theory and practice, major and minor, active and reactive there is an invitation first to see the knots (as Robin "saw" Batman's situation) and then to knot and unknot together ("just to see where it goes") – entangling in ways that craft unimaginable worlds.

But, we (Lynda, Tim, Jenny) do not wish to over-romanticise the ally relationship. Working in the field of community mental health, especially as academics, gives us the luxury of disconnection through intellectualisation. We can play word games and debate appropriate phrases – do we speak of "mental health challenges," or engage in discourses of "wellbeing", or? We can engage in critical analysis to expose how particular dynamics of power are maintained and reinforced in the construction of "mental health."

★★★

When I (Lynda) am being an ally, walking alongside someone I care about, I am forced to confront the base physical nature of people's lives as well – the consequences of stigma and discrimination that can result in a poverty of relationships, and a poverty of the material world.

And yet.

Even as I write this, I position myself above – scattering of acknowledgements to my education and employment, my careful use of language, the creation of a mental health field as though it was in some way outside of myself. I say I am an ally, as though the "other" is not ally to me. What Tim and Jenny's work, and the theory they draw from, reminds me, is that I am speaking as an element of the major apparatus. In positioning myself as the solver, the counsellor, or the academic, I have sought to provide therapy or training programs, share intellectual models, and tried to "fix" someone's life. Too often these endeavours have little to do with the people I am seeking to stand alongside, and a lot to do with my need for control in moments of uncertainty, my own safety, and my ego. In these moments, to borrow Tim's analogy, I pull the knot too tight.

So let me try again.

In the last few years I have come out twice.

When I shared with people that I was now living with a woman – after two previous marriages to men, there were a few raised eyebrows, some good-humoured digs, some all-knowing nods, and even a proposition. When I have come out about my mental health, I have received very different responses. Some responses are born of care and concern, but others are born of discomfort, uncertainty, or rejection. In thinking about what it means to be an academic, researching the experience of being psychiatrised, while myself being psychiatrised, I am reminded of Alan Kaplan's (2002) delicate image of walking on the rim of a cup. I am neither fully inside nor outside – but instead, I totter on the edge of my identity, my communities, my practice, myself.

And, with this afterword I totter. I expect the "other" to offer lived experience knowledge, not me. When inviting me to author an afterword with them, Tim and Jenny shared a few pages of ideas around knots and entanglements. "Does this stir anything in you?" Tim asked. … And so, I engage with some of my edge entanglements and the ways I dangle at the micropolitical threshold of major and minor. As you read on, we circle back to the desires that (dis)assemble in this book.

I think about the multiple times and ways in which people may be required to "come out": sexuality, health conditions, disabilities, poverty, illiteracy, histories of abuse, and a range of other potentially marginalising experiences one is required to suddenly make visible. What makes coming out particularly difficult, is that it is an exercise to be repeated ad nauseum throughout the day, whether it be confessing one's medical history on an insurance form, correcting the tradesman who asks, "Would your husband like to see the quote?", or being triggered by an everyday interaction. One must constantly make a decision about how much to disclose, when and to whom. A quote for a roof repair suddenly becomes a politically charged act.

Elraz (2018) observes the way in which "the societal view about mental illness operates as a 'blanket discourse' that overrides and colonizes other work-oriented subject positions, which is to say that the person is deemed to be, first and foremost, 'mentally ill'" (p. 729). In other words, once out – whether as a lesbian or a person with a mental health issue – this identity is so powerful as to obscure all others and to be the lens through which all other actions are viewed. Chimamanda Adichie (2009) framed it as the danger of a single story. She attests that the danger is not that this single story is incorrect, but rather, that it is incomplete.

My story has long been incomplete. Part of it is fear of stigma – but it is also about identity, respect to others, and not considering myself mentally unwell *enough*, in other words, the ongoing politics of identity. A high level of education, a loving family, a stable income, and otherwise good physical health, meant I had the resources in my life to help me get through tough times. I have never spent time in hospital. I have never been *that* mentally ill. In the mental health networks I have joined as a volunteer, and in my research for which I am paid, I spend time with people who have spent extended periods in institutions, who live with diverse perceptions, hearing voices and seeing visions, and with confusing, sometimes frightening experiences of the world around them. "They" are in constant contact with other systems: the health system, the child protection system, the criminal justice system, the housing system, the welfare system. "They" have spent time dealing with addictions, been subject to violence and incarceration, institutionalisation, homelessness, stigma and discrimination, poverty, and illness, and had their fundamental rights withheld. When I think of "mental illness," I think about the people I have met who have been so incredibly worse off than me. I know I have not been tested in the same way. In part, I am reluctant to out myself as being psychiatrised, because I see myself as having got off lightly.

So even though I have studied, researched, worked in, volunteered for, been a carer for others who experience distress, and have my own extended lived experience with distress and what has been called "mental illness", I still admit my own status reticently. I want to open up spaces for dialogue and support those around me who struggle, yet I often couch my own experiences in obfuscating ways. I want my students and peers who are vulnerable to know it is OK and that I understand what it means to struggle. But I don't want them to dismiss me as being less than, because of my "mental health" issues and to use this as an arsenal to discredit me. The hypocrisy tears at me: I am a fierce advocate for "mental health" support and normalisation, and the rights of people around me. Yet I expect more vulnerable individuals to combat a stigma I do not face personally. I am vocal about the distress and challenges of others and yet silent about my own. I can "pass" for mentally well.

This in-between space, being both in and out – is itself a site of stress and distraction. I worry about sharing with people what's going on for me, because I fear it will be used against me, seen as a limitation and a weakness in such a competitive space as academia. I worry I will not be given the opportunities I desire. I also hold the contradictory space of worrying when given opportunities that I will ultimately fail due to a mental health episode. I need people to know why I yearn to contribute, yet sometimes am overwhelmed by what seems like a reasonable workload, why I cannot recall the fine details they need at a particular moment, and why I withdraw. When well, I like to think I have insight, perception and generosity. When unwell, my judgement is poor and I am destroyed by the simplest of tasks, like filling in a form, or taking a shower.

There are times I feel deep shame for not having been braver, bolder, more self-aware. I wish I had woken-up earlier, as I find myself apart from those I might otherwise identify with or find solidarity with. Their story is not mine. Other times I can be simply accepting that these are the experiences – good and bad – that I have had, and that have brought me to this place. I walk on the rim of the cup – neither fully in nor outside. But I also know I have been, and can still easily pass for being, part of the majority.

At the same time, I have been labelled as having severe and persistent, endogenous depression, accompanied by premenstrual dysphoric disorder. I am victim to their tenacious grip on my life. And my partners have all suffered alongside me. Neumarkt (2005) says that human beings are feeling beings first and thinking beings second. Being able to analyse the social forces that construct our experiences, recognise their naming as an act of power, own our privilege, being able to imagine alternatives, or reframe them in some way – does not lessen the impact of our experiences.

Daily the jewel box of medications beckons me in the dawn and dusk light. I have struggled with their side effects, from crippling nausea, and weight gain, to insomnia, tiredness, bouts of confusion, memory loss, and an inability to do basic maths! It is difficult – particularly as an academic, over-invested in education and the journey of the intellect – to weave together the contradiction that I can be clear and clever in darkness – or I can stay half asleep, stumbling, but in light. I admit that when I hear people speak of "COVID fog" during the COVID-19 pandemic, I wickedly indulge in Schadenfreude. I am in a daily battle with my mind and my body, living with anxiety, self-harm, and deep sadness that renders me unable to do all that I long to do. There are days when I dread waking up because life is too painful and my thinking is too toxic. I am desperate for solitude and stillness – yet long for intimacy. I struggle to maintain relationships as I fear being "too much," so choose to be nothing at all. I spend thousands of dollars each year to get the support and medication I need just to function. Yet I am fortunate because my job permits me to pay my medical bills, as well as offering me a rare degree of autonomy over my time. I tie myself in knots.

Science fiction writer Hugh Howey (2013) observes that some crooked things looked even worse when straightened. This thing loosely called "mental illness" has ripped me apart so many times I can no longer trust the good times in my life. I see them as a brief oasis between spells of despair. I treasure them – but cannot afford to invest too deeply in them. Life is an endeavour requiring continual monitoring: I am forever searching for the right mix of medication, talking therapies and professional advice, theoretical insights and models, self-awareness, diet, exercise, stimulation, rest, challenge, and support. And this constant vigilance in itself is exhausting as the self is constructed as a project.

Perhaps the real danger is not in "coming out" and disclosing mental health challenges; it is the danger of coming out about something far more forbidding. Braidotti (2013) argues that far from being self-evident, life is a project – one has to work at it. She argues that we have an ontological drive to become – to reach our "potential". This seduces us to keep living and to keep becoming. And if we sustain this for long enough, then life becomes a habit. And if the habit becomes self-fulfilling then life becomes addictive. When I think about distress, trauma, and "mental health" I wonder if, at least for some of us, life has never taken this addictive form. It is often a very deliberate, daily, choice, that – at least so far – we continue to make.

I am defeat
When it knows it
Can now do nothing
By suffering.
All you lived through,
Dancing because you
No longer need it
For any deed.
I shall never be
Different. Love me.

W. H. Auden (Auden & Mendelson, 1979)

I am entangled in the lives of others who are psychiatrised. And I am not. I am knot.

★★★

In (un)imagining an affirmative future for psychiatrised people and transformative minor assemblages explored in this book, we (Lynda, Tim, Jenny) cannot ignore that edge entanglements and knots of psychiatrisation can be arduous. Idealising minor entanglements (such as the ally relationships in this book) can sometimes overlook the ways they are continually at risk of being re-knotted by the major apparatus – minor bodies may continue to struggle against subjugation and oppression, and minor health practices and research may struggle for credibility and legitimacy.

It may be that in this "world" in which I am so unplayful, I am a different person than in the "world" in which I am playful. Or it may be that the "world" in which I am unplayful is constructed in such a way that I could be playful in it. I could practice, even though that "world" is constructed in such a way that my being playful in it is kind of hard.

(María Lugones, 1987, p. 13)

The allyship entanglements discussed in this book are at the edge of playful and unplayful worlds. Sebastian De Line (2018), a trans artist and scholar of Haudenosaunee-European-Asian descent writes of the difficulty of being "playful" amidst intersecting major assemblages. "We are perceived as being too serious when we address racist humor.... We are conversely not taken seriously when being "too queer" or "too feminine" in a misogynist world" (De Line, 2018, p. 87). Minor assemblages and allyship entanglements continue to be knotted with a world in which "being playful in it is kind of hard" for psychiatrised people (Lugones, 1987, p. 13). The desires bound up in *Edge Entanglements* are for a world yet to come, where spaces are not cramped, where friends don't need to be allies, where people are not categorically ordered according to their value, where people experiencing distress "have a place to go where (they're) loved" (Shimrat, 2013, p. 156).

> The question of craziness would disappear if we lived in a humane world. Even if someone was in a state of incredible pain, the issue would not be one of diagnosis, putting a name on it, or calling it crazy or not crazy. Instead, it would be saying, "What can we do to help you?".
>
> *(Shimrat, 1997, p. 57)*

Edge Entanglements and being at the edge of things is not only an experimental encounter, but also an intentionally hopeful encounter. Rosi Braidotti's (2011) description of *hope* is mentioned in Chapter 4 as "a sort of 'dreaming forward' that permeates our lives and activates them. It is a powerful motivating force grounded in our collective imaginings" (p. 298). This postqualitative work is playful, yes, and. The creative imaginings of *Edge Entanglements* are full of desire for a world yet to come. We have experienced theory as an agitating force, turning our attention to the knots of domination and inviting us to "stop believing in trees, roots, and radicles. They've made us suffer too much" (Deleuze & Guattari, 1987, p. 15).

An invitation to sorcery

Come. Gather around the fire – its only a small one and not in the most auspicious of circumstances, but the barrel is heating up and the shadows loom large on the cityscape around us. Warm your hands. Make magic with us. Conjure sorcery that breathes fresh vitality into our communities, wield spells of welcoming that increase our collective sense of belonging, and summon the people to come – may our enchantments be monstrous and expansive, cracking the oppressive grips of the cramped spaces that we are entangled.[1]

The sorcery that we dream of, and was present in the allyship assemblages in this book, is not a metaphor – we desire the underworld to manifest, we yearn for an otherworldly force to ripple through our lives. Psychiatrised people have been subjugated by authoritative "mental health" practices, vilified in the media, discredited and diminished in the dominant spaces of our society. "People who 'go crazy' can either be given over to psychiatric care, or somehow live in a society that is uncaring and lacks love" (Shimrat, 2013, p. 156). The patriarchal, capitalist, neo-liberal, colonial, heteronormative, white, sanist, ableist world leaves little room to manoeuvre for those among us who sit outside of the categorical norm. There is no room for madness (unless it is controlled and constrained), no room for queerness (unless it can be sold or appropriated in marketing), no room for Blackness (unless it can be toned down or pumped through the speakers of a pickup truck), no room for Indigeneity (unless it is assimilated or used to signal a simulacra of inclusiveness). And so, we have worked to ally ourselves with the "other", the Mad, queers, misfits to stop believing in this world and summon new worlds (and worlds that are yet to come). The chapters of this book traversed a kind of world making sorcery that is possible in our communities and practices.

Yet, we want to hold this moment, this draw to sorcery, with delicate care. While I (Tim) have experienced periods of distress related to a cancer diagnosis and surgery, I have not been psychiatrised or been marginalised in my distress. If anything, I have received caring and loving responses to my distress. I (Jenny) have experienced trauma in relation to ongoing societal reactions to my queerness and as a person read (usually) to be a woman existing in a patriarchal society – but have never been psychiatrised. And, we (Tim, Jenny, and Lynda) have never engaged in practices of sorcery (e.g., witchcraft). I (Jenny) have never had much to do with religion. I (Lynda) am an atheist, after time on the edges of religion in a Catholic school. However, I (Tim) have been a part of practices that demonised sorcery, and I mean that quite literally. I grew up attending a conservative evangelical Christian church, and as a young person participated in (or was a spectator to) several problematic and coercive practices (that I now detest). I recall reluctantly attending a Friday night exorcism with my youth group in 1995 – a disgusting event that made a violent spectacle out of distress, trauma, madness and sorcery – conflating these with "demonic possession." My memory of the event is hazy at best, but the foul taste in my mouth remains. The church offered people an empty promise of "wholeness" and in turn paraded them on stage as sacrificial lambs or as the embodiment of evil. Sorcery and madness were not welcome in that space, sorcery and madness were dangerous in that space – if the "evil" could not be "cast out" then "satan" had won the battle for their minds. And so, we (Tim, Jenny and Lynda) do not wish to casually or flippantly speak of sorcery and magic. As we type these words, we realise that, in part, we desire the language of sorcery out of defiance against the knots of violence in Tim's and others' pasts.

Edge Entanglements tells a story of relational processes (of sorcery) for pairs of people, processes that occurred at the edge of the forest. We used the imagery of the edge of the forest to describe the coming together of difference – differing people/places/forces/intensities. The edge of the forest is where the domesticated world (such as the mental health system) starts to unravel and potentially transform into something else. Agitated by theory, we explored how the edge of things is a transformative starting point. The edge of the forest is a place for the displacement of power, softening of hierarchies and the solidarity of connection. The edge of the forest as a place of enchantment, magic, and sorcery – where unanticipated and liberating processes can occur for psychiatrised people and allies in their life. Mindful of how dominant "mental health" systems swirl and capture people with diverse experiences of trauma/distress in (sometimes oppressive) programs and treatment, and we sought to vigilantly explore movements that unsettled and broke away from habitual patterns in the "mental health" sector.

In 1994 a group of citizen advocates and community organisers in Brisbane, Australia set up a fire and gathered others around in the form of an organisation called A Place to Belong (APTB). At the threshold of the dominant, neoliberal, market-driven mental health sector and the cramped spaces of an inner-city Brisbane suburb, APTB has sought to develop networks of support for people with complex experiences of distress and "mental health" challenges. Funded by a major health provider, APTB provided individualised support services, but simultaneously facilitated the development of diffuse and expansive community networks among the psychiatrised people that accessed their services. They intentionally fostered connections between their service users and people in the community, connections that were outside of (or informally connected to) the organisation. "'A place to belong' is anywhere and everywhere – connectedness can occur through 'amateurs' getting alongside others and through seemingly small and insignificant and ordinary process" (Barringham & Barringham, 2002, p. 56). APTB was a de-centralised node of activation founded on practices of belonging. The organisation was dissolved in 2020 but the sorcery of their network continues through a loosely connected assemblage of people under the name Rhizomes, a name that came out of the project described in this book.

Belongingness has been central to the Rhizomes network and continues to keep their eyes on the horizon, desiring worlds that are welcoming of difference and "a place to go where you're loved" (Shimrat, 2013, p. 156). We'd be remiss to consider this form of belongingness as only the pursuit of kindness, acceptance, care, and all the good things – to belong (in a world that makes it difficult to belong) is also a sociopolitical enactment. Belongingness is a "counter-hegemonic" pursuit, where space is contested and pulled away from the dominating major apparatus (Eizenberg, 2004). Belongingness comes with precarity and wanders amidst the sociopolitical edge, dreaming of welcoming new worlds amidst an unwelcoming society.

Note

1 Some of the ideas in this section on sorcery were developed following conversations between Lindsay Eales and Tim. In particular, Lindsay referred to APTB as a "fire gathering" and gave permission to use this figuration in the Afterword.

REFERENCES

Abrams, T., Setchell, J., Thille, P., Mistry, B., & Gibson, B. E. (2019). Affect, intensity, and moral assemblage in rehabilitation practice. *BioSocieties*, *14*(1), 23–45. https://doi.org/10.1057/s41292-018-0115-2

Adame, A. L., & Knudson, R. M. (2007). Beyond the counter-narrative: Exploring alternative narratives of recovery from the psychiatric survivor movement. *Narrative Inquiry*, *17*(2), 57–178. https://doi.org/10.1075/ni.17.2.02ada

Adichie, C. N. (2009). The danger of single story. *Ted Global* 2009. Retrieved from: https://www.ted.com/talks/chimamanda_ngozi_adichie_the_danger_of_a_single_story?language=en

Ahmed, S. (2015). *The cultural politics of emotion*. Routledge.

Alexander, D., & Wyatt, J. (2018). In(tra)fusion: Kitchen research practices, collaborative writing, and re-conceptualising the interview. *Qualitative Inquiry*, *24*(2), 101–108. https://doi.org/10.1177/1077800416686370

Althusser, L., & Balibar, E. (1970). *Reading capital* (B. Brewster, Trans.). Verso Books.

Anglicare Australia. (2019). *Our better selves: Anglicare Australia's state of the family report*. Anglicare Australia.

Anti-Oppression Network. (n.d.). *Allyship*. Retrieved from: https://theantioppressionnetwork.com/allyship/

Arva, E. L. (2008). Writing the vanishing real: Hyperreality and magical realism. *Journal of Narrative Theory*, *38*(1), 60–85. https://doi.org/10.1353/jnt.0.0002

Auden, W. H., & Mendelson, E. (1979). *Selected poems*. Faber and Faber.

Australian Institute of Health and Welfare. (2019). *Mental health services – In brief 2019*. AIHW.

Bad Religion. (1989). I want to conquer the world. On *No Control* [CD]. Epitaph Records.

Baines, D., Charlesworth, S., & Cunningham, I. (2015). Changing care? Men and managerialism in the nonprofit sector. *Journal of Social Work*, *15*(5), 459–478. https://doi.org/10.1177/1468017314548149

Banks, S. (2011). Ethics in an age of austerity: Social work and the evolving new public management. *Journal of Social Intervention: Theory and Practice*, *20*(2), 5–23. https://doi.org/10.18352/jsi.260

Barlott, T., Adams, K., & Cook, A. (2016). Increasing participation in the information society by people with disabilities and their families in lower-income countries using mainstream technologies. *Universal Access in the Information Society*, *15*(2), 189–198. https://doi.org/10.1007/s10209-015-0418-z

Barlott, T., Adams, K., Díaz, F. R., & Molina, M. M. (2015). Using SMS as a tool to reduce exclusions experienced by caregivers of people with disabilities in a resource-limited Colombian community. *Disability and Rehabilitation: Assistive Technology*, *10*(4), 347–354. https://doi.org/10.3109/17483107.2014.974223

Barlott, T., Aplin, T., Catchpole, E., Kranz, R., Le Goullon, D., Toivanen, A., & Hutchens, S. (2020). Connectedness and ICT: Opening the door to possibilities for people with intellectual disabilities. *Journal of Intellectual Disabilities*, *24*(4), 503–521. https://doi.org/10.1177/1744629519831566

Barlott, T., Shevellar, L., & Turpin, M. (2017). Becoming minor: Mapping new territories in occupational science. *Journal of Occupational Science*, *24*(4), 524–534. https://doi.org/10.1080/14427591.2017.1378121

Barlott, T., Shevellar, L., Turpin, M., & Setchell, J. (2020a). Destabilising social inclusion and recovery, and pursuing "lines of flight" in the mental health sector. *Sociology of Health & Illness*, *42*(6), 1328–1343. https://doi.org/10.1111/1467-9566.13106

Barlott, T., Shevellar, L., Turpin, M., & Setchell, J. (2020b). The dissident interview: A deterritorialising guerrilla encounter. *Qualitative Inquiry*, *26*(6), 650–660. https://doi.org/10.1177/1077800419859041

Barlott, T., & Turpin, M. (2022). Desiring occupation: Theorising the passion, creativity and social production of everyday life. *Journal of Occupational Science* [Early online], *29*, 130–140.

Barringham, N., & Barringham, P. (2002). *Finding people to be there: Rebuilding a sense of belonging*. Anglicare.

Beckett, I. F. W. (2001). *Modern insurgencies and counter-insurgencies: Guerrillas and their opponents since 1750*. Psychology Press.

Bellingham, B., Kemp, H., Boydell, K., Isobel, S., Gill, K., & River, J. (2021). Towards epistemic justice doing: Examining the experiences and shifts in knowledge of lived experience researchers over the course of a mental health research training programme. *International Journal of Mental Health Nursing*, *30*(6), 1588–1598.

Beresford, P. (2012). From "vulnerable" to vanguard: Challenging the coalition. *Soundings*, *50*, 46–57. https://doi.org/10.3898/136266212800379509

Beresford, P. (2020). "Mad," mad studies and advancing inclusive resistance. *Disability and Society*, *35*(8), 1337–1342. https://doi.org/10.1080/09687599.2019.1692168

Beresford, P., & Russo, J. (Eds.) (2022). *The Routledge International Handbook of Mad Studies*. Routledge.

Bessa, Y. (2012). Modernity theories and mental illness: A comparative study of selected sociological theorists. *International Journal of Humanities and Social Science*, *2*(17), 31–38.

Bettencourt, G.M. (2020). "You can't be a class ally if you're an upper-class person because you don't understand": Working-class students' definitions and perceptions of social class allyship. *The Review of Higher Education*, *44*(2), 265–291. https://doi.org/10.1353/rhe.2020.0041

Bey, H. (1991). *The temporary autonomous zone*. Autonomedia.

Bignall, S. (2008). Deleuze and foucault on desire and power. *Angelaki*, *13*(1), 127–147. https://doi.org/10.1080/09697250802156125

Bila, N. J. (2019). Social workers' perspectives on the recovery-oriented mental health practice in Tshwane, South Africa. *Social Work in Mental Health*, *17*(3), 344–363.

Bishop, A. (2015). *Becoming an ally: Breaking the cycle of oppression in people.* Fernwood.

Blackman, L. (2011). Affect, performance and queer subjectivities. *Cultural studies, 25*(2), 183–199. https://doi.org/10.1080/09502386.2011.535986

Blackman, L. (2012). *Immaterial bodies: Affect, embodiment, mediation.* Sage Publications Ltd. https://doi.org/10.4135/9781446288153

Blackman, L., & Venn, C. (2010). Affect. *Body & Society, 16*(1), 7–28.

Blatt, R. (2022). "I don't need advice but I will take it": Allied labor in transgender allyship. *Sexualities.* https://doi.org/10.1177/13634607221114467

Bock, S., Woods, S., & Sock, D. (2020). 10 years, 5 queers performance at DomestiCITY. *Brisbane Festival 2020.* Retrieved from: https://www.youtube.com/watch?v=GXct25rcub4

Bogue, R. (1997). Minor writing and minor literature. *symplokē, 5*(1/2), 99–118. https://doi.org/10.1353/sym.2005.0051

Bolton, D. (2008). *What is mental disorder? An essay in philosophy, science, and values.* Oxford University Press. https://doi.org/10.1093/med/9780198565925.001.0001

Bon, Jovi. (1986). Livin' on a prayer. On *Slippery When Wet* [CD]. Mercury Records.

Boot, M. (2013). *Invisible armies: An epic history of guerrilla warfare from ancient times to the present.* W.W. Norton.

Bourke, B. (2020). Leaving behind the rhetoric of allyship. *Whiteness and Education, 5*(2), 179–194. https://doi.org/10.1080/23793406.2020.1839786

Boydell, K. M., Gladstone, B. M., & Crawford, E. S. (2002). The dialectic of friendship for people with psychiatric disabilities. *Psychiatric Rehabilitation Journal, 26*(2), 123–131. https://doi.org/10.2975/26.2002.123.131

Braidotti, R. (2011). *Nomadic theory: The portable Rosi Braidotti.* Columbia University Press.

Braidotti, R. (2013). *The posthuman.* Polity Press.

Bredewold, F., Tonkens, E., & Trappenburg, M. (2016). Solidarity and reciprocity between people with and without disabilities. *Journal of Community & Applied Social Psychology, 26*(6), 534–550. https://doi.org/10.1002/casp.2279

Bromley, E., Gabrielian, S., Brekke, B., Pahwa, R., Daly, K. A., Brekke, J. S., & Braslow, J. T. (2013). Experiencing community: Perspectives of individuals diagnosed as having serious mental illness. *Psychiatric Services, 64*(7), 672–679. https://doi.org/10.1176/appi.ps.201200235

Brown, S. P., McKesson, L. D., Robinson, J., & Jackson, A. Y. (2021). Possibles and post qualitative inquiry. *Qualitative Inquiry, 27*(2), 231–234. https://doi.org/10.1177/1077800420922266

Buchanan, I. (2008). *Deleuze and Guattari's anti-Oedipus.* Continuum.

Buhagiar, K., Templeton, G., & Osborn, D. P. (2020). Recent physical conditions and health service utilization in people with common mental disorders and severe mental illness in England: Comparative cross-sectional data from a nationally representative sample. *European Psychiatry, 63*(1), 1–8. https://doi.org/10.1192/j.eurpsy.2020.22

Bullough, V. L. (1976). Heresy, witchcraft, and sexuality. *Journal of Homosexuality, 1*(2), 183–199.

Burdekin, B. (1993). *National inquiry into the human rights of people with mental illness: Launch of report.* Australian Human Rights Commission.

Capuzza, J. C. (2015). What's in a name? Transgender identity, metareporting, and the misgendering of Chelsea Manning. In J. Capuzza, & L. Spencer (Eds.), *Transgender communication studies: Histories, trends, and trajectories* (pp. 93–110). Lexington Books.

Carlson, J., Leek, C., Casey, E., Tolman, R., & Allen, C. (2020). What's in a name? A synthesis of "allyship" elements from academic and activist literature. *Journal of Family Violence, 35*(8), 889–898. https://doi.org/10.1007/s10896-019-00073-z

Carpenter, W. T., Jr., & Kirkpatrick, B. (1988). The heterogeneity of the long-term course of schizophrenia. *Schizophrenia Bulletin, 14*(4), 645–652. https://doi.org/10.1093/schbul/14.4.645

Cassidy, M., Thompson, R., El-Nagib, R., Hickling, L. M., & Priebe, S. (2019). Motivations and experiences of volunteers and patients in mental health befriending: A thematic analysis. *BMC Psychiatry, 19*(1), 116. https://doi.org/10.1186/s12888-019-2102-y

Champetier, C. (2001). Philosophy of the gift: Jacques Derrida, Martin Heidegger. *Angelaki: Journal of Theoretical Humanities, 6*(2), 15–22. https://doi.org/10.1080/713650416

Clark, L. A., Cuthbert, B., Lewis-Fernández, R., Narrow, W. E., & Reed, G. M. (2017). Three approaches to understanding and classifying mental disorder: ICD-11, DSM-5, and the National Institute of Mental Health's Research Domain Criteria (RDoC). *Psychological Science in the Public Interest, 18*(2), 72–145. https://doi.org/10.1177/1529100617727266

Cleary, M., Horsfall, J., & Escott, P. (2014). Marginalization and associated concepts and processes in relation to mental health/illness. *Issues in Mental Health Nursing, 35*(3), 224–226. https://doi.org/10.3109/01612840.2014.883792

Cole, D. R. (2013). Lost in data space: Using nomadic analysis to perform social science. In R. Coleman, & J. Ringrose (Eds.), *Deleuze and research methodologies* (pp. 219–237). Edinburgh University Press.

Cole, T. (2012, March 21). The white-savior industrial complex. *The Atlantic.* https://www.theatlantic.com/international/archive/2012/03/the-white-savior-industrial-complex/254843/

Colebrook, C. (2002). *Gilles Deleuze.* Routledge.

Coleman, R., & Ringrose, J. (2013). *Deleuze and research methodologies.* Edinburgh University Press.

Collins Dictionary. (n.d.). Transversal. In *CollinsDictionary.com.* Retrieved December 11, 2020, from https://www.collinsdictionary.com/dictionary/english/transversal

Colman, F. (2005). Hit me harder: The transversality of becoming-adolescent. *Women: A Cultural Review, 16*(3), 356–371. https://doi.org/10.1080/09574040500321420

Corrigan, P. W., Rowan, D., Green, A., Lundin, R., River, P., Uphoff-Wasowski, K., White, K., & Kubiak, M. A. (2002). Challenging two mental illness stigmas: Personal responsibility and dangerousness. *Schizophrenia Bulletin, 28*(2), 293–309. https://doi.org/10.1093/oxfordjournals.schbul.a006939

Corstens, D., Longden, E., McCarthy-Jones, S., Waddingham, R., & Thomas, N. (2014). Emerging perspectives from the Hearing Voices Movement: Implications for research and practice. *Schizophrenia Bulletin, 40*(Suppl 4), S285–S294. https://doi.org/10.1093/schbul/sbu007

Coţofană, A. (2017). White man law versus black magic women. Racial and gender entanglements of witchcraft policies in Romania. *Kultūra ir visuomenė: socialinių tyrimų žurnalas, 8*(2), 69–95.

Coulter, C. (2020). A diffractive story. *Qualitative Inquiry, 26*(10), 1213–1221. https://doi.org/10.1177/1077800420939207

Dalgleish, M., Everett, H., & Duff, C. (2019). Subjectivity and transversality in mental health research: Towards a post-qualitative analysis of voyeurism. *Subjectivity, 12*(3), 193–209. https://doi.org/10.1057/s41286-019-00072-x

Davidson, L. (2008). "Recovery" as a response to oppressive social structures. *Chronic Illness, 4*(4), 305–306. https://doi.org/10.1177/1742395308095355

Davidson, L., Mezzina, R., Rowe, M., & Thompson, K. (2010). "A life in the community": Italian mental health reform and recovery. *Journal of Mental Health, 19*(5), 436–443. https://doi.org/10.3109/09638231003728158

Davidson, L., O'Connell, M. J., Tondora, J., Lawless, M., & Evans, A. C. (2005). Recovery in serious mental illness: A new wine or just a new bottle? *Professional Psychology: Research and Practice, 36*(5), 480–487. https://doi.org/10.1037/0735-7028.36.5.480

Davidson, L., & Roe, D. (2007). Recovery from versus recovery in serious mental illness: One strategy for lessening confusion plaguing recovery. *Journal of Mental Health, 16*(4), 459–470. https://doi.org/10.1080/09638230701482394

de la Bellacasa, M. P. (2017). *Matters of care: Speculative ethics in more than human worlds.* University of Minnesota Press.

Deegan, P. E. (1988). Recovery: The lived experience of rehabilitation. *Psychosocial Rehabilitation Journal, 11*(4), 11–19. https://doi.org/10.1037/h0099565

Dein, S. (2003). Psychogenic death: Individual effects of sorcery and taboo violation. *Mental Health, Religion & Culture, 6*(3), 195–202.

DeLanda, M. (2006). *A new philosophy of society: Assemblage theory and social complexity.* Continuum. https://doi.org/10.5040/9781350096769

Deleuze, G. (1988). *Foucault.* University of Minnesota Press.

Deleuze, G. (1989). *Cinema 2: The time-image* (H. Tomlinson, & R. Galeta, Trans.). University of Minnesota Press.

Deleuze, G. (1990) *The logic of sense* (C. J. Stivale, Trans.). Continuum.

Deleuze, G. (1995). *Negotiations, 1972–1990.* Columbia University Press.

Deleuze, G. (1996). *Gilles Deleuze from A to Z* (C. J. Stivale, Trans.). Semiotext(e).

Deleuze, G. (2000). *Proust and signs: The complete text.* The Athlone Press.

Deleuze, G. (2004). *Desert islands and other texts 1953–1974* (M. Taormina, Trans.; D. Lapoujade, Ed.). Semiotext(e).

Deleuze, G. (2006). *Nietzsche and philosophy.* Columbia University Press.

Deleuze, G. (2017). Postscript on the societies of control. In C. Norris, & D. Wilson (Eds.), *Surveillance, crime and social control* (pp. 35–39). Routledge.

Deleuze, G., & Guattari, F. (1984). *Anti-Oedipus.* Bloomsbury.

Deleuze, G., & Guattari, F. (1986). *Kafka: Toward a minor literature* (Vol. 30). University of Minnesota Press.

Deleuze, G., & Guattari, F. (1987). *A thousand plateaus.* Bloomsbury.

De Line, S. (2018). A generous and troubled Chthulucene: Contemplating Indigenous and tranimal relations in (un)settled worldings. *Graduate Journal of Social Science, 14*(2), 83–106.

Department of Health. (2017). *The Fifth National Mental Health and Suicide Prevention Plan.* https://www.mentalhealthcommission.gov.au/getmedia/0209d27b-1873-4245-b6e5-49e770084b81/Fifth-National-Mental-Health-and-Suicide-Prevention-Plan.pdf

Derrida, J. (1992). *Given time: I. Counterfeit money* (Vol. 1). University of Chicago Press.

Deuchars, R. (2011). Creating lines of flight and activating resistance: Deleuze and Guattari's war machine. *AntePodium.* 1–28.

Diamond, S. (2013). What makes us a community: Reflections on building solidarity in anti-sanist praxis. In B. A. LeFrançois, R. Menzies, & G. Reaume (Eds.), *Mad matters: A critical reader in Canadian mad studies* (pp. 269–280). Canadian Scholars' Press.

DiCicco-Bloom, B., & Crabtree, B. F. (2006). The qualitative research interview. *Medical Education, 40*(4), 314–321. https://doi.org/10.1111/j.1365-2929.2006.02418.x

Dickie, V., Cutchin, M. P., & Humphry, R. (2006). Occupation as transactional experience: A critique of individualism in occupational science. *Journal of Occupational Science, 13*(1), 83–93.

Dosse, R. (2010). *Gilles Deleuze & Félix Guattari: Intersecting lives.* Columbia University Press.

Duff, C. (2014). *Assemblages of health: Deleuze's empiricism and the ethology of life.* Springer.

Eales, L., & Peers, D. (2021). Care haunts, hurts, heals: The promiscuous poetics of queer crip Mad care. *Journal of Lesbian Studies, 25*(3), 163–181. https://doi.org/10.1080/1089 4160.2020.1778849

Eizenberg, E. (2004, October). The production of contesting space: Community gardens and the cultivation of social change. In *Proceeding of open space: People space conference,* Edinburgh, UK.

Elraz, H. (2018). Identity, mental health and work: How employees with mental health conditions recount stigma and the pejorative discourse of mental illness. *Human Relations, 71*(5), 722–741. https://doi.org/10.1177/0018726717716752

Epstein, M. (2013). *The consumer movement in Australia: A memoir of an old campaigner.* Our Consumer Place.

Erasmus, Z. (2020). Sylvia Wynter's Theory of the Human: Counter-, not Post-humanist. *Theory, Culture & Society, 37*(6), 47–65. https://doi.org/10.1177/0263276420936333

Facca, D., & Kinsella, E. A. (2021). Emergence, multiplicity and connection: Rethinking ethical discernment in qualitative research through a rhizo-ethics approach. *International Journal of Qualitative Studies in Education,* 1–15. https://doi.org/10.1080/09518398.2021 .1930248

Farias, L., & Laliberte Rudman, D. (2016). A critical interpretive synthesis of the uptake of critical perspectives in occupational science. *Journal of Occupational Science, 23*(1), 33–50. https://doi.org/10.1080/14427591.2014.989893

Faulkner, A. (2017). Survivor research and Mad Studies: The role and value of experiential knowledge in mental health research. *Disability & Society, 32*(4), 500–520. https://doi.org /10.1080/09687599.2017.1302320

Federici, S. (2004). *Caliban and the Witch.* Autonomedia.

Fisher, B., & Tronto, J. (1990). Toward a feminist theory of caring. In E. K. Abel, & M. K. Nelson (Eds.). *Circles of care: Work and identity in women's lives* (pp. 35–62). State University of New York Press.

Fletcher, E. H. (2018). Uncivilizing "mental illness": Contextualizing diverse mental states and posthuman emotional ecologies within The Icarus Project. *Journal of Medical Humanities, 39*(1), 29–43. https://doi.org/10.1007/s10912-017-9476-y

Foucault, M. (1977). Theatrum philosophicum. In D. F. Bouchard (Ed.), *Language, counter-memory, practice: Selected essays and interviews* (D. F. Bouchard, & S. Simon, Trans., pp. 165–196). Cornell University Press.

Foucault, M. (1984). Preface. In G. Deleuze, & F. Guattari, *Anti-Oedipus* (pp. xiii–xvi). Bloomsbury.

Fox, N. J., & Alldred, P. (2015). New materialist social inquiry: Designs, methods and the research-assemblage. *International Journal of Social Research Methodology, 18*(4), 399–414. https://doi.org/10.1080/13645579.2014.921458

Fox, N. J., & Alldred, P. (2017). *Sociology and the new materialism: Theory, research, action.* Sage. https://doi.org/10.4135/9781526401915

Fullagar, S. (2017). Post-qualitative inquiry and the new materialist turn: Implications for sport, health and physical culture research. *Qualitative Research in Sport, Exercise and Health, 9*(2), 247–257. https://doi.org/10.1080/2159676x.2016.1273896

Fullagar, S., O'Brien, W., & Pavlidis, A. (2019). *Feminism and a vital politics of depression and recovery.* Springer.

Genosko, G. (2002). *Félix Guattari: An aberrant introduction.* A&C Black.

Gerrard, J., Rudolph, S., & Sriprakash, A. (2016). The politics of post-qualitative inquiry: History and power. *Qualitative Inquiry, 23*(5), 384–394.

Gibson, B. E. (2019). Post-critical physiotherapy ethics: A commitment to openness. In B. E. Gibson, D. Nicholls, J. Setchell, & K. Synne-Groven (Eds.), *Manipulating practices: A critical physiotherapy reader.* (pp. 35–53). Capelen Damm.

Gibson, B. E., Fadyl, J. K., Terry, G., Waterworth, K., Mosleh, D., & Kayes, N. M. (2021). A posthuman decentring of person-centred care. *Health Sociology Review, 30*(3), 292–307. https://doi.org/10.1080/14461242.2021.1975555

Gibson, M. (2012). *Witchcraft myths in American culture.* Routledge.

Gilbert, J. (2010). Deleuzian politics? A survey and some suggestions. *New Formations, 68*(1), 10–33. https://doi.org/10.3898/newf.68.01.2009

Gold, R. L. (1958). Roles in sociological field observations. *Social Forces, 36*(3), 217–223. https://doi.org/10.2307/2573808

Goodchild, P. (1996). *Deleuze and Guattari: An introduction to the politics of desire* (Vol. 44). Sage.

Gorman, R. (2013). Mad nation? Thinking through race, class, and mad identity politics. In B. A. LeFrançois, R. Menzies, & G. Reaume (Eds.), *Mad matters: A critical reader in Canadian mad studies* (pp. 269–280). Canadian Scholars' Press.

Greene, J. C. (2013). On rhizomes, lines of flight, mangles, and other assemblages. *International Journal of Qualitative Studies in Education, 26*(6), 749–758. https://doi.org/10.1080/0951 8398.2013.788763

Gregory, P. R. (1994). Who needs to change: You, me or everyone? *Australian Occupational Therapy Journal, 41*(3), 133–136. https://doi.org/10.1111/j.1440-1630.1994.tb01299.x

Guattari, E. (2014). *I, little asylum.* Semiotext(e).

Guattari, F. (2015). *Psychoanalysis and transversality: Texts and interviews 1955–1971.* Semiotext(e).

Guevara, C. (1961). *Guerrilla warfare.* Monthly Review Press.

Gunning, T. (1989). Towards a minor cinema: Fonoroff, Herwitz, Ahwesh, Lapore, Klahr and Solomon. *Motion Picture, 3*(1–2), 2–5.

Halpern, A. R., Martin, J. S., & Reed, T. D. (2008). An ERP study of major–minor classification in melodies. *Music Perception: An Interdisciplinary Journal, 25*(3), 181–191. https://doi.org/10.1525/mp.2008.25.3.181

Hamer, H. P., Finlayson, M., & Warren, H. (2014). Insiders or outsiders? Mental health service users' journeys towards full citizenship. *International Journal of Mental Health Nursing, 23*(3), 203–211. https://doi.org/10.1111/inm.12046

Hamer, H. P., Rowe, M., & Seymour, C. A. (2019). "The right thing to do": Fostering social inclusion for mental health service users through acts of citizenship. *International Journal of Mental Health Nursing, 28*(1), 297–305. https://doi.org/10.1111/inm.12533

Hammell, K. W. (2009). Sacred texts: A sceptical exploration of the assumptions underpinning theories of occupation. *Canadian Journal of Occupational Therapy, 76*(1), 6–13. https://doi.org/10.1177/000841740907600105

Hammell, K. W. (2011). Resisting theoretical imperialism in the disciplines of occupational science and occupational therapy. *British Journal of Occupational Therapy, 74*(1), 27–33. https://doi.org/10.4276/030802211x12947686093602

Hammersley, M. (2015). Ethnography. In G. Ritzer (Ed.), *The Blackwell encyclopedia of sociology.* Wiley. https://doi.org/10.1002/9781405165518.wbeose070.pub2

Hammersley, M., & Atkinson, P. (2007). *Ethnography: Principles in practice.* Routledge.

Happell, B., Scholz, B., Gordon, S., Bocking, J., Ellis, P., Roper, C., Liggins, J., & Platania-Phung, C. (2018). "I don't think we've quite got there yet": The experience of allyship for mental health consumer researchers. *Journal of Psychiatric and Mental Health Nursing, 25*(8), 453–462. https://doi.org/10.1111/jpm.12476

Haraway, D. (1988). Situated knowledges: The science question in feminism and the privilege of partial perspective. *Feminist Studies, 14*(3), 575–599.

Haraway, D. (2016). Staying with the trouble: Making kin in the chthulucene. Duke University Press.

Harper, D. (2002). Talking about pictures: A case for photo elicitation. *Visual studies, 17*(1), 13–26.

Harper, D., & Speed, E. (2012). Uncovering recovery: The resistible rise of recovery and resilience. *Studies in Social Justice, 6*(1), 9–25. https://doi.org/10.26522/ssj.v6i1.1066

Hazelton, M. (2005). Mental health reform, citizenship and human rights in four countries. *Health Sociology Review, 14*(3), 230–241. https://doi.org/10.5172/hesr.14.3.230

Hill, F. (2000). *The Salem witch trials reader.* Da Capo Press.

Honan, E. (2007). Writing a rhizome: An (im)plausible methodology. *International Journal of Qualitative Studies in Education, 20*(5), 531–546. https://doi.org/10.1080/09518390600923735

Honan, E., & Bright, D. (2016). Writing a thesis differently. *International Journal of Qualitative Studies in Education, 29*(5), 731–743. https://doi.org/10.1080/09518398.2016.1145280

Horwitz, A. (1982). *The social control of mental illness.* Academic Press.

Howey, H. (2013). *Wool.* Cornerstone.

Irigaray, L. (1985). *Speculum of the other woman.* Cornell University Press.

Jackson, A. Y. (2017). Thinking without method. *Qualitative Inquiry, 23*(9), 666–674.

Jackson, A. Y., & Mazzei, L. A. (2013). Plugging one text into another: Thinking with theory in qualitative research. *Qualitative Inquiry, 19*(4), 261–271. https://doi.org/10.1177/1077800412471510

Jackson, R. G., Huskins, K., Skelton, S. M., & Thorius, K. A. K. (2020). *Allyship & accomplice: Two sides of the same coin.* Midwest & Plains Equity Assistance Center.

Jacobsson, K., & Åkerström, M. (2012). Interviewees with an agenda: Learning from a "failed" interview. *Qualitative Research, 13*(6), 717–734. https://doi.org/10.1177/1468794112465631

Johansson, L. (2016). Post-qualitative line of flight and the confabulative conversation: A methodological ethnography. *International Journal of Qualitative Studies in Education, 29*(4), 445–466. https://doi.org/10.1080/09518398.2015.1053157

Juntanamalaga, P., Scholz, B., Roper, C., & Happell, B. (2019). "They can't empower us": The role of allies in the consumer movement. *International Journal of Mental Health Nursing, 28*(4), 857–866. https://doi.org/10.1111/inm.12585

Kantartzis, S., & Molineux, M. (2012). Understanding the discursive development of occupation: Historico-political perspectives. In G. E. Whiteford, & C. Hocking (Eds.), *Occupational science: Society, inclusion, participation* (pp. 38–53). Wiley-Blackwell.

Kaplan. A. (2002). *Development practitioners and social process: Artists of the invisible.* Pluto Press.

Kathirvel, S., Jeyashree, K., & Patro, B. K. (2012). Social mapping: A potential teaching tool in public health. *Medical Teacher, 34*(7), e529–e531. https://doi.org/10.3109/0142159x.2012.670321

Katz, C. (1996). Towards minor theory. *Environment and Planning D: Society and Space, 14*(4), 487–499. https://doi.org/10.1068/d140487

Kermode, M., Grills, N., Singh, P., & Mathias, K. (2021). Improving social inclusion for young people affected by mental illness in Uttarakhand, India. *Community Mental Health Journal, 57*(1), 136–143.

Kessler, R. C., Barker, P. R., Colpe, L. J., Epstein, J. F., Gfroerer, J. C., Hiripi, E., Howes, M. J., Normand, S.-L. T., Manderscheid, R. W., & Walters, E. E. (2003). Screening for serious mental illness in the general population. *Archives of General Psychiatry, 60*(2), 184–189. https://doi.org/10.1001/archpsyc.60.2.184

Kirkwood, S., Goodman, S., McVittie, C., & McKinlay, A. (2016). *The language of asylum.* Palgrave Macmillan.

Kutlaca, M., Radke, H. R. M., Iyer, A., & Becker, J. C. (2020). Understanding allies' participation in social change: A multiple perspectives approach. *European Journal of Social Psychology, 50*(6), 1248–1258. https://doi.org/10.1002/ejsp.2720

Laliberte Rudman, D. (2013). Enacting the critical potential of occupational science: Problematizing the "individualizing of occupation". *Journal of Occupational Science, 20*(4), 298–313. https://doi.org/10.1080/14427591.2013.803434

Laliberte Rudman, D. (2014). Embracing and enacting an "occupational imagination": Occupational science as transformative. *Journal of Occupational Science, 21*(4), 373–388. https://doi.org/10.1080/14427591.2014.888970

Lambley, R. (2020). Small talk matters! Creating allyship in mental health research. *Qualitative Research in Psychology,* 1–15. https://doi.org/10.1080/14780887.2020.1769239

Lamont, A. (2020). *Guide to allyship.* https://guidetoallyship.com/

Lather, P. (1993). Fertile obsession: Validity after poststructuralism. *The Sociological Quarterly, 34*(4), 673–693. https://doi.org/10.1111/j.1533-8525.1993.tb00112.x

Lather, P. (2013). Methodology-21: What do we do in the afterward? *International Journal of Qualitative Studies in Education, 26*(6), 634–645. https://doi.org/10.1080/09518398.2013.788753

Lather, P., & St. Pierre, E. A. (2013). Post-qualitative research. *International Journal of Qualitative Studies in Education, 26*(6), 629–633. https://doi.org/10.1080/09518398.2013.788752

Laws, J. (2017). Magic at the margins: Towards a magical realist human geography. *Cultural Geographies, 24*(1), 3–19. https://doi.org/10.1177/1474474016647367

Le Boutillier, C., & Croucher, A. (2010). Social inclusion and mental health. *The British Journal of Occupational Therapy, 73*(3), 136–139.

Leblanc, S., & Kinsella, E. A. (2016). Toward epistemic justice: A critically reflexive examination of 'sanism' and implications for knowledge generation. *Studies in Social Justice, 10*(1), 59–78.

Lee, R. M., & Robbins, S. B. (2000). Understanding social connectedness in college women and men. *Journal of Counseling & Development, 78*(4), 484–491. https://doi.org/10.1002/j.1556-6676.2000.tb01932.x

LeFrançois, B. A., Menzies, R., & Reaume, G. (2013). *Mad matters: A critical reader in Canadian mad studies.* Canadian Scholars' Press.

Lenz Taguchi, H. (2016). "The concept as method": Tracing-and-mapping the problem of the neuro(n) in the field of education. *Cultural Studies ↔ Critical Methodologies, 16*(2), 213–223. https://doi.org/10.1177/1532708616634726

Lewis, A. (1974). Psychopathic personality: A most elusive category. *Psychological Medicine, 4*(2), 133–140. https://doi.org/10.1017/S0033291700041969

Liegghio, M. (2020). Allyship and solidarity, not therapy, in child and youth mental health: Lessons from a participatory action research project with psychiatrized youth. *Global Studies of Childhood, 10*(1), 78–89. https://doi.org/10.1177/2043610619885390

Lloyd, C., Williams, P. L., Machingura, T., & Tse, S. (2016). A focus on recovery: Using the mental health recovery star as an outcome measure. *Advances in Mental Health, 14*(1), 57–64. https://doi.org/10.1080/18387357.2015.1064341

Longo, P. (2001). Revisiting the equality/difference debate: Redefining citizenship for the new millennium. *Citizenship Studies, 5*(3), 269–284.

Loveman, B., & Davies, T. M., Jr. (1997). *Che Guevara: Guerrilla warfare*. Scholarly Resources.

Lugones, M. (1987). Playfulness, "world"-travelling, and loving perception. *Hypatia, 2*(2), 3–19. https://doi.org/10.1111/j.1527-2001.1987.tb01062.x

Lundy, C. (2013). Who are our nomads today?: Deleuze's political ontology and the revolutionary problematic. *Deleuze Studies, 7*(2), 231–249. https://doi.org/10.3366/dls.2013.0104

Lynch, J. (2020). *A whole person approach to wellbeing: Building sense of safety*. Routledge.

MacLure, M. (2013). Researching without representation? Language and materiality in post-qualitative methodology. *International Journal of Qualitative Studies in Education, 26*(6), 658–667. https://doi.org/10.1080/09518398.2013.788755

MacPhee, K., & Wilson Norrad, L. (2022). Learning and unlearning: Two social workers' autoethnographic exploration into Mad Studies. *Journal of Progressive Human Services, 33*(1), 40–61. https://doi.org/10.1080/10428232.2021.2007456

Manning, E. (2016). *The minor gesture*. Duke University Press.

Mao, T-T. (2000). *On guerrilla warfare*. (S. Griffith II, Trans.). University of Illinois Press.

Martin, A. D., & Kamberelis, G. (2013). Mapping not tracing: Qualitative educational research with political teeth. *International Journal of Qualitative Studies in Education, 26*(6), 668–679. https://doi.org/10.1080/09518398.2013.788756

Mascayano, F., Alvarado, R., Andrews, H. F., Jorquera, M. J., Lovisi, G. M., Souza, F. M. D., ... & Susser, E. (2019). Implementing the protocol of a pilot randomized controlled trial for the recovery-oriented intervention to people with psychoses in two Latin American cities. *Cadernos de Saúde Pública, 35*(4), e00108018.

Masny, D. (2013). Rhizoanalytic pathways in qualitative research. *Qualitative Inquiry, 19*(5), 339–348. https://doi.org/10.1177/1077800413479559

Massumi, B. (1987). Notes on the translation and acknowledgments. In G. Deleuze, & F. Guattari, *A thousand plateaus*. Bloomsbury.

Max, K. (2005). Chapter four: Anti-colonial research: Working as an ally with Aboriginal peoples. *Counterpoints, 252*, 79–94. https://www.jstor.org/stable/42978745

Mayan, M. J. (2009). *Essentials of qualitative inquiry*. Left Coast Press.

Mayes, R., & Horwitz, A. V. (2005). DSM-III and the revolution in the classification of mental illness. *Journal of the History of the Behavioral Sciences, 41*(3), 249–267. https://doi.org/10.1002/jhbs.20103

Mazzei, L. A. (2013). A voice without organs: Interviewing in posthumanist research. *International Journal of Qualitative Studies in Education, 26*(6), 732–740. https://doi.org/10.1080/09518398.2013.788761

Mazzei, L. A. (2016). Voice without a subject. *Cultural Studies, 16*(2), 151–161.

Mazzei, L. A. (2021). Postqualitative inquiry: Or the necessity of theory. *Qualitative Inquiry, 27*(2), 198–200. https://doi.org/10.1177/1077800420932607

Mazzei, L. A., & McCoy, K. (2010). Thinking with Deleuze in qualitative research. *International Journal of Qualitative Studies in Education, 23*(5), 503–509. https://doi.org/10.1080/09518398.2010.500634

Mbembe, A. (2001). *On the postcolony*. University of California Press.

McAuliffe, C. (2012). Graffiti or street art? Negotiating the moral geographies of the creative city. *Journal of Urban Affairs, 34*(2), 189–206. https://doi.org/10.1111/j.1467-9906.2012.00610.x

McCorkle, B. H., Dunn, E. C., Yu Mui, W., & Gagne, C. (2009). Compeer friends: A qualitative study of a volunteer friendship programme for people with serious mental illness. *International Journal of Social Psychiatry, 55*(4), 291–305. https://doi.org/10.1177/0020764008097090

McGeorge, H. J., & Ketcham, C. C. (1983). Sabotage: A strategic tool for guerrilla forces. *World Affairs, 146*(3), 249–256.

McGill, J. (1996). *Developing leisure identities: A pilot project.* Brampton Caledon Community Living.

McGinty, E. E., Webster, D. W., Jarlenski, M., & Barry, C. L. (2014). News media framing of serious mental illness and gun violence in the United States, 1997–2012. *American Journal of Public Health, 104*(3), 406–413. https://doi.org/10.2105/ajph.2013.301557

McKenzie, M. (2014). *Black girl dangerous on race, queerness, class and gender.* BGD Press.

McKnight, J. (1995). *The careless society: Community and its counterfeits.* Basic Books.

McLennan, S. (2014). Medical voluntourism in Honduras: "Helping" the poor? *Progress in Development Studies, 14*(2), 163–179. https://doi.org/10.1177/1464993413517789

McLeod, K. (2014). The missing work of collaboration: Using assemblages to rethink antidepressant action. *Contemporary Drug Problems, 41*(1), 109–142. https://doi.org/10.1177/009145091404100106

McLeod, K. (2017). *Wellbeing machine: How health emerges from the assemblages of everyday life.* Carolina Academic Press.

McPhail, B. A. (2004). Setting the record straight: Social work is not a female-dominated profession. *Social Work, 49*(2), 323–326. http://www.jstor.org/stable/23721143

McPhie, J. (2019). *Mental health and wellbeing in the Anthropocene: A posthuman inquiry.* Springer.

McWade, B. (2016). Recovery-as-policy as a form of neoliberal state making. *Intersectionalities: A Global Journal of Social Work Analysis, Research, Polity, and Practice, 5*(3), 62–81.

Minkler, M., & Wallerstein, N. (2010). *Community-based participatory research for health: From process to outcomes.* Wiley.

Mitchell, G., & Pistrang, N. (2011). Befriending for mental health problems: Processes of helping. *Psychology and Psychotherapy: Theory, Research and Practice, 84*(2), 151–169. https://doi.org/10.1348/147608310x508566

Morrow, M. (2013). Recovery: Progressive paradigm or neoliberal smokescreen? In B. A. LeFrançois, R. Menzies, & G. Reaume (Eds.), *Mad matters: A critical reader in Canadian mad studies* (pp. 323–333). Canadian Scholars' Press.

Moss, C., Warner, T., Happell, B., & Scholz, B. (2020). Motivations for allyship with mental health consumer movements. *Qualitative Research in Psychology*, 1–18. https://doi.org/10.1080/14780887.2020.1718814

Motala, S., Abo-Al-Ez, K. M., & Adonis, M. (2022). The subjectification of black engineering educators: A posthumanist cartography. *Qualitative Inquiry.* https://doi.org/10.1177/10778004221099570

Nairn, K., Munro, J., & Smith, A. B. (2005). A counter-narrative of a "failed" interview. *Qualitative Research, 5*(2), 221–244. https://doi.org/10.1177/1468794105050836

National Institute of Mental Health. (2016). *Mental illness.* https://www.nimh.nih.gov/health/statistics/mental-illness.shtml

Neumarkt, P. (2005). Challenge of self knowledge. *Journal of Evolutionary Psychology, 26*(1–2), 15–17.

Newman, A. M. (2019). Desiring the standard light skin: Black multiracial boys, masculinity and exotification. *Identities, 26*(1), 107–125. https://doi.org/10.1080/1070289X.2017.1377420

Nixon, S. A. (2019). The coin model of privilege and critical allyship: Implications for health. *BMC Public Health, 19*(1), 1–13. https://doi.org/10.1186/s12889-019-7884-9

Oades, L. G., & Anderson, J. (2012). Recovery in Australia: Marshalling strengths and living values. *International Review of Psychiatry, 24*(1), 5–10. https://doi.org/10.3109/09540261.2012.660623

O'Connell, M. (1988). *The gift of hospitality: Opening the doors of community life to people with disabilities.* The Community Life Project, Centre for Urban Affairs and Policy Research.

Olson, R. E. (2021). Emotions in human research ethics guidelines: Beyond risk, harm and pathology. *Qualitative Research.* https://doi.org/10.1177/14687941211039965

Onifade, Y. (2011). The mental health recovery star. *Mental Health and Social Inclusion, 15*(2), 78–87. https://doi.org/10.1108/20428301111140921

Ørtenblad, L., Væggemose, U., Gissel, L., & Nissen, N. K. (2019). Volunteering to care for people with severe mental illness: A qualitative study of the significance of professional and private life experience. *Community Mental Health Journal, 55*(2), 271–278. https://doi.org/10.1007/s10597-018-0243-y

Ostrow, L., & Adams, N. (2012). Recovery in the USA: From politics to peer support. *International Review of Psychiatry, 24*(1), 70–78. https://doi.org/10.3109/09540261.2012.659659

Ozarin, L. (2001). Moral insanity: A brief history. *Psychiatric News.* https://doi.org/10.1176/pn.36.10.0021

Padgett, D. K., Henwood, B., Abrams, C., & Drake, R. E. (2008). Social relationships among persons who have experienced serious mental illness, substance abuse, and homelessness: Implications for recovery. *American Journal of Orthopsychiatry, 78*(3), 333–339. https://doi.org/10.1037/a0014155

Parisi, L. (2004). *Abstract sex: Philosophy, bio-technology and the mutations of desire.* Continuum.

Patton, P. (2001). Deleuze and Guattari. Ethics and post-modernity. In G. Genosko (Ed.), *Deleuze and Guattari: Critical assessments of leading philosophers* (Vol. 2, pp. 1150–1163). Routledge.

Paulston, R. G. (2000). A spatial turn in comparative education? Constructing a social cartography of difference. In J. Schriewer (Ed.), *Discourse formation in comparative education* (pp. 297–354). Peter Lang.

Peace, R. (2001). Social exclusion: A concept in need of definition? *Social Policy Journal of New Zealand, 16*, 17–36.

Pereira, R. B., & Whiteford, G. E. (2013). Understanding social inclusion as an international discourse: Implications for enabling participation. *The British Journal of Occupational Therapy, 76*(2), 112–115. https://doi.org/10.4276/030802213x13603244419392

Perry, B. L., Frieh, E., & Wright, E. R. (2017). Therapeutic social control of people with serious mental illness: An empirical verification and extension of theory. *Society and Mental Health, 8*(2), 108–122. https://doi.org/10.1177/2156869317725891

Piat, M., & Sabetti, J. (2012). Recovery in Canada: Toward social equality. *International Review of Psychiatry, 24*(1), 19–28. https://doi.org/10.3109/09540261.2012.655712

Pilisuk, M. (2001). A job and a home: Social networks and the integration of the mentally disabled in the community. *American Journal of Orthopsychiatry, 71*(1), 49–60. https://doi.org/10.1037/0002-9432.71.1.49

Potts, A. (2004). Deleuze on Viagra (or, what can a "Viagra-body" do?). *Body & Society, 10*(1), 17–36. https://doi.org/10.1177/1357034x04041759

Priebe, S., Chevalier, A., Hamborg, T., Golden, E., King, M., & Pistrang, N. (2020). Effectiveness of a volunteer befriending programme for patients with schizophrenia: Randomised controlled trial. *The British Journal of Psychiatry, 217*(3), 477–483. https://doi.org/10.1192/bjp.2019.42

Puar, J. K. (2017). *Terrorist assemblages: Homonationalism in queer times.* Duke University Press.

Qu, S. Q., & Dumay, J. (2011). The qualitative research interview. *Qualitative Research in Accounting & Management, 8*(3), 238–264. https://doi.org/10.1108/11766091111162070

Queensland Government. (2021). *What is the mental health review tribunal?* https://www.mhrt.qld.gov.au/information-about/about-the-tribunal

Queensland Health (2018). *Community Care Unit*. https://www.health.qld.gov.au/cq/services/mental-health/services/community-care-unit

Rainsford, S. (2018). Poetic counterpoints: Emmanuelle Guattari's I, Little Asylum. *Ploughshares: Critical Essays*. https://blog.pshares.org/poetic-counterpoints-emmanuelle-guattaris-i-little-asylum/

Reaume, G. (2022). How is Mad Studies different from anti-psychiatry and critical psychiatry? In P. Beresford & J. Russo (Eds.), *The Routledge international handbook of mad studies* (pp. 98–107). Routledge.

Recovery in the Bin. (2016). *Unrecovery star*. https://recoveryinthebin.org/unrecovery-star-2/

Renold, E., & Ivinson, G. (2014). Horse-girl assemblages: Towards a post-human cartography of girls' desire in an examining valleys community. *Discourse: Studies in the Cultural Politics of Education, 35*(3), 361–376. https://doi.org/10.1080/01596306.2014.888841

Renold, E., & Ringrose, J. (2008). Regulation and rupture: Mapping tween and teenage girls' resistance to the heterosexual matrix. *Feminist Theory, 9*(3), 313–338. https://doi.org/10.1177/1464700108095854

Repper, J., & Carter, T. (2011). A review of the literature on peer support in mental health services. *Journal of Mental Health, 20*(4), 392–411. https://doi.org/10.3109/09638237.2011.583947

Resch, R. P. (1992). *Althusser and the renewal of Marxist social theory*. University of California Press.

Reville, D. (2010). https://madnesscanada.com/resources/video/toronto-activists-project/david-reville-interview/

Rockloff, S. F., & Lockie, S. (2004). Participatory tools for coastal zone management: Use of stakeholder analysis and social mapping in Australia. *Journal of Coastal Conservation, 10*(1), 81–92. https://doi.org/10.1007/bf02818944

Rose, D. (2014). The mainstreaming of recovery. *Journal of Mental Health, 23*(5), 217–218. https://doi.org/10.3109/09638237.2014.928406

Rose, D. (2017). Service user/survivor-led research in mental health: Epistemological possibilities. *Disability & Society, 32*(6), 773–789. https://doi.org/10.1080/09687599.2017.1320270

Rosen, A. (2006). The Australian experience of deinstitutionalization: Interaction of Australian culture with the development and reform of its mental health services. *Acta Psychiatrica Scandinavica, 113*(s429), 81–89. https://doi.org/10.1111/j.1600-0447.2005.00723.x

Rosiek, J. L., Snyder, J., & Pratt, S. L. (2020). The new materialisms and Indigenous theories of non-human agency: Making the case for respectful anti-colonial engagement. *Qualitative Inquiry, 26*(3–4), 331–346. https://doi.org/10.1177/1077800419830135

Ross, M. H., & Setchell, J. (2019). People who identify as LGBTIQ+ can experience assumptions, discomfort, some discrimination, and a lack of knowledge while attending physiotherapy: A survey. *Journal of Physiotherapy, 65*(2), 99–105. https://doi.org/10.1016/j.jphys.2019.02.002

Roxburgh, S. (2019). Homosexuality, witchcraft, and power: The politics of ressentiment in Cameroon. *African Studies Review, 62*(3), 89–111.

Ruggeri, M., Leese, M., Thornicroft, G., Bisoffi, G., & Tansella, M. (2000). Definition and prevalence of severe and persistent mental illness. *The British Journal of Psychiatry, 177*(2), 149–155. https://doi.org/10.1192/bjp.177.2.149

Russell, G. M., & Bohan, J. S. (2016). Institutional allyship for LGBT equality: Underlying processes and potentials for change. *Journal of Social Issues, 72*(2), 335–354. https://doi.org/10.1111/josi.12169

Saleeby, D. (2006). *The strengths perspective in social work practice*. Pearson Education.

Sayce, L. (2015). *From psychiatric patient to citizen revisited*. Palgrave Macmillan.

Scheurich, J. J. (1997). *Research method in the postmodern* (Vol. 3). Psychology Press.

Schutt, R. K. (2016). Social environment and mental illness: The progress and paradox of deinstitutionalization. In B. L. Perry (Ed.), *50 years after deinstitutionalization: Mental illness in contemporary communities* (pp. 91–118). Emerald Group. https://doi.org/10.1108/s1057-629020160000017004

Sellar, B. (2009). Assemblage theory, occupational science, and the complexity of human agency. *Journal of Occupational Science, 16*(2), 67–74. https://doi.org/10.1080/14427591.2009.9686645

Setchell, J., Nicholls, D. A., & Gibson, B. E. (2017). Objecting: Multiplicity and the practice of physiotherapy. *Health: An Interdisciplinary Journal for the Social Study of Health, Illness and Medicine*, 1–20. https://doi.org/10.1177/1363459316688519

Shevellar, L., & Barringham, N. (2016). Working in complexity: Ethics and boundaries in community work and mental health. *Journal of Australian Social Work, 69*(2), 181–193. https://doi.org/10.1080/0312407x.2015.1071861

Shimrat, I. (1997). *Call me crazy: Stories from the mad movement.* Press Gang Pub.

Shimrat, I. (2013). The tragic farce of 'community mental health care'. In B. LeFrançois, R. Menzies, & G. Reaume (Eds.), *Mad matters: A critical reader in Canadian mad studies* (pp. 144–157). Canadian Scholars' Press.

Siegel, D. E., Tracy, E. M., & Corvo, K. N. (1994). Strengthening social networks intervention strategies for mental health case managers. *Health & Social Work, 19*(3), 206–216. https://doi.org/10.1093/hsw/19.3.206

Silverstein, S. M., & Bellack, A. S. (2008). A scientific agenda for the concept of recovery as it applies to schizophrenia. *Clinical Psychology Review, 28*(7), 1108–1124. https://doi.org/10.1016/j.cpr.2008.03.004

Smith, D. (2011). Deleuze and the question of desire: Towards an immanent theory of ethics. In N. Jun, & D. Smith (Eds.), *Deleuze and ethics* (pp. 123–141). Edinburgh University Press.

Spandler, H. (2007). From social exclusion to inclusion? A critique of the inclusion imperative in mental health. *Medical Sociology Online, 2*(2), 3–16.

Springgay, S., & Truman, S. E. (2018). On the need for methods beyond proceduralism: Speculative middles, (in)tensions, and response-ability in research. *Qualitative Inquiry, 24*(3), 203–214. https://doi.org/10.1177/1077800417704464

Starkman, M. (2013). The movement. In B. A. LeFrançois, R. Menzies, & G. Reaume (Eds.), *Mad matters: A critical reader in Canadian mad studies* (pp. 269–280). Canadian Scholars' Press.

St. Pierre, E. A. (2011). Post qualitative research: The critique and the coming after. In N. K. Denzin, & Y. S. Lincoln (Eds.), *The Sage handbook of qualitative research* (4th ed., pp. 611–625). Sage.

St. Pierre, E. A. (2016). Practices for the "new" in the new empiricisms, the new materialisms, and postqualitative inquiry. In N. K. Denzin, & M. D. Giardina (Eds.), *Qualitative inquiry and the politics of research* (pp. 75–96). Routledge.

St. Pierre, E. A. (2017). Writing post qualitative inquiry. *Qualitative Inquiry, 24*(9), 603–608. https://doi.org/10.1177/1077800417734567

St. Pierre, E. A., & Jackson, A. Y. (2014). *Qualitative data analysis after coding.* Sage.

St. Pierre, E. A., Jackson, A. Y., & Mazzei, L. A. (2016). *New empiricisms and new materialisms: Conditions for new inquiry.* Sage.

Stewart, J. L. (2019). The ghettoization of persons with severe mental illnesses. *Mental Health and Social Inclusion, 23*(1), 53–57. https://doi.org/10.1108/mhsi-10-2018-0036

Stewart, V., Roennfeldt, H., Slattery, M., & Wheeler, A. J. (2019). Generating mutual recovery in creative spaces. *Mental Health and Social Inclusion, 23*(1), 16–22. https://doi.org/10.1108/mhsi-08-2018-0029

Stickley, T., Higgins, A., Meade, O., Sitvast, J., Doyle, L., Ellilä, H., Jormfeldt, H., Keogh, B., Lahti, M., Skärsäter, I., Vuokila-Oikkonen, P., & Kilkku, N. (2016). From the rhetoric to the real: A critical review of how the concepts of recovery and social inclusion may inform mental health nurse advanced level curricula – The eMenthe project. *Nurse Education Today, 37*, 155–163. https://doi.org/10.1016/j.nedt.2015.11.015

Stivale, C. J. (1984). The literary element in "Mille Plateaux": The new cartography of Deleuze and Guattari. *SubStance, 13*(3/4), 20–34. https://doi.org/10.2307/3684772

Taguchi, H. L., & Palmer, A. (2014). Reading a Deleuzio-Guattarian cartography of young girls' "school-related" ill-/well-being. *Qualitative Inquiry, 20*(6), 764–771. https://doi.org/10.1177/1077800414530259

Tamboukou, M. (2010). Charting cartographies of resistance: Lines of flight in women artists' narratives. *Gender and Education, 22*(6), 679–696. https://doi.org/10.1080/0954025 3.2010.519604

Taylor, J. (1969). Carolina in my mind. On *James Taylor* [CD]. Apple Records.

The Icarus Project. (2019). Retrieved January 13, 2019, from https://theicarusproject.net/

Thompson, K. S., & Rowe, M. (2010). Social inclusion. *Psychiatric Services, 61*(8), 735. https://doi.org/10.1176/ps.2010.61.8.735

Thompson, R., Valenti, E., Siette, J., & Priebe, S. (2016). To befriend or to be a friend: A systematic review of the meaning and practice of "befriending" in mental health care. *Journal of Mental Health, 25*(1), 71–77. https://doi.org/10.3109/09638237.2015.1021901

Townley, G. (2015). "It helps you not feel so bad – Feel like you again": The importance of community for individuals with psychiatric disabilities. *Journal of Psychosocial Rehabilitation and Mental Health, 2*(2), 113–124. https://doi.org/10.1007/s40737-015-0036-3

Tracy, E. M., & Whittaker, J. K. (1990). The social network map: Assessing social support in clinical practice. *Families in Society, 71*(8), 461–470.

Truman, S. E. (2019). Feminist new materialisms. In P. Atkinson, S. Delamont, A. Cernat, J. W. Sakshaug, & R. A. Williams (Eds.), *SAGE Research Methods Foundations*. SAGE Publications Ltd. https://dx.doi.org/10.4135/9781526421036808740

Tse, S., Ran, M. S., Huang, Y., & Zhu, S. (2013). Mental health care reforms in Asia: the urgency of now: Building a recovery-oriented, community mental health service in China. *Psychiatric Services, 64*(7), 613–616.

Tucker, I. (2010). Mental health service user territories: Enacting "safe spaces" in the community. *Health, 14*(4), 434–448. https://doi.org/10.1177/1363459309357485

Turner, D. W., III. (2010). Qualitative interview design: A practical guide for novice investigators. *The Qualitative Report, 15*(3), 754–760.

Ulmer, J. B., & Koro-Ljungberg, M. (2015). Writing visually through (methodological) events and cartography. *Qualitative Inquiry, 21*(2), 138–152. https://doi.org/10.1177/1077800414542706

Uromi, S. M. (2014). Violence against persons with albinism and older women: Tackling witchcraft accusations in Tanzania. *Cell, 782*, 503638.

Van der Tuin, I., & Dolphijn, R. (2010). The transversality of new materialism. *Women: A Cultural Review, 21*(2), 153–171. https://doi.org/10.1080/09574042.2010.488377

Vandekinderen, C., Roets, G., Roose, R., & Van Hove, G. (2012). Rediscovering recovery: Reconceptualizing underlying assumptions of citizenship and interrelated notions of care and support. *The Scientific World Journal, 2012*, 1–7. https://doi.org/10.1100/2012/496579

Ware, N. C., Hopper, K., Tugenberg, T., Dickey, B., & Fisher, D. (2007). Connectedness and citizenship: Redefining social integration. *Psychiatric Services, 58*(4), 469–474. https://doi.org/10.1176/ps.2007.58.4.469

Watkins, R. (2012). *Black power, yellow power, and the making of revolutionary identities*. University Press of Mississippi.

White Accomplices. (2020). Retrieved December 21, 2020, from https://www. whiteaccomplices.org/

White, C. & Sock, D. (2020). Discussion on housing at DomestiCITY, *Brisbane Festival 2020.* Retrieved from https://www.youtube.com/watch?v=m8jvIa3JCyU

Whiteford, G. (2001). The occupational agenda of the future. *Journal of Occupational Science,* *8*(1), 13–16. https://doi.org/10.1080/14427591.2001.9686480

Whiteford, G. E., & Hocking, C. (Eds.). (2012). *Occupational science: Society, inclusion, participation.* John Wiley & Sons.

Whitehead, T. L. (2005). *Basic classical ethnographic research methods.* Cultural Ecology of Health and Change.

Widder, N. (2010). Desire. In M. Bevir (Ed.), *Encyclopaedia of political theory.* Sage Publications.

Williams, C. C., Almeida, M., & Knyahnytska, Y. (2015). Towards a biopsychosociopolitical frame for recovery in the context of mental illness. *British Journal of Social Work, 45*(Supp. 1), i9–i26. https://doi.org/10.1093/bjsw/bcv100

Wilson, R. A. (2012). *The illuminati papers.* Ronin.

Wilson, S. (2008). *Research is ceremony: Indigenous research methods.* Fernwood Publishing.

Wilton, R. (2004). Putting policy into practice? Poverty and people with serious mental illness. *Social Science & Medicine, 58*(1), 25–39.

Wong, Y.-L. I., Matejkowski, J., & Lee, S. (2011). Social integration of people with serious mental illness: Network transactions and satisfaction. *The Journal of Behavioral Health Services & Research, 38*(1), 51–67. https://doi.org/10.1007/s11414-009-9203-1

Wong, Y.-L. I., Stanton, M. C., & Sands, R. G. (2014). Rethinking social inclusion: Experiences of persons in recovery from mental illness. *American Journal of Orthopsychiatry, 84*(6), 685–695. https://doi.org/10.1037/ort0000034

Wright, N., & Stickley, T. (2013). Concepts of social inclusion, exclusion and mental health: A review of the international literature. *Journal of Psychiatric and Mental Health Nursing, 20*(1), 71–81. https://doi.org/10.1111/j.1365-2850.2012.01889.x

Wyder, M., Roennfeldt, H., Rosello, R. F., Stewart, B., Maher, J., Taylor, R., Pfeffer, A., Bell, P., & Barringham, N. (2018). Our sunshine place: A collective narrative and reflection on the experiences of a mental health crisis leading to an admission to a psychiatric inpatient unit. *International Journal of Mental Health Nursing, 27*(4), 1240–1249. https:// doi.org/10.1111/inm.12487

Yen, A. (2020). Slack rope performance for DomestiCITY, *Brisbane Festival 2020.* Retrieved from https://www.youtube.com/watch?v=N1CTBoFcydY

Zemke, R. (2016). Extending occupational science education. *Journal of Occupational Science, 23*(4), 510–513. https://doi.org/10.1080/14427591.2016.1224010

Zourabichvili, F., & Aarons, K. (2012). *Deleuze: A philosophy of the event: Together with the vocabulary of Deleuze* (G. Lambert, & D. Smith, Eds.). Edinburgh University Press.

INDEX

Pages in *italics* refer to figures, **bold** refer to tables, and pages followed by n refer to notes.

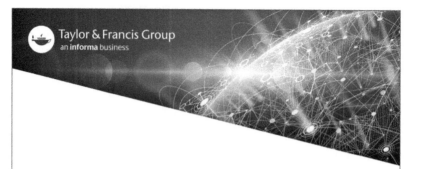